VISUAL QUICKSTART GUIDE

InDesign 2

FOR MACINTOSH AND WINDOWS

Sandee Cohen

Peachpit Press

Visual QuickStart Guide
InDesign 2 for Macintosh and Windows
Copyright © 2002 by Sandee Cohen

Peachpit Press

1249 Eighth Street
Berkeley, CA 94710
800 283 9444 • 510 524 2178
fax 510 524 2221
Find us on the Web at http://www.peachpit.com.
To report errors, please send a note to errata@peachpit.com

Peachpit Press is a division of Pearson Education

Notice of Rights

Notice of Liability

Trademarks

Editor: Cary Norsworthy
Production Coordinator: Kate Reber
Compositor & Interior Design: Sandee Cohen
Cover Design: The Visual Group
Copy Editor: Pam Pfiffner
Indexer: Steve Rath

ISBN 0-201-79478-0

0 9 8 7 6 5 4 3 2 1

Printed and bound in the United States of America

JAN 14 2003

DEDICATED TO

My students
Your questions help me keep it green and
your finished projects amaze me.

THANKS TO

Nancy Ruenzel, publisher of Peachpit Press.

Cary Norsworthy, my editor at Peachpit Press. Cary is a triple threat—an artist who can edit and write.

Pam Pififfner of **CreativePro.com** who took the time out of her busy schedule to copy edit the book—and did a great job!

Kate Reber of Peachpit Press, who does a great job of production.

The staff of Peachpit Press, all of whom make me proud to be a Peachpit author.

Steve Rath, who does the best index in the business. Steve is the reason I don't need to use InDesign's Index features.

David Evans of Adobe, who wrote the foreword to this edition. David has been an exceptional source of information on the development of InDesign as well as a wonderful dinner companion.

Maria Yap of Adobe, who gave me so much support for the first version of my book and kindly provided a quote for the back cover of this edition.

Tim Cole of Adobe, who helped me understand the new features and count the ticks on Nigel.

Eliot Harper of the InDesign beta program who patiently answered all our questions and fielded our complaints.

Noha Edell and **Ashwini Jambotkar** who are my New York City Adobe support team.

Scott Citron of The New York InDesign Users Group.

David Blatner who took time to help me write this book on InDesign as he was busy with his own.

Olav Martin Kvern who is the most brilliant InDesign scripter.

The staff at **Photospin.com** who were kind enough to provide all the half-tone images used in this book.

The InDesign team in Seattle, who listened to everyone's comments about the first two versions and did a tremendous job in making the changes for version 2.

Michael Randasso and the staff of the New School for Social Research Computer Instruction Center.

Pixel, my cat, who has gotten very blasé about these books and doesn't watch me work anymore.

and a very special thanks to

David Lerner of **Tekserve,** who personally helped me get my G4 Powerbook running Macintosh OS X. Tekserve (www.tekserve.com) is the best place to buy, fix, or enhance Macintosh computers.

Colophon

This book was created using InDesign 1.5 and InDesign 2.0. Screen shots were taken using Ambrosia SW Snapz Pro and Snapz Pro X. The computers used were a Macintosh G4 450 Mhz running Mac OS 9, and a G4 Powerbook running Mac OS X. InDesign 2 for Windows ran on the Macintosh OS 9 platform using Virtual PC 5 (no Intel inside). Fonts used were Minion and Futura from Adobe, Circle Negative from Myfonts.com, and a specialty "tip" font I created using FontLab from FontLab Inc.

TABLE OF CONTENTS

Table of Contents

Table of Contents

FOREWORD

Back in my "good old days," as a college student learning the ins and outs of graphic design, I bought a Macintosh Plus, Aldus Pagemaker, and an Apple LaserWriter printer.

Apple's Macintosh, with its WYSIWYG display, plus Adobe's PostScript page description language (that drove the LaserWriter), and Aldus Corporation's PageMaker with its approachable interface, brought the ability to create visually dynamic printed pages to the masses and democratized graphic design and typesetting. It also changed a centuries-old industry around professional printing.

These tools were dismissed as toys by many industry veterans, lacking the true professional-level typographic and color controls needed to produce professional results. And these industry veterans were, for the most part, right. But times change.

The processor that was in my first (beloved) Mac Plus is now out-gunned by your garden-variety Nintendo GameBoy (no kidding!). I now carry around a six-pound laptop in my backpack that the U.S. government classifies as a supercomputer.

Interestingly, if you look at advances in software compared to the advances in computing power, publishing software simply has not kept up. In fact, even 15 years into the desktop-publishing revolution, page-layout software still could not match the professional-quality typography provided by the high-end type-setters of the early 1980s — that is, until Adobe released InDesign.

Adobe Systems first started working on the product that would eventually be known as InDesign almost eight years ago, based on the recognition that the computing power restrictions of the "early days" were rapidly coming to a close, and that a modern application was needed to take full advantage of this new horsepower. And in releasing InDesign 1.0, Adobe took a quantum leap forward in advancing the state of the art. InDesign 1.0 provided, for the first time on the desktop, real precision typography that rivaled dedicated typesetters.

It provided other advancements as well, like the ability to work in high resolution on screen by providing a display model based on our next-generation Display Postscript (called AGM). And we broke through the barriers imposed by "lowest-common-denominator" file formats like TIFF and EPS by supporting native Adobe Illustrator, Adobe Photoshop and Adobe PDF documents, and all the intelligence they afford. InDesign 1.0 changed the rules of the game, but we (and our customers) recognized that it still needed some work.

One of our goals was to create a program that would allow artists and designers more freedom and power than they had with the traditional electronic publishing tools — one that took advantage of the advances in computing power, and one that would significantly advance the state of the art in terms of productivity and creative freedom.

We also wanted to build it using modern programming conventions that would allow us to react quickly to changing market conditions (like the onslaught of the Internet) and

allow the program to grow quickly as computers became more and more powerful. So, one of the first things we did was change how the program code works.

Instead of one large application that contains all the commands, menus, tools, and dialog boxes (called "spaghetti code" by programmers, because of the sloppy way pieces of the software interact), we created a highly-modular code base that is controlled by a powerful plug-in interface. The actual program is only a small 2.3 megabytes in size — but the plug-in folder contains over 30 megabytes of modules, and each of these modules controls different parts of the application. This makes it easy for us — and third-party developers — to enrich InDesign's capabilities very rapidly.

Of course, this makes life for our engineers much easier, but it also has a great benefit to InDesign users: instead of taking years between updates and new versions, we are able to respond very quickly to our customers' requests and bring new, powerful capabilities to graphic designers and production artists in a very short period of time.

InDesign was first released in August of 1999. Just six months later, in the spring of 2000, we released InDesign 1.5 — which added over 80 new features and tools. Later in the fall, we released version 1.5.2 which added support for non-PostScript printers and made other enhancements (and fixed some bugs that needed to be squashed!).

Now, less than three years from the release of InDesign 1.0, Adobe is proud to release InDesign 2.0. We've added an impressive list of new features to InDesign (over 800 new features with version 2!) that takes creative freedom to new levels and allows designers to create stunning artwork that is simply impossible to do with any other application.

We would never have been able to do all this without the vision of the product team that designed our software architecture almost eight years ago.

The reward for this vision is yours: Adobe InDesign 2 is without any question the most powerful, flexible, capable and professional page layout application available today.

InDesign offers designers, art directors, and production managers an impressive array of features. Some features, such as optical margin alignment, support for the OpenType font format, and the Adobe Paragraph Composition engine allow designers to control type in ways that have not been seen in other desktop-publishing programs.

Other features, such as book coordination, table of contents, and indexing, make InDesign useful for book production. The tables in InDesign 2 give designers more choices for importing information from Microsoft Word or Microsoft Excel. Beyond that, tables also can be used to structure page designs in ways that will change how designers approach creating pages.

Most exciting to me is InDesign's ability to create transparency effects like drop shadows, soft feathered edges, and blend elements on a page in simply spectacular fashion. Of course InDesign also integrates very well with other Adobe applications, with full support for native Adobe Photoshop, Adobe PDF and Adobe Illustrator files. Even better, InDesign recognizes the transparency in those files, allowing InDesign users to create effects that have been extremely difficult (or impossible!) to create using previous desktop publishing tools—and previously painful tasks like managing clipping paths simply go away with these capabilities.

I am pleased to see Sandee Cohen has created the third edition of the InDesign Visual Quickstart Guide. Sandee has been actively involved in writing about InDesign since the very first version. She also was an alpha tester with the InDesign team since before 1.0 shipped—her feedback has shaped the software in profound ways, and her expertise, wisdom, and keen intuitive sense about "how things should work" have helped us improve the product with every release. Just like the program itself, her book just gets better with each version.

Sandee really knows what she's talking about, as evidenced by her regular contributions to *Macworld*, CreativePro.com, and other leading industry publications that follow the professional publishing industry. She's a regular speaker on panels at influential tradeshows and industry associations, and as a trainer, she has influenced and tutored some of the very best and brightest design stars in the world. I think you'll find Sandee's writing style appoachable, comprehensive and just plain fun.

InDesign 2 provides unprecedented capabilities for professional graphic design and production, and this book can help you come up to speed on all the powerful tools InDesign 2 affords.

Best realization of your creative dreams,

David Evans
Senior Evangelist
Cross-Media Publishing Adobe Systems, Inc.
Seattle, Washington
February, 2002

INTRODUCTION

Welcome to the *InDesign 2 Visual QuickStart Guide*, my third version of the book. (If you're counting, the first book was InDesign, the second was InDesign 1.0/1.5, and the third is InDesign 2.) I can't believe it's been just two years since I wrote the first edition and a year and a half since the second. In that short period of time Adobe has turned InDesign into a ground-breaking application. I feel very lucky to have been working with and teaching InDesign since its very first version.

Rarely has an application caused as much excitement as InDesign. The first version, released in April 2000, was hailed for its innovative typographic features. Version 1.5, which came out in December of 2000, added more tools and text controls.

Now, with version 2, InDesign has once again broken new ground with transparency effects, drop shadows, feather effects, and support for transparency in files imported from Photoshop and Illustrator. InDesign 2 has also added support for long document construction with its book coordination, table of contents, and indexing features.

Using This Book

If you have used any of the Visual QuickStart Guides, you will find this book to be similar. Each chapter is divided into different sections that deal with a specific topic—usually a tool or command. For instance, the chapter on text has sections on creating text frames, typing text, selecting text, and so on.

Each of the sections contains numbered exercises that show you how to perform a specific technique. As you work through the steps, you gain an understanding of the technique or feature. The illustrations help you judge if you are following the steps correctly.

I've also sprinkled sidebars, printed in gray boxes, throughout the chapters. Some of these sidebars give you a bit of history or background for a specific feature. Other times, I've written out humorous stories about desktop publishing. These sidebars are the same as the little stories and anecdotes I tell my students in the classes I teach.

Instructions

You will find it easier to use this book once you understand the terms I am using. This is especially important since some other computer books use terms differently. Therefore, here are the terms I use in the book and explanations of what they mean.

Click refers to pressing down and releasing the mouse button on the Macintosh, or the left mouse button on Windows. You must release the mouse button or it is not a click.

Press means to hold down the mouse button, or a keyboard key.

Press and drag means to hold the mouse button down and then move the mouse. I also use the shorthand term *drag*. Just remember that you have to press and hold as you drag the mouse.

Menu Commands

InDesign has menu commands that you follow to open dialog boxes, change artwork, and initiate certain actions. These menu commands are listed in bold type. The typical direction to choose a menu command might be written as **Object > Arrange > Bring to Front**. This means that you should first choose the Object menu, then choose the Arrange submenu, and then choose the Bring to Front command.

Keyboard Shortcuts

Most of the menu commands for InDesign have keyboard shortcuts that help you work faster. For instance, instead of choosing New from the File menu, it is faster and easier to use the keyboard shortcut (Cmd-N on the Macintosh and Ctrl-N on Windows). Often these shortcuts use multiple keystroke combinations.

The modifier keys used in keyboard shortcuts are sometimes listed in different orders by different software companies or authors. For example, I always list the Cmd or Ctrl keys first, then the Opt or Alt key, and then the Shift key. Other people may list the Shift key first. The order that you press those modifier keys is not important. However, it is very important that you always add the last key (the letter or number key) after you press the other keys.

Learning Keyboard Shortcuts

While keyboard shortcuts help you work faster, you really do not have to start using them right away. In fact, you will most likely learn more about InDesign by using the menus. As you look for one command, you may see another feature that you would like to explore.

Once you feel comfortable working with InDesign, you can start adding keyboard shortcuts to your repertoire. My suggestion is to look at which menu commands you use a lot. Then each day choose to use one of those shortcuts. For instance, if you import a lot of art from other programs, you might decide to learn the shortcut for the Place command. For the rest of that day use the Place shortcut every time you import text or art. Even if you have to look at the menu to refresh your memory, use the keyboard shortcut to actually open the Place dialog box. By the end of the day you will have memorized the Place shortcut. The next day you can learn a new one.

Cross-Platform Issues

One of the great strengths of InDesign is that it is almost identical on both the Macintosh and Windows platforms. In fact, at first glance it is hard to tell which platform you are working on. However, because there are some differences between the platforms, there are some things you should keep in mind.

Modifier Keys

Modifier keys are always listed with the Macintosh key first and then the Windows key second. So the direction "Hold the Cmd/ Ctrl key" means hold the Cmd key on the Macintosh platform or the Ctrl key on the Windows platform. When the key is the same on both computers, such as the Shift key, only one key is listed.

Generally the Cmd key on the Macintosh (sometimes called the Apple key) corresponds to the Ctrl key on Windows. The Opt key on the Macintosh corresponds to the Alt key on Windows. The Control key on the Macintosh does not have an equivalent on Windows. Notice that the Control key for the Macintosh is always spelled out while the Ctrl key for Windows is not.

Platform-Specific Features

A few times in the book, I have written separate exercises for the Macintosh and Windows platforms. These exercises are indicated by (Mac) and (Win).

Most of the time this is because the procedures are so different that they need to be written separately. Some features exist only on one platform. Those features are then labeled as to their platform.

Whether you're learning InDesign in a class or on your own, I hope this book helps you master the program. Just don't forget to have fun!

Sandee Cohen

(Sandee@vectorbabe.com)
February 2002

GETTING STARTED 1

When I start learning a new application, I'm always in a rush to get started. So when I pick up a book about the application, I never read the first chapter.

I don't want to read about buttons, fields, and controls—especially if I'm already familiar with other programs from the company, such as Photoshop and Illustrator.

I rush right into the middle chapters of the book.

However, after a few hours of slogging helplessly through my documents, I realize there are things I don't understand about the program. I realize I'm a bit confused. So I come back to the first chapter to learn the foundation of the program.

Of course, since you're much more patient than I am, you're already here—reading the first chapter.

Using Palettes

Most of the commands and features that control InDesign are found in the 19 onscreen palettes. Each of the palettes covers special features. The palettes are similar to those found in other Adobe applications.

Align palette

The Align palette ❶ (**Window** > **Align**) aligns and distributes objects on a page (*see Chapter 4, "Working with Objects"*).

Attributes palette

The Attributes palette ❷ (**Window** > **Attributes**) allows you to set fills and strokes to overprint (*see Chapter 6, "Working in Color"*). It also lets you create non-printing objects (*see Chapter 17, "Output"*).

Character palette

The Character palette ❸ (**Window** > **Type** > **Character**) controls character-level attributes such as the typeface and point size (*see Chapter 3, "Basic Text"*).

❶ *Use the* **Align palette** *to align the edges and centers of objects or to distribute the space between objects.*

❷ *The* **Attributes palette** *lets you set the overprinting controls for fills and strokes or to set objects to not print.*

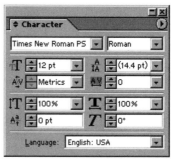

❸ *Use the* **Character palette** *to format the attributes of text characters.*

Using Palettes

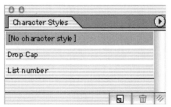

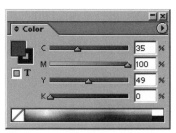

❹ *Use the* **Character Styles palette** *to automate the formatting of text characters.*

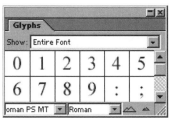

❺ *The* **Color palette** *is used to mix colors to apply to text and objects.*

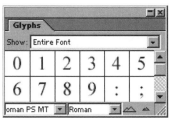

❻ *The* **Glyphs palette** *lets you insert characters from a font.*

Character Styles palette

The Character Styles palette **❹** (**Window** > **Type** > **Character Styles**)lets you define and work with character styles *(see Chapter 14, "Automating Text").*

Color palette

The Color palette **❺** (**Window** > **Color**) allows you to mix or apply colors *(see Chapter 5, "Working in Color").*

Glyphs palette

The Glyphs palette **❻** (**Window** > **Type** > **Insert Glyphs**) lets you insert or replace characters from a font *(see Chapter 3, Basic Text)*. The Glyphs palette also helps you work with OpenType features *(see Chapter 15, "Typography Controls").*

Screen Real Estate

Your workspace may feel cramped with so many palettes on your screen. One way to handle the problem is to invest in a small, second monitor.

Then you can set up InDesign so that the palettes are displayed in the second monitor while the Toolbox and the document window are displayed on your main monitor.

This gives you much more room to work on your document.

Gradient palette

The Gradient palette ❼ (**Window > Gradient**) lets you define and control the appearance of gradients *(see Chapter 5, "Working in Color")*.

Hyperlinks palette

The Hyperlinks palette ❽ (**Window > Hyperlinks**) is used to create links that let you easily navigate around PDF and HTML documents *(see Chapter 10, "Pages and Books")*.

Index palette

The Index palette ❾ (**Window > Index**) lets you create cross-referenced index entries for a document or book *(see Chapter 10, "Pages and Books")*.

Even More Palettes?

Your copy of InDesign may display still more palettes, such as those with extra features for scripting and working with XML tags.

Still more palettes may appear that are part of third-party plug-ins that give you features not found in the basic InDesign program.

Third-party palettes are not available in the ordinary installation. You need to install the plug-ins for those features. *(See Chapter 19, "Customizing InDesign" for information on installing plug-ins.)*

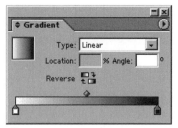

❼ *The* **Gradient palette** *lets you create color blends.*

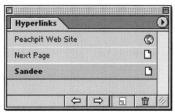

❽ *Use the* **Hyperlinks palette** *to create and store links to other pages in the document or on the Web.*

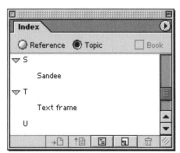

❾ *The* **Index palette** *lets you create a manage index entries for a document or book.*

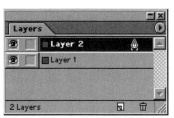

10 *Use the* **Layers palette** *to add layers and change their display.*

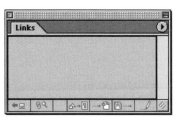

11 *Create a* **Library palette** *to store commonly used items and add them to documents.*

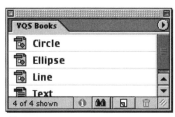

12 *The* **Links palette** *displays a list of all the imported graphics and text files.*

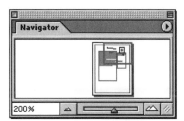

13 *Use the* **Navigator palette** *to see a preview of your document and move around the pages.*

Layers palette

The Layers palette **10** (Window > Layers) controls the stacking order and visibility of different layers *(see Chapter 11, "Layers").*

Library palette

The Library palette **11** (File > New > Library) lets you store and use elements *(see Chapter 12, "Libraries").*

Links palette

The Links palette **12** (Window > Links) controls the status of placed images *(see Chapter 8, "Imported Graphics").*

Navigator palette

The Navigator palette **13** (Window > Navigator) lets you see the layout of pages *(see Chapter 2, "Document Setup").*

Using Palettes

Pages palette

The Pages palette ⓮ (**Window** > **Pages**) lets you add and control pages and master pages as well as move from one page to another *(see Chapter 10, "Pages and Books")*.

Paragraph palette

The Paragraph palette ⓯ (**Window** > **Type** > **Paragraph**) controls paragraph-level attributes such as the alignment and margin indents *(see Chapter 3, "Basic Text")*.

Paragraph Styles palette

The Paragraph Styles palette ⓰ (**Window** > **Type** > **Paragraph Styles**) lets you define and apply paragraph styles *(see Chapter 14, "Automating Text")*.

Story palette

The Story palette ⓱ (**Window** > **Type** > **Story**) lets you change the automatic margin alignment to an optical margin alignment that adjusts the position of punctuation and serifs *(see Chapter 15, "Typography Controls")*.

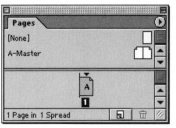

⓮ *The* **Pages palette** *lets you add and delete pages, apply master pages, and move through the document.*

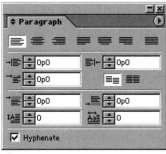

⓯ *The* **Paragraph palette** *contains all the formatting controls for text paragraphs.*

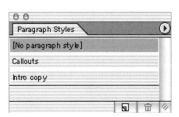

⓰ *The* **Paragraph Styles palette** *makes it easy to apply complex paragraph formatting to paragraphs.*

⓱ *Use the* **Story palette** *to apply the optical margin alignment for hanging punctuation.*

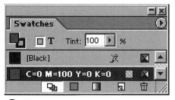

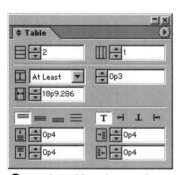

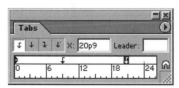

Stroke palette

The Stroke palette ⓲ (**Window > Stroke**) controls attributes such as stroke width, dashes, and end arrows and symbols *(see Chapter 6, "Styling Objects")*.

Swatches palette

The Swatches palette ⓳ (**Window > Swatches**) stores the colors and gradients use in a document *(see Chapter 5, "Working in Color")*.

Table palette

The Table palette ⓴ (**Window > Table**) contains the formatting and controls for creating tables within text frames *(see Chapter 13, "Tabs and Tables")*.

Tabs palette

The Tabs palette ㉑ (**Window > Tabs**) controls the position of the tab stops for text *(see Chapter 13, "Tabs and Tables")*.

⓲ *The* **Stroke palette** *controls the appearance of rules and lines around objects.*

⓳ *The* **Swatches palette** *stores colors and gradients.*

⓴ *Use the* **Table palette** *to format tables and table cells.*

㉑ *The* **Tabs palette** *lets you position and format tabs within text.*

Using Palettes

Text Wrap palette

The Text Wrap palette ㉒ (**Window > Text Wrap**) controls how text wraps around objects and placed images *(see Chapter 9, "Text Effects")*.

Transform palette

The Transform palette ㉓ (**Window > Transform**) lets you see the size and position of objects. You can also use the Transform palette to apply transformations such as scaling and rotation *(see Chapter 4, "Working with Objects")*.

Transparency palette

The Transparency palette ㉔ (**Window > Transparency**) contains the controls for opacity and blend modes *(see Chapter 6, "Styling Objects")*.

Trap Styles palette

The Trap Styles palette ㉕ (**Window > Trap Styles**) is used to store different settings for how colors are trapped between one object and another *(see Chapter 17, "Output")*.

If you can't afford a second monitor, you can quickly hide your palettes and Toolbox.

To hide palettes:

1. Make sure an insertion point is not within a text frame to avoid inserting a tab character into your text.

2. Press Shift+Tab key. This hides all the palettes.

   or

   Press the Tab key. This hides all the palettes including the Toolbox.

   TIP Press the commands again or choose the palette command from the Window menu to reveal the palettes.

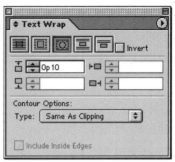

㉒ *Use the* **Text Wrap palette** *to control how text wraps around objects and images.*

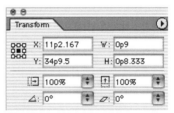

㉓ *The* **Transform palette** *lets you control the position and size of objects.*

㉔ *Use the* **Transparency palette** *to control how text wraps around objects and images.*

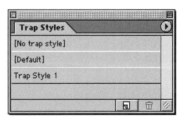

㉕ *The* **Trap Styles palette** *lets you store trapping settings to apply to various objects.*

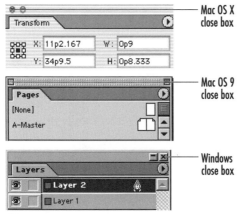

Mac OS X close box

Mac OS 9 close box

Windows close box

26 *Click the close box to close a palette.*

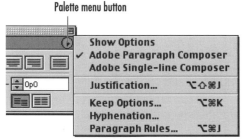

Palette menu button

27 *Click the* **palette menu button** *to display the menu for a palette.*

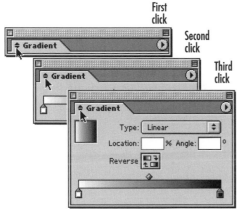

First click

Second click

Third click

28 *Each click on the palette options arrow changes the display of a palette.*

Working with Palettes

If you don't see a palette onscreen, you can open it by choosing the command in the Window menu.

To open a palette:

◆ Choose the name of the palette from the Window menu.

TIP The palettes that control type, such as Character and Paragraph, are listed under **Window > Type** as well as the Type menu

To close a palette:

◆ Click the close box in the title bar **26**.

In addition to the palette buttons and fields, each palette contains a menu.

To display the palette menus:

1. Click the palette menu button to open the palette menu **27**.
2. Choose a command from the menu.

Some palettes display only certain features when first opened. You show the optional features by clicking the options arrows in the palette tab.

To reveal the palette options:

1. Click the arrow in the palette tab to expand the palette to reveal the option for the palette **28**.
2. Continue to click the arrow to toggle through each of the palette display states.

TIP The palette menu also contains a Show Options command that toggles between the palette display states.

You can also shrink a palette so that it only displays the palette tab.

To shrink a palette display:

◆ Click the collapse box (also called the minimize button) **29** to collapse the palette.

To expand a palette display:

◆ If the palette is collapsed, click the collapse box **29** to expand the palette.

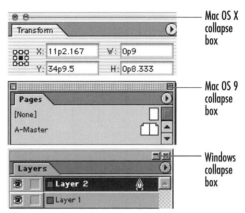

Mac OS X collapse box

Mac OS 9 collapse box

Windows collapse box

Some of the palettes allow you to display small palette rows which helps you save screen space.

29 *Click the* **collapse box** *to shorten the display of a palette.*

To display small palette rows:

◆ Choose Small Palette Rows from the palette menu to display the smaller text and symbols **30** for that palette.

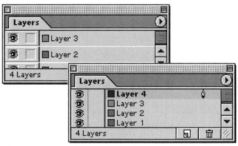

30 **Small palette rows** *(lower window) display more information in the same size palette.*

Another way to save screen space is to move one palette so that it is located within the boundaries of another. This is called *nesting*.

To nest palettes:

1. Position the cursor over the palette tab.

2. Drag the tab so that the outline is inside another palette. A black rectangle around the inside perimeter of the palette indicates that the two palettes will be nested **31**.

3. Release the mouse button. The palette appears next to the other palette **32**.

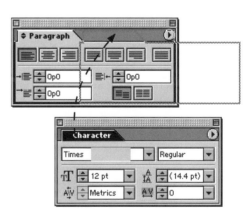

31 *Drag the palette tab into another palette area to* **nest palettes.**

Working with Palettes

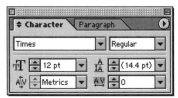

32 *The results of nesting one palette into another.*

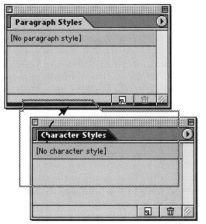

33 *Drag the palette tab to the bottom edge of another palette to* **dock the palettes** *together.*

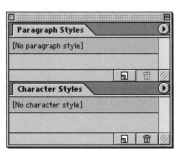

34 *Docked palettes are displayed together.*

To unnest palettes:

1. Drag the palette tab so that the outline is completely outside the other palette.

2. Release the mouse button. The palette appears as a separate palette.

You can also dock palettes so they open, close and move together. The palettes take up less space than if they were separated, yet unlike nested palettes, both can be seen at once.

To dock a palette:

1. Drag one palette tab to the bottom edge of another palette **33**. A dark line appears at the bottom of the palette area.

2. Release the mouse. This docks the palette underneath the top palette **34**.

To undock palettes:

1. Drag one palette tab so that the outline is completely outside the other palette.

2. Release the mouse button. The palette appears as a separate palette.

Working with Interface Elements

Each of the dialog boxes and palettes has interface elements to control the features.

Button

Click to activate a button **35**.

Checkbox

Click to activate a checkbox **36**. If there are multiple checkboxes, you can select more than one box.

Field

Highlight the value and type a new number in a field **37**.

Field arrows

Click the up or down arrows next to a field **38** to increase or decrease the values.

TIP Click the field name to activate the field. You can then use the up or down keyboard arrows to increase or decrease the values in the field.

Icon button

Click the icon button that represents the feature you want to choose **39**.

Pop-up combo box

Click to choose the items in the list **40**.

Pop-up menu

Click to choose the items in the list **41**.

Radio button

Click to select a radio button **42**. You can only choose one radio button in a group.

Slider

Drag a slider to increase or decrease the value in a field **43**.

35 *Click to activate a* button.

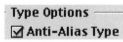

36 *Click to activate a* checkbox.

37 *Enter values in a* field.

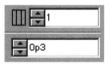

38 *Click the* field arrows *to increase or decrease the values.*

39 *Click to choose an* icon button.

40 *Click to choose an entry in* a list.

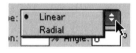

41 *Click to choose an entry in a* pop-up menu.

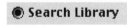

42 *Click to select a* radio button.

43 *Drag to change the values of a* slider.

Working with Interface Elements

44 *An example of the Mac OS X interface elements.*

The Mac OS X Interface

It wouldn't be fair not to mention the new Macintosh Aqua interface that is seen when InDesign runs on OS X. The buttons, checkboxes, and radio buttons all have the glassy Aqua appearance **44**.

As yummy as the interface looks, the features all work the same as their more pedestrian OS 9 counterparts.

Using the Toolbox

The Toolbox contains 27 tools as well as controls for the colors of fills and strokes **45**. Some of the tools have fly-out controls that let you access the other tools in the category.

To choose a tool:

◆   Click the tool in the Toolbox.

or

Tap the individual keyboard shortcuts for each of the tools. *(See the Appendix for a list of all the default keyboard commands.)*

To see the tool keyboard shortcuts:

◆   Move the cursor over the tool and pause. A tool tip appears with the name of the tool and the keyboard shortcut **46**.

TIP If you don't see the tool tip after pausing for a moment, make sure the Tool Tips control is turned on in the application preferences *(see Chapter 19, "Customizing InDesign")*.

TIP You can change or add keyboard shortcuts for tools using the keyboard shortcut controls *(see Chapter 19, "Customizing InDesign")*.

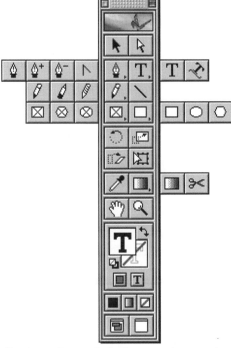

45 *The Toolbox with the fly-out tools exposed.*

46 *Pause over a tool to see the tool tip containing the tool name and keyboard shortcut.*

Tools that have a small triangle in their box have other tools hidden in a fly-out panel.

To open the related:

1. Press the tool slot with the fly-out triangle.

2. Choose one of the tools listed in the fly-out panel 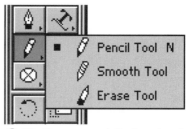.

Using Contextual Menus

Contextual menus are menus that change depending on the type of object selected or where the mouse is positioned ④⑧. The benefit of contextual menus is that you don't have to move all the way up to the menu bar to invoke a command. Also the menu changes to provide you commands that are appropriate for the type of object chosen.

To display contextual menus:

◆ (Mac) Hold the Control key and click the mouse button.

or

(Win) Click the right mouse button.

TIP The contextual menu cursor appears as you hold the Control key.

④⑦ *The* **fly-out panel** *displays the additional tools for that slot in the Toolbox.*

Contextual cursor

④⑧ *The* **contextual menu** *changes depending on what type of object is selected.*

DOCUMENT SETUP 2

Billions of years ago, when dinosaurs ruled the earth—or just seventeen years ago, before the beginning of desktop publishing—people prepared documents for printing using pieces of stiff board. They marked up the boards with special blue pencils to indicate the edges of the pages. They drew marks that specified where the margins and columns should be and how the pages should be trimmed. This board, called a *mechanical,* was used as the layout for the document.

Unlike the board mechanicals of the past, InDesign documents are electronic layouts. Just as with the board mechanicals, you need to set the page sizes, margins, and column widths. However, since you are not using a pencil but a computer, you have additional controls for how the document is laid out.

It helps enormously if you know most of the details about the document's layout before you begin work. For instance, you might find out in the middle of a project that the margins are too wide and the text won't fit the alloted space. While you can always change the margin width later, it helps if you have an idea of what size they should be before you do too much work. Of course, changing an electronic layout takes far less time than it did with board mechanicals that old dinosaurs like me used to use.

Starting Documents

When you create a new document, you have to answer a lot of questions in the Document Setup dialog box.

To start a new document:

1. Choose **File** > **New** > **Document**. This opens the Document Setup dialog box ❶.

2. Type the number of pages in your document in the Number of Pages field.

3. Check Facing Pages to set your document with left-hand and right-hand pages. *(See the next page for more information on facing pages.)*

4. Check Master Text Frame to make it easy to automatically add text to pages. *(See page 201 for more information on master text frames.)*

5. Use the Page Size pop-up list to set the size of your page. *(See the next page for more information on the page size.)*

6. Set the Orientation to portrait or landscape. *(See page 18 for more information on the page orientation.)*

7. Enter the size of the margins in the Margins fields. *(See page 18 for more information on setting the margins.)*

8. Set the number of columns and the gutter width in the Columns Number and Gutter fields. *(See page 19 for more information on columns and gutters.)*

9. Click OK. The document appears in the window ❷.

TIP The pages are surrounded by an area called the pasteboard. Like a drawing table, you can set items there for later use. Items on the pasteboard do not print.

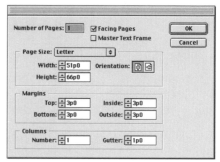

❶ *The* **Document Setup dialog box** *offers basic layout options.*

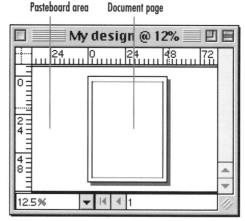

❷ *Each document page is surrounded by the pasteboard area where you can temporarily store objects for use later.*

Left margin   Right margin

③ *The left and right margins on* **nonfacing pages.**

Outside margin   Inside margins   Outside margin

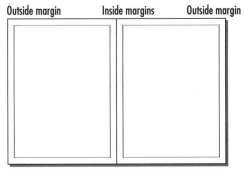

④ *The outside and inside margins on* **facing pages.**

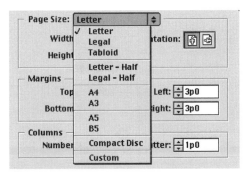

⑤ *The* **Page Size** *menu offers standard U.S. and international paper sizes, as well as customization controls.*

Choosing Layout Options

The term *facing pages* refers to documents such as this book where pages on one side of its spine face the pages on the other side. (This is also called a *spread.*) Single pages, such as advertisements, are set with facing pages turned off.

To set facing pages:

◆ With the Document Setup dialog box open, click Facing Pages. This gives you left- and right-hand pages in your document **③**.

TIP When a document is set for facing pages, the left and right margins change to inside and outside margins **④**.

The page size is the size of the individual pages of the document.

To set the size of the page:

◆ Choose of one of the following 11 choices from the Page Size menu **⑤**:

- **Letter**, 8 1/2 by 11 inches.
- **Legal**, 8 1/2 by 14 inches.
- **Tabloid**, 11 by 17 inches.
- **Letter–Half**, 8 1/2 by 5 1/2 inches.
- **Legal–Half**, 8 1/2 by 7 inches.
- **A4**, 21 by 29.7 centimeters.
- **A3**, 29.7 by 42 centimeters.
- **A5**, 14.8 by 21 centimeters.
- **B5**, 17.6 by 25 centimeters.
- **Compact Disc**, 4.7222 by 4.75 inches.
- **Custom**, which allows you to enter your own specific values.

TIP The A4, A3, A5, and B5 sizes are used primarily outside of the United States.

TIP If you change the values in the Width or the Height fields, the Page Size automatically switches to the Custom setting.

The term *orientation* refers to how the page is positioned, either up and down or sideways.

To set the orientation:

◆ Click the Portrait orientation to create a document where the width is always less than the height ❻.

or

Click the Landscape orientation to create a document where the width is always greater than the height ❻.

To set the margins:

1. Click the field arrows or enter an amount for the Top and Bottom fields.

2. If the document is set for facing pages, click the field arrows or enter an amount for the Inside and Outside fields ❼.

or

If the document is not set for facing pages, click the field arrows or enter an amount for the Left and Right margins ❽.

To set the columns and gutters:

1. Click the field arrows or enter an amount for the number of columns ❾.

2. Click the field arrows or enter an amount for the *gutter,* or the space between the columns ❾.

TIP The columns and gutters act as guidelines on your page ❿. You can still place text or graphics across the columns or gutters.

To set the document defaults:

◆ Change the document setup or any of the other attributes with no page open, to make all new pages have the same settings when opened.

Portrait   Landscape

❻ *The* **Orientation** choices *let you set the position of the page.*

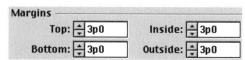

❼ *The margin settings for a document with facing pages.*

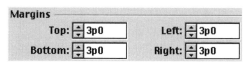

❽ *The margin settings for a document with non-facing pages.*

❾ *The* **column settings** *let you set the number of columns and the amount of space in the gutter between the columns.*

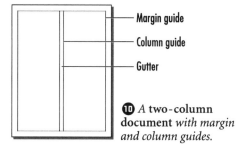

❿ *A two-column document with margin and column guides.*

⓫ *The* **Document Setup dialog box** *for an existing document.*

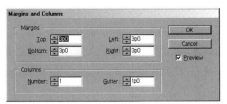

⓬ *The* **Margins and Columns dialog box** *for an existing document.*

Changing Layout Options

You may discover that you need to change some of the settings of a document. When you start a new document, all the settings appear in one dialog box. However, after you begin working on the document you must use two separate controls to make changes to the document.

To change the document setup:

1. Choose **File > Document Setup** to open the Document Setup dialog box **⓫**.

2. Make whatever changes you want to the following settings:
   - Number of Pages
   - Facing Pages
   - Page Size
   - Orientation

3. Click OK to apply the changes to the document.

To change the margins and columns:

1. Choose **Layout > Margins and Columns** to open the Margins and Columns dialog box **⓬**.

2. Make whatever changes you want to the following settings:
   - Margins
   - Number of columns
   - Gutter or the width of the space between the columns

3. Click OK to apply the changes to the document.

TIP Changing the margins and columns while on a page or spread changes the settings only for that page or spread. To change the settings for all the pages, you need to work with the Master Page. *(See Chapter 10, "Pages and Books" for more information on master pages.)*

Using Document Rulers

Rather than hold a ruler up to your monitor, InDesign gives you electronic rulers you can customize or hide.

To show and hide the document rulers:

◆ To see the rulers along the top and left edges of the document window 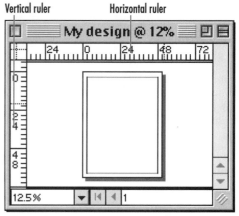, choose **View > Show Rulers.**

or

To hide the rulers, choose **View > Hide Rulers.**

⓭ *The horizontal and vertical rulers.*

Vertical ruler   Horizontal ruler

You can change the rulers to different units of measurement. This is especially helpful if you receive instructions written in measurements with which you are not familiar.

To change the unit of measurement:

1. Choose **Edit > Preferences > Units & Increments.** This opens the Units & Increments dialog box. (In Mac OS X choose **InDesign > Preferences > Units & Increments.**)

2. For the Horizontal and Vertical settings, choose one of the measurements from the pop-up lists 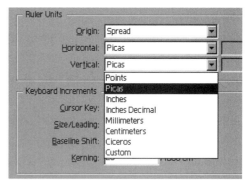.

TIP You can have different units for the horizontal and the vertical rulers. For instance, the vertical ruler can match the document's leading so that each unit equals each line of copy. The horizontal unit can be in inches or picas.

3. If you choose Custom, enter the number of points for each unit on the ruler.

TIP You can also change the units with the ruler contextual menus . *(See page 14 for more information on how to access contextual menus.)*

⓮ *The choices for the rulers units of measurement.*

⓯ *The contextual menu when clicked over a ruler.*

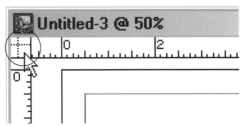

16 *The* zero point indicator *of the rulers.*

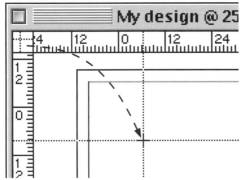

17 *You set the ruler's zero point by dragging the zero point indicator to a new position on the page.*

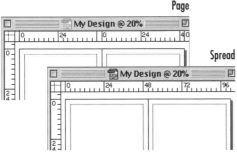

18 *You can set the rulers for a document to reset for each page or to cross each spread.*

The rulers start numbering at the top-left corner of the page. You may want to move this point, called a *zero point,* to a different position. This might help you judge how much space you have from one spot of the page to another.

To reposition the zero point:

1. Position the cursor over the zero point crosshairs at the upper-left corner of the rulers **16**.

2. Drag the zero point to the new position on the page **17**.

3. Release the mouse button to position the zero point.

TIP Double-click the zero point crosshairs in the corner of the rulers to reset the zero point to the upper-left corner.

If you are working on a project such as an advertising spread, it may be easier to position objects if the rulers continue across the spine of the pages. InDesign lets you customize the origin of the rulers **18**.

To set the origin of the rulers:

1. Choose **Edit** > **Preferences** > **Units & Increments.** (In Mac OS X choose **Edit** > **Preferences** > **Units & Increments.**)

2. Set the Ruler Units Origin menu to Page, Spread, or Spine **14**.

   or

   Choose a setting from the ruler contextual menu **15**.

TIP There is no difference between the page or spine settings unless there are more than three pages to the spread.

Setting Margin and Column Guides

Guides are nonprinting lines that help you position text and graphics on the page. InDesign has different types of guides: Margin guides can be used to indicate where elements, such as page numbers, belong; column guides can be used to divide text from graphics.

To show and hide guides:

◆ To see the margin, column, and ruler guides, choose **View** > **Show Guides.**

   or

   To hide the guides, choose **View** > **Hide Guides.**

TIP The Show Guides command also displays the ruler guides. *(For more information on ruler guides, see the following page.)*

If you have not changed the default settings, InDesign displays the margin guides in pink and the column guides in blue. You may want to change those colors, especially if you have objects on the page that use similar colors.

To change the appearance of margin and column guides:

1. Choose **Edit** > **Preferences** > **Guides** (Mac OS 9 and Win) or **InDesign** > **Preferences** > **Guides** (Mac OS X) to open the Guides Preferences dialog box ⑲.

2. Use the Margins pop-up list to set the color of the margin guides.

3. Use the Columns pop-up list to set the color of the column guides.

4. Check Guides in Back to position the guides behind text and graphics on the page ⑳.

⑲ *The dialog box for the* guides preferences.

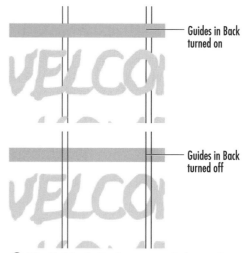

Guides in Back turned on

Guides in Back turned off

⑳ *The* **Guides in Back** command *changes how guides are displayed as they pass through text and artwork.*

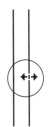

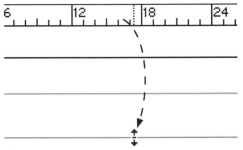

㉑ *The* **two-headed arrow** *indicates that a column guide can be moved.*

㉒ *You can drag ruler guides out from the horizontal ruler or vertical ruler.*

There may be times when you want to move the column guides manually. This gives you a custom guide setting.

To move column guides:

1. Position the cursor over the guide you want to move.

2. Press the mouse button. The cursor turns into a two-headed arrow that indicates that the column has been selected **㉑**.

3. Drag the column guide to the new position.

TIP You cannot change the width of the gutter space between the columns by moving a column guide. But you can change it in the Margins and Columns dialog box *(see page 19)*.

Using Ruler Guides

Another type of guide is the ruler guide. Ruler guides are more flexible than margin or column guides and can be positioned anywhere on the page to help with object placement. You create individual ruler guides by pulling a guide out from the ruler.

To pull a guide from the ruler:

1. Position the cursor over the horizontal or vertical ruler. *(See page 20 for how to display the rulers.)*

2. Press the mouse button. The cursor turns into a two-headed arrow.

3. Drag to pull the guide out onto the page **㉒**.

Using Ruler Guides

Rather than pulling guides out one at a time, you can also create a series of ruler guides in rows and columns.

To create rows and columns using guides:

1. Choose **Layout** > **Create Guides**. This opens the Create Guides dialog box 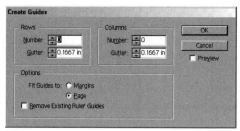.

2. Type the number of rows (horizontal guides) in the Rows Number field.

3. Type the amount for the space between the rows in the Rows Gutter field.

4. Type the number of columns (vertical guides) in the Columns Number field.

5. Type the amount for the space between the columns in the Columns Gutter field.

6. Choose between Fit Guides to Margins or Page 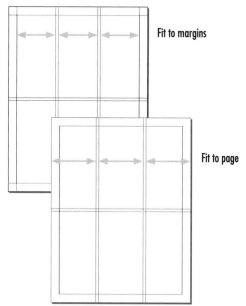.

7. Check Remove Existing Ruler Guides to delete all the ruler guides that were previously on the page.

8. Click OK to apply the guides.

TIP Check Preview to see the guides on the page change as you enter the values within the dialog box.

To reposition ruler guides:

1. Position the cursor over the guide you want to move.

2. Press the mouse button. The cursor turns into a two-headed arrow and the guide changes to a darker color. This indicates that the guide has been selected.

3. Drag the ruler guide to a new position.

You may want to lock your guides so they don't move inadvertently.

To lock guides:

♦ Choose **View** > **Lock Guides**.

TIP Choose the command again to unlock the guides.

㉓ *The* **Create Guides** *dialog box lets you automatically add many guides on a page.*

Fit to margins

Fit to page

㉔ **Fit Guides to Margin** *spaces the guides inside the page margins.* **Fit Guides to Page** *spaces the guide inside the page trim.*

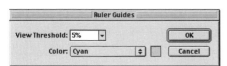

25 *Use the* **Ruler Guides dialog box** *to change the color of the ruler guides. You can also set at what magnification the guides are seen.*

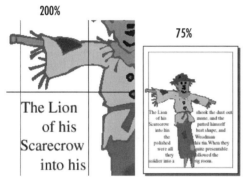

26 *A* **view threshold** *of 200% means the guides are visible only when the magnification is 200% or higher.*

Just as you can change margin guides, you can change the color of ruler guides. You can also set the magnification at which the guides are not visible.

To change the appearance of ruler guides:

1. Choose **Layout** > **Ruler Guides** to open the dialog box **25**.
2. Use the Color pop-up list to pick the color for the ruler guides.
3. Set a percentage for the View Threshold. This sets the amount of magnification below which the ruler guides are not displayed **26**.

TIP Increase the View Threshold if you have many guides on the page. This hides the guides at low magnifications and shows them at higher ones. *(See page 27 for setting the view magnifications.)*

Objects can be set to automatically snap to guides as you move them. This makes it easier to align objects to guides.

To make objects snap to guides:

◆ Choose **View** > **Snap to Guides**.

TIP Choose the command again to turn off the feature.

To change the snap-to distance:

1. Choose **File** > **Preferences** > **Guides**.
2. Enter an amount in the Snap to Zone in the Guides preferences **19**. This is how close to a guide (in pixels) the cursor dragging an object must be before it snaps to the guide.

Using Ruler Guides

Working With Document Grids

Ruler guides aren't the only way to align object. The document grid can be used as a structure for designing pages. The baseline grid is used to keep lines of text even. *(See page 296 for how to align text to the baseline grid.)*

To display the grids:

◆ Choose View > Show Document Grid 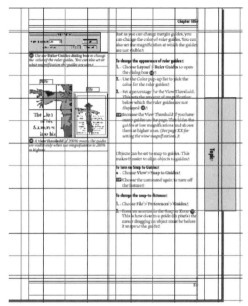 or View > Show Baseline Grid.

To hide the grids:

◆ Choose View > Hide Document Grid or View > Hide Baseline Grid.

To change the grid apperance:

1. Choose Edit > Preferences > Grids to open the Grids Preferences dialog box ㉘. In Mac OS X, choose InDesign > Preferences > Grids.

2. Use the Color pop-up list to change the grid color.

3. Enter an amount in the Horizontal and Vertical Gridline Every field to set the distance between the main gridlines.

4. Enter an amount in the Subdivisions field to create lighter gridlines between the main gridlines.

5. Enter an amount in the Start field to set where the baseline grid should start.

6. Enter a percentage in the View Threshold field. This sets the lowest magnification at which the grid is visible.

7. Check Grids in Back to position the gridlines behind objects on the page ㉙.

To turn on Snap to Grid:

◆ Choose View > Snap to Document Grid. If Snap to Document Grid is checked, the feature is already turned on.

㉗ *Choose* **Show Document Grid** *to see the horizontal and vertical gridlines.*

㉘ *The* **Grids Preferences dialog box** *lets you control the display and arrangement of the document grid.*

㉙ *The* **Fit Entire Pasteboard command** *shows the page as well as the pasteboard.*

InDesign's "Smart" View Commands

If you have used other page layout programs, you may not realize how smart some of InDesign's View commands are. These are the commands Fit Page in Window, Fit Spread in Window, and Entire Pasteboard.

In other programs if you choose the Fit Page in Window command, the magnification changes to show the entire page. If you then change the size of the window, the magnification is no longer the correct size to show the entire page.

InDesign, however, is much smarter. When you choose those three View commands, InDesign continues to display the page, spread, or pasteboard even if you resize the window. The magnification dynamically changes as you change the size of the window.

The command will stay active until you choose a new view or manually change the magnification. That's pretty smart!

Changing the Magnification

Magnification refers to the size of the document as it appears on your screen. InDesign gives you many ways to change the magnification setting. Some of the quickest and easiest ways to change the magnification settings are to use View commands.

To zoom with the view commands:

1. To increase the magnification, choose **View > Zoom In**.

2. To decrease the magnification, choose **View > Zoom Out**.

3. To see all of the current page, choose **View > Fit Page In Window**. This changes the magnification setting to whatever amount is necessary to see the entire page.

TIP Small monitors force you to use small magnifications to see the entire page. Larger monitors show the entire page at magnifications that are easier to read.

4. To see all of the current spread, choose **View > Fit Spread In Window**. *(See page 21 for more information on working with spreads.)*

5. To see the document at a 100% magnification, choose **View > Actual Size**.

6. To see the entire pasteboard area, choose **View > Entire Pasteboard** **㉙**.

InDesign lets you view the page with a wide range of magnification settings. You can set the page to a specific magnification amount by selecting from the magnification list.

To use the magnification list:
1. Click the control at the bottom-left corner of the document window to display the magnification list ③⓪.
2. Choose one of the magnifications in the list.

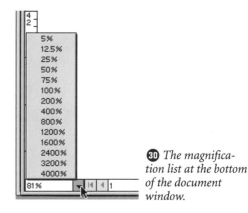

③⓪ *The magnification list at the bottom of the document window.*

You can also view specific magnifications not in the list.

To enter a specific magnification amount :
1. Double-click or drag across the magnification shown in the bottom-left corner of the document window.
2. Type a number between 5 and 4000.
   TIP It is not necessary to type the % sign.
3. Press Return or Enter to apply the setting.

Magnification Shortcuts

Because the View commands are used so often, the keyboard shortcuts are listed here. You can also find those shortcuts listed on the View menu.

Mac Commands

Zoom In	Cmd-=
Zoom Out	Cmd-hyphen
Fit Page in Window	Cmd-0
Fit Spread in Window	Cmd-Opt-0
Actual Size	Cmd-1

Windows Commands

Zoom In	Ctrl-=
Zoom Out	Ctrl-hyphen
Fit Page in Window	Ctrl-0
Fit Spread in Window	Ctrl-Alt-0
Actual Size	Ctrl-1

31 *Use the* **Zoom tool** *to change the magnification of the page.*

32 *Drag the Zoom tool diagonally to magnify a specific area. The marquee indicates the area to be selected.*

33 *The selected area fills the window after you release the mouse button.*

Using the Zoom and Hand Tools

The Zoom tool lets you jump to a specific magnification and position on the page. The Hand tool moves the view to a new position.

To use the Zoom tool:

1. Click the Zoom tool in the Toolbox **31**. The cursor turns into a magnifying glass.

2. Click the Zoom tool on the area you want to zoom in on. Click as many times as is necessary to change the magnification.

TIP Press Cmd/Ctrl and Spacebar to access the Zoom tool without leaving the tool that is currently selected.

TIP Each click of the Zoom tool changes the magnification to the next setting in the magnification list.

TIP Press the Opt/Alt key while in the Zoom tool to decrease magnification. The icon changes from a plus sign (+) to a minus sign (–).

TIP Double-click the Zoom tool in the Toolbox to set the view to the actual size (100%).

A *marquee zoom* allows you to zoom quickly to a certain magnification and position.

To create a marquee zoom:

- Drag the Zoom tool diagonally across the area you want to see. Release the mouse button to zoom in **32** – **33**.

You can also use the Hand tool (sometimes called the *Grabber* tool) to move around within the area of the document. This is more flexible than using the scrollbars.

34 *Use the* **Hand tool** *to move the page around the window.*

To use the Hand tool:

1. Click the Hand tool in the Toolbox **34**.

2. Drag the Hand tool to move around the page.

TIP Double-click the Hand tool in the Toolbox to fit the entire page in the window.

TIP Hold the Spacebar to access the Hand tool without leaving the tool currently selected.

As stated above, you can access the Hand tool by pressing the Spacebar. If you are inside a text frame, the Spacebar adds spaces inside the text. Fortunately there is a special technique to access the Hand tool without creating extra spaces.

To access the Hand tool in a text block:

1. Hold the Cmd/Ctrl key. This changes the cursor to the either the Selection or the Direct Selection tool.

2. Add the Spacebar to the Cmd/Ctrl key. This changes the cursor to the Zoom tool.

3. Release the Cmd/Ctrl key. This leaves the Spacebar pressed and the Hand tool active.

Playing the Keyboard "Bass Notes"

I confess! I haven't chosen the Zoom or Hand tools in years. Rather than move the mouse all the way over to the toolbox, I use the keyboard shortcuts.

On the Mac, I keep my fingers lightly resting on the Cmd, Opt, and Spacebar keys. By changing which keys are pressed, I alternate between the Zoom In, Zoom Out, and Hand tools.

On Windows, I do the same thing with the Ctrl, Alt, and Spacebar keys.

So, as my right hand moves the mouse around and taps other keys on the keyboard, my left hand is always playing the three bass notes of the keyboard.

Using the Zoom and Hand Tools

Zoom out

Magnification field   Zoom slider

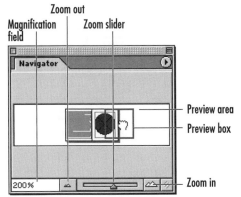

Preview area

Preview box

Zoom in

200%

35 *The elements of the Navigator palette.*

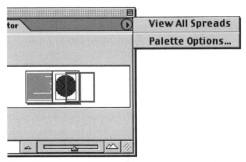

View All Spreads

Palette Options...

36 *The Navigator palette menu lets you change the number of spreads displayed.*

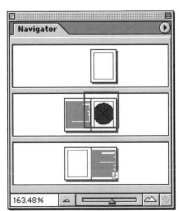

Navigator

163.48%

37 *When View All Spreads is chosen, the Navigator displays all the spreads in the document.*

Using the Navigator Palette

The Navigator palette combines the functions of both the Zoom and Hand tools.

To use the Navigator zoom buttons:

1. If the Navigator palette is not already open, choose **Window > Navigator**. This opens the Navigator palette **35**.

2. Click the Zoom In button to increase the magnification.

3. Click the Zoom Out button to decrease the magnification.

To set a specific magnification:

1. Highlight the value in the Magnification field and enter the specific magnification.

2. Press Return or Enter.

The Zoom slider in the Navigator palette lets you increase or decrease the magnification.

To use the Zoom slider:

◆ Drag the Zoom slider to the right to increase the magnification.

or

Drag the slider to the left to decrease the magnification.

The Navigator palette can display a single spread or all the spreads in the document.

To change the view spread options:

◆ Choose View All Spreads from the Navigator palette menu **36**. This displays all the spreads in the document **37**.

TIP When you choose View All Spreads, the menu choice changes to View Active Spread. This displays only the currently selected spread. *(See Chapter 10, "Pages and Books" for more information on working with spreads.)*

The Preview Area within the Navigator palette can also be used to move around the document.

To move using the Navigator Preview Area:

1. Position the cursor inside the Preview Area of the Navigator palette. The cursor changes into a hand 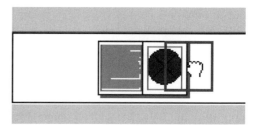.

2. Drag the Hand around the Preview Area. The Preview Box moves to change the area displayed within the document window.

➌➑ *The* **Hand cursor** *inside the Preview Area of the Navigator palette.*

The View Box is the rectangle that shows the size of the area displayed in the document window. You can change the color of that rectangle.

To change the color of the View Box:

1. Choose Palette Options from the Navigator menu. This opens the Palette Options dialog box **➌➒**.

2. Use the Color list to pick a new color.

➌➒ *The* **Palette Options** *let you change the color of the View Box inside the Navigator palette.*

Controlling Windows

The window commands let you view one document in two windows and control the display of multiple windows.

To see a document in two windows:

1. Choose **Window > New Window.** This creates a second window containing the document.

2. Choose **Window > Tile.** This changes the size of the two windows and positions them side by side on your screen **➍➋**.

   or

   Choose **Window > Cascade.** This stacks all the open windows so that their title bars are visible.

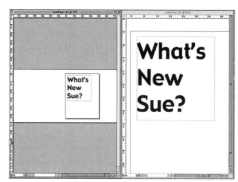

➍➋ *Two views of the same document set as tiled windows.*

41 The **Save As** dialog box (Win).

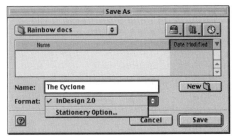

42 The **Save As** dialog box (Mac).

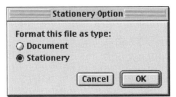

43 The **Stationery Option** dialog box (Mac).

Saving Documents

After you work on a document for even a little while, you must save your work as a file to a hard drive or disk. This is vital so that you don't lose important information should your computer crash.

To save and name a file (Win):

1. Choose **File** > **Save** or **File** > **Save As**. This opens the Save As dialog box **41**.

2. Use the Save In field to choose a destination disk and folder for the file.

3. Use the File Name field to name the file.

4. Use the Save As Type field to choose between an InDesign document or an InDesign Template.

TIP The template format saves the file so that each time it is opened, it opens as an untitled document. This protects the document from inadvertant changes.

5. Click Save to save the file and close the dialog box.

To save and name a file (Mac):

1. Choose **File** > **Save** or **File** > **Save As**. This opens the Save As dialog box **42**.

2. Use the Macintosh navigational elements to choose a destination disk and folder for the file.

3. Use the Name field to name the file.

4. Use the Format pop-up list to choose between an InDesign document or the Stationery option.

5. If you choose the Stationery option, click Stationery in the Stationery Option dialog box **43**.

TIP The Stationery format saves the file so that each time it is opened, it opens as an untitled document. This protects the document from inadvertent changes.

As you work, you may want to spin off a copy of your document under another name. The Save a Copy command makes this easy to do.

To create a copy of a document:

1. Choose **File** > **Save a Copy**. This opens the Save As dialog box.

2. Use the same steps as described in the two previous exercises to save the file.

3. Click Save. The copy of the document is saved while you can continue to work on your current file.

Like many other programs, InDesign lets you revert to the previously saved version of a document.

To revert a document:

◆ Choose **File** > **Revert**. The document is closed and then re-opened at the state when you last saved it.

It happens—someday, somehow your computer will crash or you will be forced to restart it without saving your work. Fortunately InDesign has an automatic recovery option that can save your work.

To recover a file:

1. Restart the computer after the crash or data loss.

2. Start InDesign. Any files that were open when the crash occurred will be automatically opened.

3. Choose **File** > **Save As** to save the file with a new name and destination.

TIP The restored data is a temporary version of the file and must be saved in order to ensure the integrity of the data.

The Three Different Save Commands

The first time you look under the File menu you may be a little confused by the three different commands for saving documents. What are the differences between Save, Save As, and Save a Copy?

The first time you save an untitled document, there is no difference between choosing **File** > **Save** and **File** > **Save As**. Both commands bring up the Save As dialog box.

Once you have named a file, the Save command adds new work to the file without changing the file's name. The Save As command will always open the dialog box where you can change the file's name or location.

I use the Save command almost all the time. That way I only have to remember one keystroke: Cmd/Ctrl-S. The only time I use the Save As command is if I want to change the name of a document or save it somewhere else.

The Save a Copy command is different. When you save a copy, you can save the file under a new name. However, unlike the Save As command, you continue to work on the file you were working on.

I use the Save a Copy command when I am about to do something strange or bizarre to my work. The Save a Copy command lets me create a version of the file that I know I can fall back on.

Saving Documents

Opening and Closing Files

InDesign gives you options for opening and closing files.

To open a file within InDesign:

1. Choose File > Open.

2. Use the navigation controls to select the file you want to open.

TIP You can also open a document by double-clicking its icon.

To open recently saved documents:

◆ Choose File > Open Recent and then choose one of the files listed in the submenu.

TIP InDesign lists the ten last opened documents in the submenu.

To close a document:

◆ Choose File > Close.

or

Click the Close box in the document window.

Opening QuarkXPress or PageMaker Files

InDesign can convert documents and templates from QuarkXPress 3.3 or later and Adobe PageMaker 6.5 or later. Simply choose **File > Open** and choose the file. InDesign converts the file into a new InDesign document.

How good is the conversion? It's great for templates which consist of the layout without any text. All the master pages *(see page 201)* are converted along with the style sheets *(see page 272)* and colors *(see Chapter 5)*. This lets you use your old templates to produce new work in InDesign. Graphics pasted—not placed—into QuarkXPress or PageMaker are not converted.

The conversion may change documents with lots of text. For instance, InDesign arranges type with a very sophisticated composition engine *(see page 289)*. This means that text could move to new lines when it appears in the InDesign document.

If you need to make just one or two small changes to an old document, you're better off opening the file in QuarkXPress or PageMaker and making the changes to the original files.

However, if you need to completely redo a document, export the text from the file, and then use InDesign to convert the template into an InDesign file. You can then use that template for all new documents.

BASIC TEXT 3

When I started in advertising around twenty-five years ago, setting type was an involved process. First, the copywriter typed out the text on pieces of paper. The art director or typographer then marked up the page of copy with a red pencil to indicate the typeface, point size, leading, and so on. Then, the copy was sent to a typesetting house where a typesetter retyped the text into a special typesetting machine. The text was printed onto special photographic paper and sent back the next morning. The copywriter then had to proof the text to make sure that there were no errors.

That's why I am amazed every time I use a program such as InDesign to set text. I don't type the copy onto a piece of paper; I type right onto my actual layout. I don't have to send the copy out overnight; it's right there on my computer screen. And I know that the only mistakes are the ones I make myself!

Creating Text Frames

InDesign holds text in objects called *frames*.

TIP You can resize or reshape text frames like you can other objects. *(See Chapter 4, "Working with Objects" for more details on creating and working with objects.)*

To create a text frame with the Type tool:

1. Click the Type tool in the Toolbox ❶.
2. Move the cursor to the page. The cursor changes to the Type tool cursor ❷.
3. Drag diagonally to create the frame ❸.

TIP The frame starts from the horizontal line that intersects the text frame cursor.

4. Release the mouse button. The text frame appears with an insertion point that indicates you can type in the frame.

The Text tool will always create rectangular frames. However, you can use the frame tools to create other geometric shapes to hold text.

TIP The frame tools also lets you use numerical settings to specify the exact dimensions of a frame *(see page 67)*.

To draw an elliptical frames:

1. Click the Ellipse tool in the Toolbox ❹.
2. Drag diagonally to create the ellipse ❺.
3. Release the mouse button when the ellipse is the correct size.

❶ *Choose the* **Type tool** *in the Toolbox to work with text.*

❷ *The cursor set to create a text frame.*

❸ *Drag diagonally with the Text tool to create a text frame.*

❹ *The* **Ellipse tool** *in the Toolbox.*

❺ *Drag diagonally to create an ellipse.*

Creating Text Frames

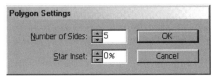

❻ *The* **Polygon tool** *in the Toolbox.*

❼ *Use the* **Polygon Settings dialog box** *to change the shape and the number of sides of a polygon.*

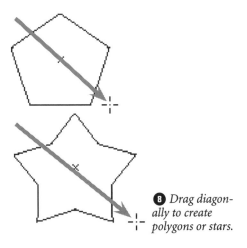

❽ *Drag diagonally to create polygons or stars.*

Unassigned Frames

The Ellipse, Polygon, and Rectangle tools create frames that are unassigned. This means they hold neither text nor graphics. But don't let the unassigned designation mislead you. It doesn't really matter if a frame is unassigned or not.

You can convert unassigned frames to hold text *(see page 40)*, or you can convert unassigned frames to hold graphics *(see page 149)*.

The Polygon tool also lets you draw stars as well as ordinary polygons.

To draw a polygon frame:

1. Double-click the Polygon tool in the Toolbox **❻**. This opens the Polygon Settings dialog box **❼**.
2. Enter a number in the field for the number of sides.
3. Leave the Star Inset amount as 0%. If you increase the star inset, you create a star. *(See the next exercise.)*
4. Drag across the page to create the polygon **❽**.

TIP Press the up or down arrow keys as you drag to increase or decrease the number of sides of the polygon.

5. Release the mouse button when the polygon or star is the correct size.

To create a star frame:

1. Double-click the Polygon tool in the Toolbox to open the Polygon Settings dialog box **❼**.
2. Enter a number in the Number of Sides field for the number of outer points.
3. Enter a value for the Star Inset amount. The greater the amount, the sharper the points will be.
4. Drag to create the star **❽**.

TIP Press the up or down arrow keys as you drag to increase or decrease the number of points of the star.

TIP Press the left or right arrow keys as you drag to increase or decrease the star inset.

5. Release the mouse button when the star is the correct size.

Creating Text Frames

You can create rectangular frames using the Rectangle tool.

9 The **Rectangle tool** *in the Toolbox.*

To draw a rectangular frame:

1. Click the Rectangle tool in the Toolbox **9**.

2. Drag diagonally to create the rectangle **10**.

3. Release the mouse button when the rectangle is the correct size.

10 *Drag diagonally to create a rectangle.*

The Elliptical and Rectangular frame tools let you numerically specify the frame size.

To set the size of a frame numerically:

1. Choose the Ellipse or Rectangle tool from the Toolbox.

2. Position the cursor where you want to create the frame.

3. Click. A dialog box appears **11**.

4. Set the Width and Height of the frame.

5. Click OK. The frame appears with its upper-left point where you first clicked.

TIP Hold the Opt/Alt key as you click to create position the centerpoint of the frame at that point.

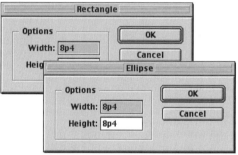

11 *The* **Ellipse and Rectangle dialog boxes** *let you specify the width and height of a frame.*

Frames created with the Ellipse, Polygon, and Rectangle tools must be converted to use as text frames.

To convert unassigned frames:

1. Select the frame you want to convert.

2. Choose the Type tool and click inside the frame.

   or

   Choose **Object > Content > Text**. An insertion point appears indicating that you can begin typing.

Tips for Drawing Frames

There are several keyboard shortcuts you can press as you draw frames:

- Hold the **Shift key** to constrain the frame to a square, circle, or uniform polygon.

- Hold the **Opt/Alt key** to draw the frame from the center outward.

- Hold the **Spacebar** to reposition the frame as you draw.

Creating Text Frames

.ghtened to see the Witch
away like brown sugar
yes.
now water would be the ⊞

⓬ *The* **overflow symbol** *indicates that there is more text in the frame than is visible.*

"See what you have done
screamed. "In a minute I sh
"I'm very sorry, indeed,"

⓭ *The* **blinking insertion point** *indicates where text will be added.*

Typing Text

The two most important parts of working with text are typing the text and then selecting the text to make changes.

To type text:

1. Click with the Type tool in a frame.
2. Begin typing.
3. Press Return to begin a new paragraph.

   or

   Press Shift-Return to begin a new line without starting a new paragraph.

TIP InDesign automatically wraps text within the text frame.

TIP If the text frame is too small to display all the text, an overflow symbol appears **⓬**. You can reshape the box *(see page 74)* or flow the text into a new frame *(see page 59)* to eliminate the overflow.

To add text into a passage you have already typed, you move the *insertion point* to where you want to place the new material. The point blinks to help you find it **⓭**.

To move the insertion point:

1. Position the Type tool cursor where you want the insertion point.
2. Click to set the insertion point.

To move the point using the keyboard:

1. Use the arrow keys to move the insertion point left or right one character at a time or one line at a time.
2. Use the Cmd/Ctrl key with the arrow keys to move the insertion point one word or one paragraph at a time.

Typing Text

Selecting Text

The simplest way to select text is to use the mouse.

To select text using the mouse:

◆ Press and drag across the text. The highlight indicates which text is being selected.

TIP You don't have to drag from left to right to select multiple lines. Simply drag down.

Like other programs, InDesign has special techniques to select words, lines, and paragraphs with the mouse.

To select a single word:

◆ Double-click within a word to select it and the space following it ⓲.

TIP A double-click selects both halves of a hyphenated word.

To select a single line:

◆ Triple-click within the line ⓳.

TIP Turn on *Triple Click to Select a Line* in the Text preferences *(see page 358)*.

To select a paragraph:

◆ If *Triple Click to Select a Line* is turned off, triple-click within the paragraph ⓴.

or

If *Triple Click to Select a Line* is turned on, quadruple-click in the paragraph.

To select all the text in a frame or story:

◆ If *Triple Click to Select a Line* is turned off, quadruple-click within any paragraph.

or

If *Triple Click to Select a Line* is turned on, quintuple-click in any paragraph.

Dorothy began to sob for she felt lonely among all these strange people. The kind-hearted Munchkins immediately took out their handkerchiefs and began to weep also.

⓲ *Double-click to* **select a single word** *which is then highligted.*

Dorothy began to sob for she felt lonely among all these strange people. The kind-hearted Munchkins immediately took out their handkerchiefs and began to weep also.

⓳ *A triple-click* **selects a single line** *in a paragraph*

Dorothy began to sob for she felt lonely among all these strange people. The kind-hearted Munchkins immediately took out their handkerchiefs and began to weep also.

⓴ *An example of how a triple-click or quadruple-click can* **select a paragraph.**

Selecting Text

Keyboard, Mouse, or Menu?

One of the hot topics in working with software is the keyboard-versus-mouse debate. If you are a fast typist, you certainly work faster using keyboard shortcuts. There are times, however, when you should consider using a mouse. I use the following guidelines.

If my hands are already on the keyboard, I try to keep them there to select text or apply a formatting change.

But if my hands are on the mouse, I try to use it. So if I've just finished moving a text frame to a new position, I can easily highlight the text with the mouse.

Menu commands are another matter entirely. I try whenever possible to learn the keyboard shortcuts for menu commands.

That way I don't have to move the mouse all the way up to the top of the page to choose a command such as Cut, Copy, or Paste *(see page 72)*.

Quick Guide to the Shortcuts

Here are some easy ways to understand the selection shortcuts.

The up, down, left, and right arrow keys all jump around the text.

Add the Cmd/Ctrl keys to make the bigger jumps. Instead of a character, you jump a word. Instead of a line, you jump a paragraph. (Remember: you have more power when you take *Command* or *Control!*)

Adding the Shift key lets you select the text. The *S* in *Shift* stands for *Select*.

If you spend a lot of time typing and modifying text, you should learn the following techniques for selecting text.

To select text using keyboard shortcuts:

1. Use the following keyboard commands for selecting text using the keyboard:
    - Press the Shift key and tap the left or right arrow key to select a single character.
    - Press the Shift key and tap the up or down arrow key to select one line of text. Repeat to select additional lines.
    - Press the Cmd/Ctrl+Shift keys and tap the left or right arrow key to select one word and the space following it.
    - Press the Cmd/Ctrl+Shift keys and tap the up or down arrow key to select a paragraph.
    - Press the Shift key and tap the Home or End key to select all the text to the beginning or end of a line.
    - Press the Cmd/Ctrl+Shift keys and tap the Home or End key to select all the text to the beginning or end of a text frame or story.
    - Choose Cmd/Ctrl+A to select all the text within an entire text frame or story.

2. Repeat any of the above commands to select additional text.

TIP You can switch commands to first select a line and then the following word.

TIP Once text is selected, you can use the above commands in reverse to deselect the text.

Selecting Text

Moving and Deleting Text

You can copy or move text from one place and then paste it into another. Text that is copied or cut is stored on the computer *clipboard. (See the sidebar, "What is the Computer Clipboard" for an explanation of how the clipboard works.)*

To copy and paste text:

1. Select the text or text frame **17**.
2. Choose **Edit > Copy** or **Cut**.

TIP If you choose Cut, the highlighted text disappears and the remaining text reflows.

3. Position the insertion point where you want to put the copied or cut text **18**.
4. Choose **Edit > Paste**. The text is inserted into the new position **19**.

TIP You can select text before pasting to replace the selected text with the copied text.

The Duplicate command copies and pastes in one step. It also leaves the contents of the clipboard untouched.

To duplicate text:

1. Select the text or text frame.
2. Choose **Edit > Duplicate**. The copied text is duplicated as follows:
   - A text frame is created slightly offset from the original object.
   - Text inside a frame is pasted immediately following the original text.

TIP The Duplicate command does not replace the contents of the clipboard.

17 *Select text in order to copy or cut it from one position to another.*

18 *Click to put the insertion point where you want to insert the copied or cut text.*

19 *The Paste command inserts the copied or cut text into the insertion point.*

What is the Computer Clipboard?

The Copy command places the copied objects into an area of the computer memory called the clipboard. The contents of the clipboard stay within the memory until a new copy or cut command is executed or the computer is turned off.

The clipboard can hold only one set of information at a time. So if you copy one sentence, you will lose it from the clipboard if you copy or cut something else later on.

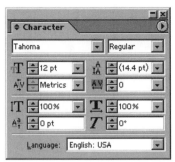

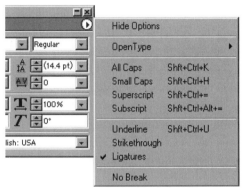

⑳ *The* **Character palette** *lets you change the character attributes.*

㉑ *The* **Character palette menu** *contains additional controls for formatting text.*

Using the Character Palette

Character formatting refers to attributes that can be applied to a single character or *glyph* in a paragraph. The Character palette controls character attributes.

To work with the Character palette:

1. If the Character palette is not visible, choose **Window > Type > Character** or **Type > Character.** This opens the Character palette **⑳**.

   or

   Click the Character palette tab to move it to the front of a set of nested palettes.

2. Click the palette tab to reveal all the palette options.

   or

   Choose Show Options from the Character palette menu **㉑**.

TIP The Character palette menu also contains additional controls for formatting text.

Setting the Typeface and Point Size

The design of type is called the *typeface*. The typeface you are reading now is called Minion. The typeface of the subhead below is called Futura Condensed Bold.

To choose a font (typeface):

1. Choose **Type** > **Font** and then choose the typeface from the font submenu.

    or

    In the Character palette, choose a typeface from the font menu **22**.

2. If necessary, choose the styling for the font from the sub-menu next to the name of the font.

    or

    Use the style list in the Character palette to choose the styling **23**.

    TIP The typestyle list changes depending on the typeface and the parts of the typeface you have installed. If you do not have the bold version of a font, it will not be listed.

    TIP You can use the keyboard commands to apply styling such as regular, bold, italic, and bold italic *(see the Appendix)*.

The size of type is measured using a system called *points*. There are 72 points per inch. The point size of this text is 10.25.

TIP Traditional typesetting measured 72.27 points per inch. However, most electronic desktop publishing programs round that size off to 72 points per inch.

To change the point size:

◆ Choose **Type** > **Size** and then choose a point size from the list **24**.

    or

    Use the point size field controls to enter a custom point size.

Sub-menu

22 *The* **font menu** *in the Character palette lets you choose the typeface for text. The sub-menu displays the style choices.*

23 *The* **style menu** *in the Character palette lets you choose the proper style choices for a typeface.*

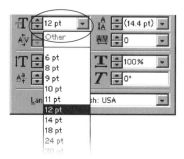

24 *The* **point size menu** *in the Character palette lets you choose common point sizes or enter a specific size in the field.*

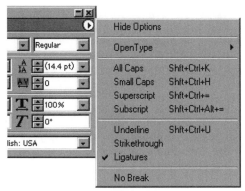

25 *The* **electronic style options** *in the Character palette menu.*

Dorothy and TOTO   All caps

L. FRANK BAUM   Small caps

Emerald City®   Superscript

H₂0   Subscript

~~Cowardly~~ Lion   Strikethrough

<u>Tin</u> Woodman   Underline

26 *Examples of the electronic styles applied to text.*

first flick

first flick

27 *The ligatures setting replaces specific pairs of letters with combination letter forms such as those circled.*

Styling Text

InDesign also lets you apply electronic styling such as All Caps, Small Caps, Subscript, and Superscript. *(See page 51 for a discussion about electronic styling.)*

To apply electronic styles:

◆ Choose one of the styles listed in the Character palette menu **25**. The text changes to the style chosen **26**.

- **All Caps** converts lowercase letters to all capital letters.
- **Small Caps** converts lowercase letters to reduced capital.
- **Superscript** reduces and raises the text above the baseline.
- **Subscript** reduces and lowers the text below the baseline.
- **Underline** draws a line under the text.
- **Strikethrough** draws a line through the text.
- **Ligatures** automatically substitutes the combined letterforms for characters such as fi and fl **27**.

TIP The All Caps style has no effect on text typed with the Caps Lock or Shift key held down.

TIP The sizes of the Small Caps, Subscript, and Superscript are controlled in the text preferences *(see page 358)*.

Setting Line and Character Spacing

Leading is the space between lines of type within a paragraph **28**. (It is pronounced *ledding,* which refers to the metal formerly used to set type.) Leading is specified as an absolute point size or as auto leading. The leading of this paragraph is 10.75 points.

To set the leading:

1. Select the paragraph of text.

2. Use the leading controls in the Character palette to enter an amount of leading **29**.

    or

    Set the leading to auto to have the leading automatically change to an amount based on the point size.

TIP The amount of the auto leading is set in the Paragraph palette Justification submenu *(see page 293).*

Kerning is the space between two letters. It is applied so letters fit snugly together **30**.

To set kerning:

1. To use the basic metric kerning pairs built into the typeface, choose Metrics from the kerning list in the Character palette **31**.

    or

    Choose Optical to adjust the kerning using the visual representation of the text.

TIP Use optical kerning when there are no built-in font metrics, for instance, when you combine two different typefaces.

2. To apply absolute kerning, use the kerning controls or pop-up menu to apply a numerical amount.

TIP Positive numbers increase the space between letters. Negative numbers decrease the space. Zero indicates no kerning is applied.

Setting Line and Character Spacing

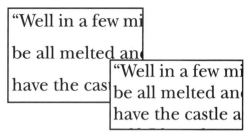

28 *The 24-point leading (top) has more line space than the 16-point leading (bottom).*

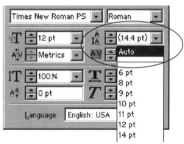

29 *The **Leading controls** in the Character palette let you change the amount of space between lines.*

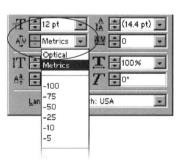

30 *A comparsion of the different kerning settings: 0 (top), Metrics (middle), Optical (bottom).*

31 *The **Kerning controls** in the Character palette to change the space between characters.*

The Emerald City
The Emerald City

32 *Tracking of 100 increases the space along all the letters.*

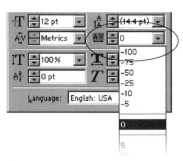

33 *The* **Tracking controls** *in the Character palette change the space across a sequence of letters.*

Wonderful Wizard

34 *A negative baseline shift lowers the capital letters from the rest of the characters.*

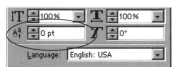

35 *The* **Baseline shift controls** *in the Character palette move text up or down along the line.*

Tracking is similar to kerning; however, unlike kerning, tracking is applied to a range of letters **32**. Tracking is very useful because as you increase the space between the letters you don't lose the relative spacing that is applied by kerning.

To set tracking:

1. Select the text you want to track.
2. Use the tracking field controls in the Character palette to set the amount of tracking **33**.

TIP Positive numbers increase the space between letters. Negative numbers decrease the space. Zero indicates no tracking is applied.

Baseline shift moves text up or down from the baseline, or the imaginary line that the letters sit on. Baseline shift is often applied to shift bullets or parentheses so they sit better next to text. It can also be used for special effects in display or headline text **34**.

To set the baseline shift:

1. Select the text that you want to reposition.
2. Use the baseline shift controls in the Character palette to move the text away from the baseline **35**.

TIP Positive numbers move the text up. Negative numbers move the text down.

Applying Text Distortions

InDesign also lets you apply horizontal or vertical scaling to text. This distorts the text to increase its height or width **36**. This changes the type from the original design of the characters. Typographic purists (such as this author) disdain distorting text.

To apply horizontal scaling:

1. Select the text that you want to distort.
2. Use the horizontal scale field controls in the Character palette to change the width of the text **37**.

To apply vertical scaling:

1. Select the text that you want to distort.
2. Use the vertical scale field controls in the Character palette **38**.

Skewing allows you to slant or tilt text **39**. This is also called *false italic* because it resembles the slant of italic text.

To skew text:

1. Select the text that you want to skew.
2. Enter an angle in the skew field in the Character palette of how much the text should be slanted **40**.

TIP Positive numbers to 180 degrees tilt the text to the left. Negative numbers to 180 degrees tilt the text to the right.

DOROTHY   Vertical scale
DOROTHY   Normal
DOROTHY   Horizontal scale

36 *The effects of applying either vertical scaling or horizontal scaling to text.*

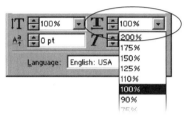

37 *Use the **Horizontal scale controls** in the Character palette to distort the width of text.*

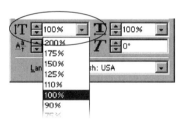

38 *The **Vertical scale controls** in the Character palette let you distort text height.*

CYCLONE!

39 *Negative and positive skew applied to create a special text effect.*

40 *The **Skew controls** in the Character palette to create fake oblique and slanted text.*

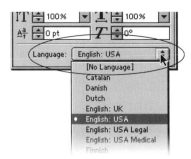

① *The* **Language menu** *lets you set the language used for spelling checks as well as typographer quotes.*

Setting the Language

You can also set the language. This ensures that foreign words are spell checked and hyphenated using the proper dictionary.

TIP If you have [No Language] selected, InDesign can't substitute typographer's quotes ("curly" quotes) for the ordinary typewriter quotes ("dumb" quotes).

To set the language:

1. Select the text that you want to set the language for.

2. Choose the language from the pop-up menu in the Character palette **①**.

Electronic Styling: Myths and Realities

As you set type using programs such as InDesign, people may tell you *never* to style fonts electronically. So if you use the Roman version of a font (such as Minion), you should never press the keyboard shortcut for italic. You should only choose the actual typeface (Minion Italic) from the font menu.

The rule emerged because some typefaces do not have an italic or bold version. The styling shows on the screen, but it doesn't print. Techno or Zapf Dingbats are examples of fonts that should not be styled electronically. When people see their printed samples they are disappointed that there is no bold or italic appearance.

Fortunately, InDesign prevents you from making errors like that. If you apply the shortcut for italic, InDesign applies the actual italic version. If there is no version, InDesign does not change the font. So there is no harm using keyboard shortcuts using InDesign.

I've also hear people advise to avoid all caps, subscript, small caps, and other electronic styles on type. In most cases, there is nothing wrong with applying those styles, and InDesign allows you to apply those electronic styles to text.

In some cases you'll have better results with a small-caps version of a font than with the electronic style for small caps. However, using a special small-caps font is a nuance and few people recognize the difference. *(For an excellent discussion on how to use electronic small caps, see* The Non-Designer's Type Book *by Robin Williams.)*

I personally hate the electronic styling for Vertical and Horizontal Scale. They distort the type horribly. The Skew command is even worse! However, I do accept that there might be times (grotesque Halloween cards?) where those distortions are acceptable.

Applying Paragraph Formatting

Paragraph formatting refers to the attributes that are applied to the paragraph as a whole. For instance, you cannot have half of the paragraph centered and the other half on the left size of the page. The alignment must be applied to the whole paragraph. InDesign paragraph formatting is applied using the Paragraph palette.

To work with the Paragraph palette:

1. If the Paragraph palette is not visible, choose **Window > Type > Paragraph** or **Type > Paragraph.** This opens the Paragraph palette 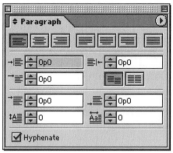.

   or

   Click the Paragraph palette tab to move it to the front of a set of tabbed palettes.

2. To display all the paragraph formatting controls, choose Show Options from the Paragraph palette pop-up menu.

TIP The Paragraph palette menu also contains additional controls for formatting text 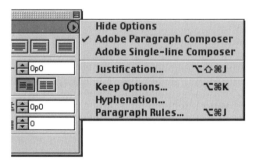. *(See Chapter 15, "Typography Controls" for working with the Paragraph palette menu.)*

TIP The following techniques are useful when applying paragraph attributes:

- To apply attributes to a single paragraph, click to place an insertion point within the paragraph.
- To apply attributes to more than one paragraph, select a portion of the first and last paragraph and the paragraphs in between.

*The **Paragraph palette** controls attributes that are applied to the whole paragraph.*

*The **Paragraph palette menu** contains additional controls for paragraph attributes.*

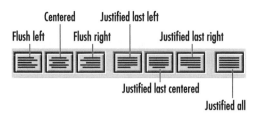

Flush left | Centered | Justified last left | Flush right | Justified last right | Justified last centered | Justified all

❹ The **Alignment buttons** *on the Paragraph palette control how the type is aligned to the frame edges.*

Well in a few minutes I shall be all melted and you shall have the castle all to yourself. I have been wicked in my day but I never thought a little girl like you would be able to melt me and end my life.	Flush left
Well in a few minutes I shall be all melted and you shall have the castle all to yourself. I have been wicked in my day but I never thought a little girl like you would be able to melt me and end my life.	Centered
Well in a few minutes I shall be all melted and you shall have the castle all to yourself. I have been wicked in my day but I never thought a little girl like you would be able to melt me and end my life.	Flush right
Well in a few minutes I shall be all melted and you shall have the castle all to yourself. I have been wicked in my day but I never thought a little girl like you would be able to melt me and end my life.	Justified last left
Well in a few minutes I shall be all melted and you shall have the castle all to yourself. I have been wicked in my day but I never thought a little girl like you would be able to melt me and end my life.	Justified last centered
Well in a few minutes I shall be all melted and you shall have the castle all to yourself. I have been wicked in my day but I never thought a little girl like you would be able to melt me and end my life.	Justified last right
Well in a few minutes I shall be all melted and you shall have the castle all to yourself. I have been wicked in my day but I never thought a little girl like you would be able to melt me and end my life.	Justified all

❺ The **seven alignment options** *position text within the text frame.*

Setting Alignment and Indents

In addition to the common alignment controls found in page layout or word processing, InDesign offers some new controls for setting alignment.

To set paragraph alignment:

1. Select the paragraphs.
2. Click one of the seven Alignment buttons **❹** to set the alignment as follows **❺**:
   - **Flush Left** sets the text to align at the left margin.
   - **Centered** sets the text to align at the center of the paragraph.
   - **Flush Right** sets the text to align at the right margin.
   - **Justified Last Left** sets the text to align at both the left and right margins, but aligns the last line flush left.
   - **Justified Last Centered** sets the text to align at both the left and right margins, but centers the last line.
   - **Justified Last Right** sets the text to align at both the left and right margins, but aligns the last line flush right.
   - **Justified All** sets all the text to align at both the left and right margins.

TIP Look closely and you'll see that the lines in the alignment buttons resemble how the alignment changes the position of the text.

Setting Alignment and Indesnts

Text doesn't have to completely fill the width of a text frame. You might want to indent a paragraph so that it stands out from the rest of the text. Or you might want to indent just the first line of each paragraph to make text easier to read. These looks are created by the margin indents.

To set the margin indents:

1. Select the paragraphs.

2. Use the margin indent controls **46** to move the text as follows **47**:

    *   **Left** moves the left side of the para-graph away from the left side of the text frame.
    *   **First Line** moves the first line of the paragraph away from the rest of the paragraph.
    *   **Right** moves the right side of the para-graph away from the right side of the text frame.

Another look you can create using the margin indents is to hang elements on the first line outside the rest of the paragraph. This is the look used for numbered and bul-leted lists such as the ones I've used through-out this book **48**.

To create a hanging bullet or numbered list:

1. Select the paragraphs.

2. Set the Left indent to the amount that the body of the paragraph should be indent.

3. Set the First Line indent to a negative amount. This hangs the first line outside the main body of the paragraph.

4. Insert a tab character *(see page 238)* to separate the bullet or number from the rest of the first line.

TIP The order of these steps is important since the First Line Indent cannot have a negative amount until the Left indent has been created.

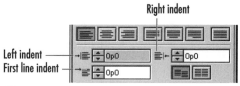

46 *The* **Margin Indents** *control the amount of space around a paragraph and its first line.*

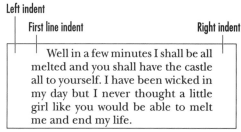

47 *The effect of applying margin indents to text inside a text frame.*

First line indent (-1p6)

Left indent (1p6)

*   Take balloon out of storage and inflate.

*   Wind clock and set the correct time.

48 *The margin indent settings for a* **hanging bullet***. Notice that the First Line indent has a negative value.*

Setting Alignment and Indents

D**o**rothy·lived·in·th
Kansas·prairies,·
who·was·a·farme
was·the·farmer's·
was·small,·for·th

49 *The* **Indent to Here character** *is indicated by the small dagger symbol. It automatically creates a hanging indent for the drop cap.*

Pros and Cons of Indent to Here Character

When should you use the Indent to Here character? When should you use the paragraph margin indents?

The Indent to Here character is an excellent solution for setting off a drop cap. Because it is not set by a measurement, it doesn't need to be adjusted if you change the drop cap letter from a wide letter such as *M* to a thin one such as *I* or *J*.

However, the Indent to Here character is not a good solution for long documents with numbered or bulleted lists. Margin indents applied to style sheets *(see page 212)* are more useful for those situations.

Inserting a Manual Indent

The Indent to Here character allows you to set an indent command that is tied to the position of the character.

TIP The Indent to Here character makes it easy to set a hanging indent for a drop cap or bulleted list.

To use the Indent to Here character:

1. Click inside a text frame where you would like the indent to occur.

2. Type Cmd/Ctrl-\ (backslash).

   or

   Choose **Type** > **Special Character** > **Indent to Here.** This inserts a character that creates an indent at that point **49**.

TIP The Indent to Here character is indicated by a dagger symbol when the Show Hidden Characters command is chosen *(see page 57)*.

To remove the Indent to Here character:

1. Place the insertion point to the right of the Indent to Here character.

2. Press the Delete/Backspace key.

Setting Paragraph Effects

The paragraph effects are available when Show Options is chosen in the Paragraph palette. One of the paragraph effects is to add space above and below a paragraph ⑤⓪. For instance, the space between this paragraph and the one following is controlled by adding space below.

To add space between paragraphs:

1. Select the paragraphs that you want to add space above or below.

2. Use the Space Before field controls to add space before the paragraphs ⑤①.

3. Use the Space After field controls to add space after the paragraphs ⑤①.

TIP Never insert paragraph returns to add space between paragraphs. That can cause problems later if text reflows!

A drop cap increases the first character's or characters' size and positions them so that they drop down into the rest of the paragraph ⑤②. The opening page for each chapter of this book contains a paragraph that has a drop cap applied.

To create drop caps:

1. Select the paragraph you want to set with a drop cap.

2. Use the Drop Cap Number of Lines field to set the number of lines that the letter should occupy ⑤③.

3. Use the Drop Cap Number of Characters field to set how many characters of the text should have the drop cap applied ⑤③.

TIP If you want the drop cap to have a different typeface, you need to select and change the letter manually.

"At the East, not far from here," said one, "there is a great desert, and none could live to cross it." ———————————— Paragraph space

"It is the same at the South," said another, "for I have been there and seen it. The South is the country of the Quadlings."

"I am told," said the third man, "that it is the same at the West and that country, where the Winkies live, is ruled by the Wicked Witch of the West, who would make you her slave if you passed her way."

⑤⓪ *An example of adding space between paragraphs..*

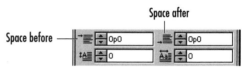

Space before ——— | Space after

⑤① *Use the **Paragraph Space controls** to add space before or after a paragraph.*

Dorothy lived in the midst of the great Kansas prairies, with Uncle Henry, who was a farmer, and Aunt Em, who was the farmer's wife.

⑤② *An example of a drop cap set for one character and three lines.*

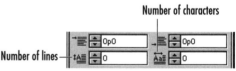

Number of lines ——— | Number of characters

⑤③ *Use the **Drop Cap controls** to change the appearance of a paragraph drop cap.*

Setting Paragraph Effects

The Munchkins immediately took out their handkerchiefs and began to weep.

The Munchkins immediately took out their handkerchiefs and began to weep.

54 *The effects of the* **Hyphenate command** *turned off (top) and turned on (bottom).*

55 *Use the* **Hyphenate checkbox** *to hyphenate words at the ends of lines.*

Tab   Space

» I · have ⎪been· wicked·but·I·never· thought·a·little·girl· like·you·would·end⌐   New line
my·life.¶———————— End of paragraph
#———————————— End of story

56 *An assortment of the* **hidden characters** *displayed within text.*

You can also control if the text within a paragraph should be hyphenated **54**.

To turn on hyphenation:

1. Select the paragraphs you want to set the hyphenation for.

2. To turn on hyphenation, click the Hyphenate checkbox in the Paragraph palette **55**. Depending on what words are hyphenated, the text may reflow. *(See Chapter 15, "Typography Controls" for information on controlling the amount of hyphens in a paragraph.)*

Using the Text Utilities

There are several utilities you can use to make it easier to work with text. For instance, you can display the hidden characters (sometimes called *invisibles*) that let you see where spaces, tab characters, and paragraph returns fall in the text.

To display hidden characters:

◆ Choose **Type** > **Show Hidden Characters.** This displays the characters in the same color as the highlight for the layer **56**.

To change the colors of the hidden characters:

◆ Change the Layer color in the Layers palette *(see page 228).*

The Glyphs palette lets you easily see all the elements in a typeface. This includes characters that are accessed using special modifiers. You can also use the palette to display the alternate letterforms that are part of Open-Type fonts *(see page 297)*.

To insert characters:

1. Place the insertion point where you would like the character to be inserted.

2. Choose **Type** > **Insert Glyphs.** This opens the Glyphs palette 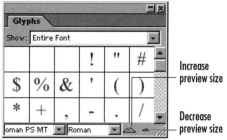.

3. Choose the typeface and style of the character you want to insert.

4. Scroll through the Preview area to find the character you want to insert.

TIP Use the Preview Size controls to increase or decrease the size of the preview.

5. Double-click the character you want to insert.

6. Repeat step 5 to insert any additional characters.

TIP The Glyphs palette allows you to insert characters that are not usually available for certain operating systems. For instance, Macintosh users can insert fractions and Windows users can insert ligatures.

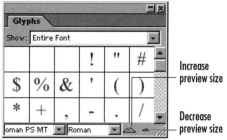

Increase preview size

Decrease preview size

57 *Use the **Glyphs palette** to insert characters from different fonts.*

So What's a Glyph?

If you're like me, you're probably wondering about the word glyph—especially if you used InDesign 1.5 and remember the Insert Character dialog box. Why use the word glyph; why not call it the Insert Character palette?

The answer has to do with being precise. You know what a letter is; a, b, c, X, Y, or Z. You wouldn't call things like 1, @, ? or $ letters, though. They're characters.

Well, glyphs are the proper name for everything including letters, characters, and alternate letterforms for things like ligatures and swashes.

So rather than call it the Insert Letters/ Characters/Alternate Letterforms palette, Adobe calls it the Glyphs palette.

⑤⑧ *The* **load text cursor** *indicates that you can continue the overflow text in another story.*

⑤⑨ *The* **link text cursor** *indicates you can click to fill the next frame with text.*

⑥⓪ *The* **link indicators** *show that the text flows into and out of the text frame.*

⑥① *The* **text threads** *show the links between frames.*

Working with Text Flow

As mentioned earlier *(see page 41)*, if text overflows its text frame, you can link the text into another frame.

To link text between frames:

1. Click the overflow symbol. The cursor changes to the load text cursor **⑤⑧**.

2. Move the cursor over to the frame you want to flow the text into. The cursor changes to the link cursor **⑤⑨**.

   TIP Unlike QuarkXPress, the second text frame does not have to be empty.

3. Click in the text frame. The link indicators show that the text in the frame flows to or from another frame **⑥⓪**.

   TIP You can use the same steps to link empty text frames. This makes it easy to flow text into the layout later.

To change the link between frames:

1. Click the link indicator in the frame where you want to break the link. The cursor turns into a link cursor.

2. Click in a new text frame to flow the text into a new frame.

   or

   Click inside the text frame to keep all the text within that frame. (The overflow symbol appears.)

InDesign also displays *text threads* which shown you the links between text frames.

To show the links between frames:

1. Select the text frame that you want to see the links for.

2. Choose **View > Show Text Threads.** This displays lines that show which frames are linked together **⑥①**.

Working with Text Flow

Setting Text Frame Controls

Once you create a text frame, you can still control the flow of text within the frame. This is similar to creating a mini-layout within the text frame.

To create text frame columns:

1. Select the text frame.

2. Choose **Object** > **Text Frame Options**. This opens the Text Frame Options dialog box **62**.

3. Set the following options in the Columns areas **63**:
   - **Number** sets the number of columns.
   - **Width** sets the column width of the columns.
   - **Gutter** controls the space between the columns.

4. Click the Preview checkbox to see the effects of the changes.

5. Click OK to apply the amounts.

InDesign also has a powerful feature that helps you maintain a fixed column width when working with a text frame. This is very helpful for magazine and newspaper layouts where all text is in the same column width.

To use the fixed column width:

1. Click Fixed Column Width in the Text Frame Options dialog box.

2. Drag to resize the frame width. The width automatically jumps to whatever size can contain an additional column **64**.

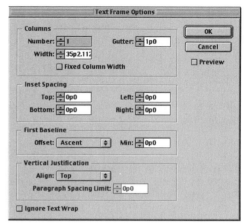

62 *The* **Text Frame Options** *dialog box controls the flow of text within a frame.*

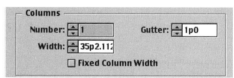

63 *The* **Columns** *settings for the Text Frame Options dialog box.*

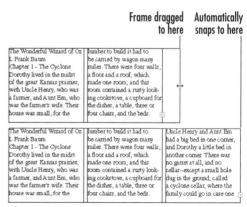

64 *Applying the* **Fixed Column Width** *ensures that the columns in a text frame are always the same size.*

Setting Text Frame Controls

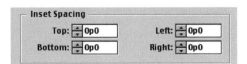

65 *The* **Inset Spacing** *settings for the Text Frame Options dialog box.*

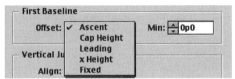

66 *A text frame with inset spacing has space between the text frame and the text.*

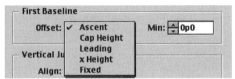

67 *The* **First Baseline Offset menu** *controls the position of the first line of text.*

Uncle Henry	Ascent
Uncle Henry	Cap Height
Uncle Henry	Leading
Uncle Henry	x Height
Uncle Henry	Fixed Height (1p)

68 *Examples of the five choices for the first line offset settings.*

In addition to the indents *(see page 54)* you can also add space between the text and the frame. This is called the *inset spacing*.

To control the frame inset:

1. Select the text frame and open the Text Frame Options dialog box.

2. Enter the values in the Inset Spacing controls to control the amount of space between the top, bottom, left, and right edges of the frame **65**.

3. Click the Preview checkbox to see the effects of the changes **66**.

4. Click OK to apply the changes to the column.

You can also control where the first baseline of the frame is positioned. (The *baseline* is the line on which the letters of the text rest.)

To control the first baseline:

1. Select the text frame and open the Text Frame Options dialog box *(see page 60)*.

2. Choose one of the five options in the Offset pop-up list **67**:

   - **Ascent** positions the first baseline so that the tops of the ascending characters (such as h, t, and d) are at the top edge of the text frame **68**.
   - **Cap Height** positions the first baseline so that the tops of capital letters are at the top edge of the frame **68**.
   - **Leading** positions the first baseline from the top edge at a distance equal to the leading *(see page 48)* assigned to the text **68**.
   - **x Height** positions the first baseline so that the top of the letter x is touches the top of the frame **68**.
   - **Fixed** allows you to set the position of the first baseline from the top edge **68**.

3. If desired, set an amount in the Min field to increase the space between the baseline and the top of the frame.

Setting Text Frame Controls

The vertical justification of a text frame controls where the text is positioned from the top to the bottom of the frame.

To set the vertical justification:

1. Select the text frame and open the Text Frame Options dialog box *(see page 60)*.

2. Choose one of the four options in the Align pop-up list 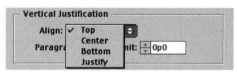:

   - **Top** positions the text so that it sits at the top of the frame .
   - **Center** positions the text so it is centered between the top and bottom of the frame .
   - **Bottom** positions the text so that the last line sits at the bottom of the frame .
   - **Justify** positions the text so that it fills the entire frame .

When you set the vertical alignment to Justify, you can set how the space between paragraphs is applied.

To set the paragraph spacing limit:

1. Set the vertical alignment to Justify.

2. Set an amount in the Paragraph Spacing Limit field 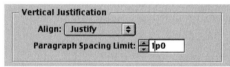. The higher the number, the more space between paragraphs and the less likely the leading between the lines will be affected by justifying the text vertically.

TIP Set an amount equal to the height of the text frame to only add space between the paragraphs, not between the lines 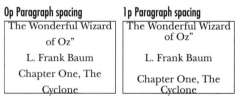.

69 *The* **Vertical Justification Align menu** *lets you choose where text is positioned vertically.*

70 *The four vertical alignment settings change the position of text within a frame.*

71 *The* **Paragraph Spacing Limit** *for justified vertical alignment controls how much space will be between paragraphs before the leading is increased.*

72 *A paragraph spacing limit of 0p causes the leading to increase. A limit of 1p only adds space between the paragraphs, not the leading.*

How Wide are the Spaces?

While some of the white space character widths are obvious, others need some definition.

An *em space* is the size of the letter M at that point size. In traditional typesetting, an em space was often used as the indent for a paragraph.

An *en space* is one-half of an em space. An en space is often used as a fixed-width space between bullets and the next character of text.

A *thin space* is one-eighth of an em space. I use a thin space on either side of an em dash or the > sign in menu commands such as **File > New**.

A *hair space* is one-twenty-fourth of an em space. A hair space is used when extremely small spaces are needed.

A *figure space* is the width of a number in the same typeface. This is used to help align numbers in financial tables.

A *punctuation space* is the width of a period or comma.

The Case of the Missing Shortcuts

As I was writing this chapter, I experienced a few very confusing days.

One day I saw the keyboard shortcuts in the menu for the special characters and white spaces. But the next day, the shortcuts were gone from the menu! I was completely confused.

It took me four days of searching to discover that if you choose commands from the Type menu, you do see the keyboard shortcuts. But if you use the contextual menu, you don't.

Using Special Text Characters

Text does not consist of just alphabetical characters. There are special characters and spaces that are used as part of professional typography. InDesign lets you insert those characters into your documents.

TIP See the next page for a list of the special characters and white space characters and their default keyboard shortcuts.

To insert special characters:

1. Place the insertion point where you want to insert the special character.

2. Choose **Type > Insert Special Character**.
   or
   Control-click (Mac) or right-mouse click (Win) and choose Insert Special Character from the contextual menu.

3. Choose a character listing from the submenu.

You can also insert white space characters which are fixed spaces such as em and en spaces. You can also insert a nonbreaking space that forces two words to stay together.

To insert special space characters:

1. Place the insertion point where you want to insert the special character.

TIP You can highlight a regular space to replace it with a white space character.

2. Choose **Type > Insert White Space**.
   or
   Control-click (Mac) or right-mouse click (Win) and choose Insert White Space from the contextual menu.

3. Choose a white space character listing from the submenu.

Windows Commands

These are the default keyboard commands in Windows for the special characters and white spaces.

Insert Special Character Commands

Auto Page Number	Ctrl+Alt+N
Bullet Character	Alt+8
Copyright Symbol	Alt+G
Discretionary Hyphen	Ctrl+Shift+-
Double Left Quotation	Alt+[
Double Right Quotation	Shift+Alt+[
Ellipsis	Alt+;
Em Dash	Shift+Alt+-
En Dash	Alt+-
Indent to Here	Ctrl+\
Next Page Number	Ctrl+Shift+Alt+]
Nonbreaking Hyphen	Ctrl+Alt+-
Paragraph Symbol	Alt+7
Previous Page Number	Ctrl+Shift+Alt+[
Registered Trademark Symbol	Alt+R
Right Indent Tab	Shift+Tab
Section Name	Ctrl+Shift+Alt+N
Section Symbol	Alt+6
Single Left Quotation	Alt+]
Single Right Quotation	Shift+Alt+]
Tab	Tab
Trademark Symbol	Alt+2

Insert White Space

Em Space	Ctrl+Shift+M
En Space	Ctrl+Shift+N
Figure Space	Ctrl+Shift+Alt+8
Hair Space	Ctrl+Shift+Alt+I
Nonbreaking Space	Ctrl+Alt+X
Thin Space	Ctrl+Shift+Alt+M

Macintosh Commands

These are the default keyboard commands on the Mac for the special characters and white spaces.

Insert Special Character Commands

Auto Page Number	Cmd+Opt+N
Bullet Character	Opt+8
Copyright Symbol	Opt+G
Discretionary Hyphen	Cmd+Shift+-
Double Left Quotation	Opt+[
Double Right Quotation	Opt+Shift+[
Ellipsis	Opt+;
Em Dash	Opt+Shift+-
En Dash	Opt+-
Indent to Here	Cmd+\
Next Page Number	Cmd+Opt+Shift+]
Nonbreaking Hyphen	Cmd+Opt+-
Paragraph Symbol	Opt+7
Previous Page Number	Cmd+Opt+Shift+[
Registered Trademark Symbol	Opt+R
Right Indent Tab	Shift+Tab
Section Name	Cmd+Opt+Shift+N
Section Symbol	Opt+6
Single Left Quotation	Opt+]
Single Right Quotation	Opt+Shift+]
Tab	Tab
Trademark Symbol	Opt+2

Insert White Space

Em Space	Cmd+Shift+M
En Space	Cmd+Shift+N
Figure Space	Cmd+Opt+Shift+8
Hair Space	Cmd+Opt+Shift+I
Nonbreaking Space	Opt+Space, Cmd+Opt+X
Thin Space	Cmd+Opt+Shift+M

WORKING WITH OBJECTS 4

Back in the old days of board mechanicals, advertising agencies and design studios had a production area called the *bullpen*. It was the people in the bullpen—called bullpen artists—who actually created the mechanical. Most of them were kids just out of design school; the bullpen was usually their first step up the ladder in advertising or design.

If we needed a simple shape—a line, a circle, a box—on the layout, it was no problem to ask the bullpen artist to draw the shape. Sometimes we asked for more complicated artwork, but at certain point our requests outpaced the skills of the bullpen artists. We had to hire more experienced artists to do the sophisticated illustrations.

The same is true with InDesign. While you can certainly use the program for drawing basic shapes, InDesign is not a full-fledged drawing program. For that you need a real illustration tool, such as Adobe Illustrator, CorelDraw or Macromedia FreeHand.

Types of Frames

Frames are the containers in which you place graphics or text. Frames can also be used as graphic shapes. There are three types of frames you can create: unassigned, graphic, and text.

Unassigned frames

Unassigned frames are created with the Rectangle, Ellipse, and Polygon tools *(see pages 67–68)*. These frames are very useful if you want to add color or a stroke around an area without inserting a graphic or text *(see page 112 and 116)*. Unassigned frames display a bounding box with handles when selected ❶.

Graphic frames

Graphic frames are created with the Rectangle Frame, Ellipse Frame, and Polygon Frame tools *(see the following section)*. When you create a graphic frame, diagonal lines inside the frame indicate that you can insert a graphic inside the frame ❶.

TIP Although most people insert images inside graphic frames, there is nothing to prevent you from flowing text inside a graphic frame.

Text frames

Text frames are created using the Text tool or by converting frames *(see page 40)*. When you create a text frame, two link boxes appear on the sides of the frame in addition to the bounding box handles. Text frames also display a blinking insertion point when they are selected ❶.

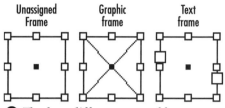

❶ *The* **three different types of frames:** *unassigned, graphic, and text.*

Diagonal Lines in Graphic Frames?

The diagonal lines inside a graphic frame come from a convention used in traditional pasteboard mechanicals.

When pasteboard artists drew the lines on mechanicals, they would often block off an area with diagonal lines to indicate that a picture or graphic was to go in that area.

Electronic page-layout programs such as QuarkXPress and Adobe InDesign use the same convention. The diagonal lines indicate where scanned images or graphics need to be inserted.

However, there is absolutely no rule that says you can only place images in graphic frames. You can place text in graphic frames or images in unassigned frames. The choice is yours.

2 *The* **Rectangle Frame tool** *in the Toolbox creates rectangular graphic frames.*

3 *The* **Ellipse Frame tool** *in the Toolbox creates elliptical graphic frames.*

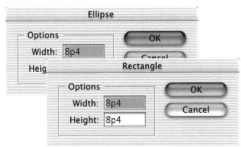

4 *The* **Ellipse and Rectangle dialog boxes** *let you create frames with precise width and height.*

Creating Basic Shapes

You use the rectangle, elliptical, and polygon frame tools to create graphic frames. These tools occupy the same slot in the toolbox.

TIP If another tool is visible, press the corner triangle to reveal the toolset *(see page 14).*

To create a rectangular graphic frame:

1. Click the Rectangle Frame tool in the Toolbox **2**.

2. Drag across the page to create the rectangle.

TIP Hold the Opt/Alt key to draw the object from the center.

3. Release the mouse button when the rectangle is the correct size.

TIP Hold the Shift key to constrain the rectangle into a square.

To create an elliptical graphic frame:

1. Click the Ellipse Frame tool in the Toolbox **3**.

2. Drag across the page to create the ellipse.

TIP Hold the Opt/Alt key to draw the object from the center.

3. Release the mouse button when the ellipse is the correct size.

TIP Hold the Shift key to constrain the ellipse into a circle.

You can also create rectangles and ellipses by specifying a numeric size.

To create objects numerically:

1. Click with either the rectangle or ellipse tools. A dialog box appears **3**.

2. Enter the width and height amounts.

3. Click OK. The object appears where the mouse was clicked.

To create a polygon graphic frame:

1. Double-click the Polygon Frame tool in the Toolbox **⑤**. This opens the Polygon Settings dialog box **⑥**.

2. Enter a number in the field for the number of sides.

3. To create a star, change the amount in the Star Inset field from 0% to a higher number.

TIP A star inset of 0% creates a polygon. As you increase the percentage, the points of the star become more obvious.

4. Drag across the page to create the polygon or star.

TIP Hold the Opt/Alt key to draw the object from the center.

TIP Hold the Shift key to constrain the width and height of the object to the same amount.

5. Release the mouse button when the polygon or star is the correct size.

⑤ *Use the* **Polygon Frame tool** *to create polygon and star graphic frames.*

⑥ *The* **Polygon Settings dialog box** *creates either polygons or stars.*

⑦ *The* **Line tool** *in the Toolbox creates straight lines.*

InDesign is definitely the program for anyone who says they can't even draw a straight line. The Line tool makes it easy.

To create straight lines:

1. Click the Line tool in the Toolbox **⑦**.

2. Position the cursor where you want the line to start.

TIP Hold the Opt/Alt key to draw the line from its centerpoint.

3. Drag to create a line.

4. Release the mouse where you want the line to end.

TIP Hold the Shift key to constrain the lines to 45-degree angles.

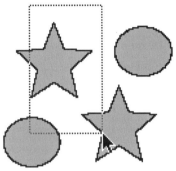

8 *The **Selection tool** in the Toolbox selects entire objects.*

9 *Drag to create a marquee to select objects.*

Selecting Objects

Once you have created objects, you can use different techniques to select those objects.

To select by clicking:

1. Choose the Selection tool (black arrow) in the Toolbox **8**.
2. Click the object you want to select.
3. Hold the Shift key to select any additional objects.

TIP Hold the Shift key and click on a selected object to deselect that object.

TIP To select objects behind others, hold the Command/Ctrl key as you click the mouse button.

You can also select objects by dragging an area, or *selection marquee,* around the object.

To select by dragging a marquee:

1. Choose the Selection tool.
2. Drag along a diagonal angle to create a marquee around the objects you want to select **9**.

TIP You do not need to marquee the entire object to select it. Objects are selected if any portion is within the marquee.

TIP Hold the Shift key and drag around another area to add to a selection.

You can also use a menu command to select all the objects on a page.

To select all the objects on a page:

◆ Choose **Edit > Select All.**

TIP This command works only if you do not have an insertion point blinking inside a text frame *(see page 41).*

Moving Objects

The simplest way to position an object on a page is to drag it to a new position.

To move an object by dragging:

1. Choose the Selection tool in the Toolbox.

2. Click the object you want to move. A bounding box with eight handles appears around the object. This indicates the object is selected.

3. Position the Selection tool on the edges of the bounding box (but not the handles of the bounding box).

TIP If an object has a fill color, gradient, or image inside it, you can drag the Selection tool directly inside the object. Otherwise, you must drag the stroke or bounding box.

4. Drag to move the object. If you drag quickly, you will see only a bounding box preview of the object being moved **10**.

   or

   Press and pause for a moment before you drag the object. The pause lets you see a preview of the actual object as you move it **11**.

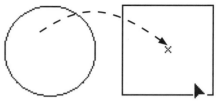

10 *Quickly drag to see a bounding box of the object being moved.*

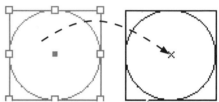

11 *Pause before you drag to see a preview of the object being moved.*

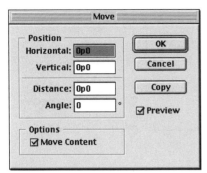

*The **Move dialog box** gives you numerical controls for moving objects.*

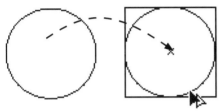

*The **double-headed arrow** indicates that a copy is being created of the moved object.*

You can also move an object more precisely. One way to do this is with the Move command in the Transform submenu.

To use the Move command:

1. Select an object or objects.

2. Choose **Object > Transform > Move**. This opens the Move dialog box **12**.

TIP This command is also available in a contextual menu *(see page 14)*.

TIP Click the Preview checkbox to see the results of your actions as you enter numbers in the dialog box.

3. Use the Horizontal and Vertical fields to move the object along those axis.

4. Use the Distance field to move the object an absolute distance.

5. Use the Angle field to set the angle along which the object moves.

6. Check Move Content to also move any placed graphics.

7. Click OK to move the original object.

   or

   Click Copy to create a duplicate of the object in the new position.

To copy an object as you drag:

1. Hold the Opt/Alt key before you start the move.

2. Move the object as described on the opposite page. A double-headed curved arrow indicates that a copy is being created **13**.

3. Release the mouse button. The copy will appear in the new position.

Moving Objects

Replicating Objects

There are several commands you can use to create duplicates of objects. Use the Copy command when you want to put the object on the clipboard *(see page 44)* so you can paste it somewhere else.

To copy objects:

1. Select an object to copy.
2. Choose **Edit** > **Copy**.

Use the Cut command to remove the object from the page so it can be pasted elsewhere.

To cut objects:

1. Select an object to cut.
2. Choose **Edit** > **Cut**.

Use the Paste command to see the contents of the clipboard.

To paste objects:

♦ Choose **Edit** > **Paste**. The contents of the clipboard appear in the center of the window area 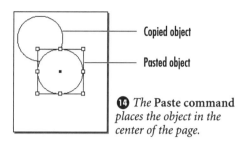.

or

Choose **Edit** > **Paste In Place**. The contents of the clipboard appear in the same location as they were when originally selected.

The Duplicate command makes a copy without changing the clipboard.

To duplicate objects:

1. Choose the object to duplicate.
2. Choose **Edit** > **Duplicate**. The selected object appears on the page slightly offset from the original 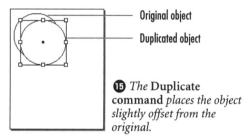.

— Copied object

— Pasted object

14 *The* **Paste command** *places the object in the center of the page.*

— Original object

— Duplicated object

15 *The* **Duplicate command** *places the object slightly offset from the original.*

Using Paste in Place

I always wondered just how useful the Paste in Place command is. After all, if you already have a copy of an object in one place, why would you need a second copy right over it?

That's not the point of Paste in Place. The power of the command is that you can paste an object in the same place on different pages. You can even paste in the same place on different documents.

PageMaker users will recognize this as the Powerpaste command. Quark-XPress users will wonder how they ever got along without it.

Replicating Objects (vertical sidebar text)

16 *Use the* **Step and Repeat dialog box** *to make multiple copies of an object positioned at specific horizontal and vertical intervals.*

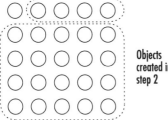

17 *The Step and Repeat command created five copies of the first circle.*

Objects created in step 1

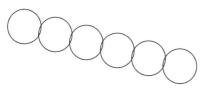

Objects created in step 2

18 *An example of how to use the Step and Repeat command to create a grid of objects.*

You can also make many duplicates at once.

To duplicate multiple objects:

1. Choose an object.
2. Choose **Edit > Step and Repeat.** The Step and Repeat dialog box appears **16**.
3. In the Repeat Count field, enter the number of duplicates to create.
4. In the Horizontal Offset field, enter a distance for the horizontal space between duplicates.
5. In the Vertical Offset field, enter a distance for the vertical space between duplicates.

TIP If you want space between the objects, make the offset at least the width or height of the object plus the amount of space between the objects.

6. Click OK. The selected object is duplicated in the desired positions **17**.

You might want to duplicate many objects so they form a horizontal and vertical grid. Although the Step and Repeat command can't do this in one step, you can use the command to create a grid **18**.

To create a grid of objects:

1. Set the Step and Repeat dialog box as follows:
   - In the Repeat Count field, enter the number of duplicates for the top row.
   - Enter the distance for the Horizontal Offset.
   - Leave the Vertical Offset as zero.
2. Select all the objects, and set the Step and Repeat dialog box as follows:
   - In the Repeat Count field, enter the number for the addition number of rows.
   - Leave the Horizontal Offset as zero.
   - Enter a distance for the Vertical Offset.

Resizing Objects

Very often, things need to be made bigger or smaller. InDesign gives you several different ways to scale objects. You can also use the bounding box handles to change the dimensions of the object visually. This is the easiest way to quickly resize an object.

To resize using the bounding box handles:

1. Choose the Selection tool.

2. Choose which handle to drag based on the following options ⑲:

   - Drag the corner handles to change both the width and height.
   - Drag the top or bottom handles to change the height only.
   - Drag the left or right handles to change the width only.

3. Drag the handle. If you drag quickly, you will see only the bounding box of the object ⑳.

   or

   Press and hold for a moment and then drag the handle. This shows a preview of the object as you resize the bounding box ㉑.

   TIP Hold down the Shift key as you drag a corner to keep the original proportions of the width and height.

   TIP Hold the Cmd/Ctrl key as you drag to resize any images placed inside the object *(see page148)*.

4. Release the mouse button when the object is the correct size.

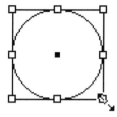

⑲ *Use the bounding box handles to resize an object.*

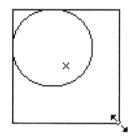

⑳ *If you drag quickly, you **only see a box** as you resize an object.*

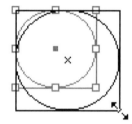

㉑ *If you press and pause a moment, you **see an actual preview** as you resize an object.*

㉒ Objects selected with the Selection tool *have both the object and its content transformed by the transform tools.*

㉓ Objects selected with the Group Selection tool *have only the object transformed by the transform tools.*

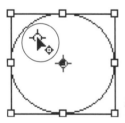

㉔ *The indicator that the transformation point can be moved to a new position.*

Using the Transform Tools

The transform tools resize and distort objects. You can transform the object itself or the object as well as any content. How you select objects changes the effect of the transform tools.

To control the effect of the transform tools:

◆ Select the object using the Selection tool. This type of selection causes the transform tools to affect both the object and any text or images inside it **㉒**.

or

Hold the Opt/Alt key as you click with the Direct Selection tool. This causes the transformation to affect only the object, not any text or images inside the object **㉓**.

TIP The plus (+) sign next to the Direct Selection tool indicates that the tool is the Group Selection tool.

All the transformations take place in relation to a transformation point. Each object has a default transformation point, but you can change it if necessary.

To control the transformation point:

1. Select the object to be transformed.
2. Choose one of the transform tools. A transform point appears inside the object.
3. Move the cursor near the transform point. A small icon appears next to the cursor that indicates you can move the transform point **㉔**.
4. Drag the transformation point to a new position.

or

Click to position the transformation point in a new position.

The Scale tool lets you increase or decrease the size of objects.

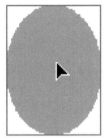

25 *The* **Scale tool** *in the Toolbox is used to change the size of objects.*

To scale objects visually using the Scale tool:

1. Select the object you want to scale.
2. Choose the Scale tool in the Toolbox **25**.
3. If necessary, change the position of the transformation point *(see previous page)*.
4. Move the cursor away from the transformation point, and drag to scale the object **26**.

TIP Hold down the Shift key to constrain the tool to horizontal, vertical, or proportional scaling.

TIP To see a preview of the image as you scale, press and hold the mouse button for a moment before you start to drag.

TIP Hold down the Opt/Alt key to copy the object as you scale it.

26 *The* **curved arrowhead** *appears while scaling an object.*

If you prefer, you can enter the resize objects numerically using the scale command.

To scale objects using the scale command:

1. Select an object or objects.
2. Choose **Object > Transform > Scale.** This opens the Scale dialog box **27**.
3. Use the Uniform Scale field to scale the object proportionally.

   or

   Use the Non-Uniform Horizontal and Vertical fields to scale the object non-proportionally.
4. Check Scale Content to also scale any placed graphics *(see Chapter 8, "Imported Graphics")* **28**.
5. Click OK to scale the object.

   or

   Click Copy to create a scaled copy of the object.

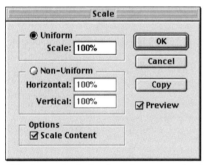

27 *The* **Scale dialog box** *lets you scale objects using numerical values.*

28 *When* **Scale Content** *is turned on, the placed image scales along with the frame.*

Using the Transform Tools

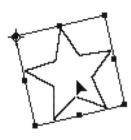

29 *The* **Rotate tool** *in the Toolbox is used to change the orientation of objects.*

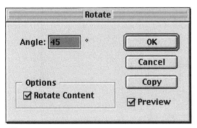

30 *Rotating an object around its transformation point.*

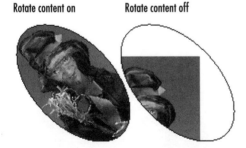

31 *The* **Rotate dialog box** *lets you rotate objects using numerical values.*

Rotate content on   Rotate content off

32 *When* **Rotate Content is turned on,** *the placed image rotates along with the frame.*

To scale objects numerically using the Scale tool:

1. Select the object or objects.
2. Choose the Scale tool in the Toolbox.
3. Hold the Opt/Alt key and click to designate the position of the transformation point. This opens the Scale dialog box **27**.
4. Set the dialog box controls as described in the previous exercise.

The Rotation tool changes the orientation of objects.

To rotate objects visually using the Rotation tool:

1. Select an object or objects.
2. Click the Rotation tool in the Toolbox **29**.
3. If necessary, change the default transformation point *(see page 75)*.
4. Move the cursor away from the transformation point, and drag to rotate the object **30**.

TIP Hold down the Shift key to constrain the rotation to 45-degree increments.

TIP Hold down the Opt/Alt key *after* you start the rotation to copy the object as you rotate it.

To rotate objects using the rotate command:

1. Select an object or objects.
2. Choose **Object** > **Transform** > **Rotate**. This opens the Rotate dialog box **31**.
3. Use the Angle field to set how much the object should rotate.
4. Check Rotate Content to also rotate any placed graphics **32**.
5. Click OK to rotate the object.

   or

   Click Copy to a rotated copy of the object.

Using the Transform Tools

To rotate objects numerically using the Rotate tool:

1. Select the object or objects.
2. Choose the Rotate tool in the Toolbox.
3. Hold the Opt/Alt key and click to set the position of the transformation point. This opens the Rotate dialog box ㉛.
4. Set the dialog box controls as described in the previous exercise.

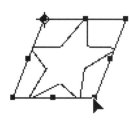

㉝ *Use the* **Shear tool** *in the Toolbox to distort objects.*

The Shear tool distorts the shape of objects.

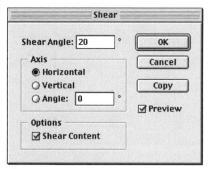

㉞ *Shearing an object around the transformation point.*

To shear objects visually using the Shear tool:

1. Select an object or objects.
2. Click the Shear tool in the Toolbox ㉝.
3. If necessary, change the transformation point by dragging it to a new position *(see page 75)*. The cursor indicates the transformation point can be moved.
4. Move the cursor away from the transformation point, and drag to shear the object ㉞.

Shear

Shear Angle: 20 ° [OK]

Axis [Cancel]
● Horizontal
○ Vertical [Copy]
○ Angle: 0 °
☑ Preview

Options
☑ Shear Content

㉟ *The* **Shear dialog box** *lets you distort objects using numerical values.*

To shear objects using the shear command:

1. Select an object or objects.
2. Choose **Object** > **Transform** > **Shear.** This opens the Shear dialog box ㉟.
3. Use the Shear Angle field to set the amount of distortion.
4. Check one of the Axis options:
   - **Horizontal** shears along the horizontal axis.
   - **Vertical** shears along the vertical axis.
   - **Angle** shears along a specific angle.
5. Check Shear Content to also distort any placed graphics ㊱.
6. Click OK to shear the object.

   or

   Click Copy to create a sheared copy of the object.

Shear content on   Shear content off

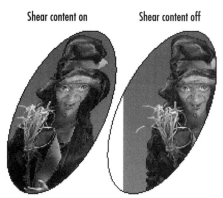

㊱ *The difference between shearing an object with Shear content on and off.*

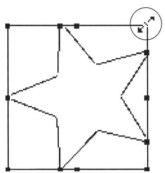

37 *Choose the* **Free Trans-form tool** *in the Toolbox to both scale and rotate objects.*

38 *The double-headed arrow indicates that the Free Transform tool is in the scale mode.*

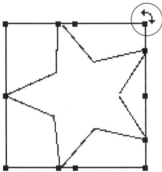

39 *The curved double-headed arrow indicates that the Free Transform tool is in the rotation mode.*

To shear objects numerically using the Shear tool:

1. Select the object or objects.

2. Choose the Shear tool in the Toolbox.

3. Hold the Opt/Alt key and click to set the position of the transformation point. This opens the Shear dialog box **35**.

4. Set the dialog box controls as described in the previous exercise.

Rather than switching between the Scale and Rotate tools, you can use the Free Transform tool to both scale and rotate.

To scale using the Free Transform tool:

1. Select an object or objects.

2. Click the Free Transform tool in the Toolbox **37**. A bounding box appears around the object.

3. Place the cursor on one of the handles of the bounding box. The cursor changes to a double-headed arrow **38**.

4. Drag to increase or decrease the size of the object.

To rotate using the Free Transform tool:

1. Select an object or objects.

2. Click the Free Transform tool in the Toolbox **37**. A bounding box appears around the object.

3. Place the cursor outside one of the handles of the bounding box. The cursor changes to a curved double-headed arrow **39**.

4. Drag to rotate the object clockwise or counter-clockwise.

Using the Transform Tools

Using the Transform Palette

The Transform palette allows you to move, scale, rotate, and shear objects precisely, using numerical values.

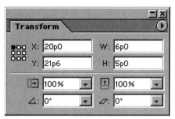

To open the Transform palette:

♦ Choose **Window** > **Transform** to open the palette ⓪.

or

If the Transform palette is behind other palettes, click the Transform palette tab.

⓪ *The* **Transform palette** *is a command center for positioning and transforming objects.*

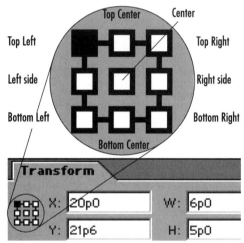

As you work with the Transform palette, it is important to know its reference point on the object.

To set the Transform palette reference point:

1. Select the object you want to transform.
2. Click the reference point control on the Transform palette to choose the point around which the object moves ㊶.

㊶ *The* **Reference point** *controls where in the object the transformation occurs.*

You can use the Transform palette to move objects numerically.

To move an object with the Transform palette:

1. Select the object you want to move.
2. To move the object horizontally, enter an amount in the X field ㊷.
   TIP As you increase the numbers, the object moves to the right.
3. To move the object vertically, enter an amount in the Y field ㊷.
   TIP As you increase the numbers, the object moves down.
4. Press Enter or Return to apply the changes.

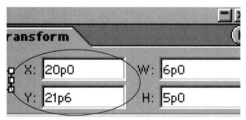

㊷ *The* **X** *and* **Y** *fields in the Transform palette control the position of an object.*

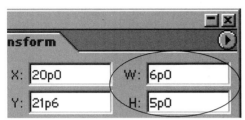

43 *The* **W and H fields in the Transform** palette *control the width and height of objects.*

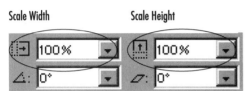

44 *The* **Scale width and height fields in the** **Transform palette** *let you apply percentage amounts to scale objects.*

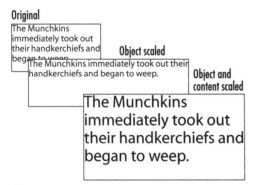

45 *The difference between scaling an object or scaling an object and its content.*

You can also resize objects using the Transform palette.

To resize with the Transform palette:

1. Select an object or objects.

2. If necessary, change the reference point as explained on the preceding page.

3. To change the width of the object, enter an amount in the W field **43**.

4. To change the height of the object, enter an amount in the H field **43**.

5. Press Enter or Return to apply the changes.

You can also scale objects using the Transform palette. *(See the warning about scaling objects in the sidebar on page 118.)*

To scale with the Transform palette:

1. Select an object or objects.

TIP The Selection tool scales the object and its contents. The Direct Selection tool scales only the object. *(See page 155 for selecting objects.)*

2. If necessary, change the reference point as explained on the preceding page.

3. To change the horizontal size, enter a percentage in the **scale X** field **44**.

4. To change the height of the object, enter a percentage in the **scale Y** field **44**.

TIP The **scale** X and Y fields also have pop-up lists to choose for the scaling.

5. Press Enter or Return to apply the changes **45**.

You can also rotate objects using the Transform palette.

To rotate with the Transform palette:

1. Select the object or objects.

TIP The Selection tool scales the object and its contents. The Direct Selection tool scales only the object. *(See page 155 for selecting objects.)*

2. If necessary, change the transformation point, as explained on page 75.

3. Enter the amount of rotation in the rotation field **46**.

TIP The rotation field also has a pop-up list to choose for the rotation.

4. Press Enter or Return to apply the changes **47**.

You can also shear objects using the Transform palette.

To shear with the Transform palette:

1. Select the object or objects you want to shear.

TIP The Selection tool scales the object and its contents. The Direct Selection tool scales only the object. *(See page 155 for selecting objects.)*

2. If necessary, change the reference point, as explained on pages 75.

3. Enter the amount of distortion in the shear field **48**.

TIP The shear field also has a pop-up list of amounts to choose for the distortion.

4. Press Enter or Return to apply the changes **49**.

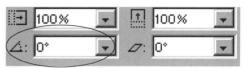

46 *The* **Rotate** *field in the Transform palette lets you change the alignment of objects.*

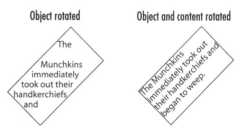

47 *The difference between rotating an object or rotating an object and its content.*

48 *The* **Shear** *field in the Transform palette let you distort the shape of objects.*

49 *The difference between shearing an object or shearing an object and its content.*

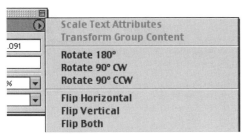

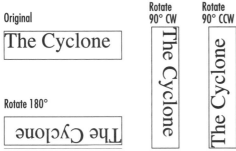

50 *The rotate and flip commands in the Transform palette menu.*

Original

The Cyclone

Rotate 180°

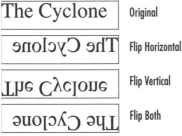

51 The effects of rotating objects using the Transform submenu.

The Cyclone — Original

Flip Horizontal

Flip Vertical

Flip Both

52 The effects of flipping objects using the Transform submenu.

Using the Transform Palette Menu

The Transform palette menu also gives you commands that make it easy to perform commonly used transformations, such as rotating and flipping objects.

To rotate with the Transform palette menu:

1. Select an object or objects.

2. Click to open the Transformation palette menu **50**.

3. Choose one of the rotation settings as follows **51**:
   - Rotate 180°.
   - Rotate 90° CW (clockwise).
   - Rotate 90° CCW (counter-clockwise).

To flip objects using the Transform palette menu:

1. Select an object or objects.

2. Click to open the Transformation palette menu :

3. Choose one of the flip settings as follows **52**:
   - Flip Horizontal.
   - Flip Vertical.
   - Flip Both.

Using the Transform Palette Menu

Using the Arrange Commands

Objects in InDesign are layered on top of one other in the same order they were created. (This is sometimes called the *stacking order.*) The first object created is layered behind the second, and so on. Though you may not see the layering when objects are side by side, it is apparent when they overlap ⊞.

⊞ The layering of objects is not the same as the layers of a document. *(See Chapter 11, "Layers" for more information on working with layers.)*

⊞ *When two objects overlap, it is obvious which object is in front of the other.*

The Arrange commands allow you to move objects through the stacking order.

To move up or down one level in a layer:

1. Select the object you want to move.
2. Choose **Object** > **Arrange** > **Bring Forward** to move the object in front of the next object in the stacking order ⊞.

   or

   Choose **Object** > **Arrange** > **Send Backward** to move the object behind the next object in the stacking order ⊞.

To move up or down the entire layer:

1. Select an object you want to move.
2. Choose **Object** > **Arrange** > **Bring to Front** to move the object in front of all the others in its layer ⊞.

   or

   Choose **Object** > **Arrange** > **Send to Back** to move the object behind all the others in its layer ⊞.

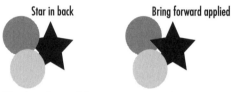

Star in back   Bring forward applied

⊞ *The effects of the* **Bring Forward command**.

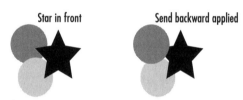

Star in front   Send backward applied

⊞ *The effects of the* **Send Backward** command.

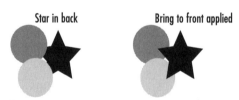

Star in back   Bring to front applied

⊞ *The effects of the* **Bring to Front command**.

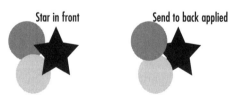

Star in front   Send to back applied

⊞ *The effects of the* **Send to Back command**.

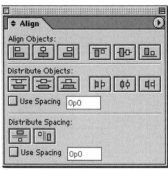

⑤⑧ *Use the **Align palette** to arrange objects in an orderly fashion.*

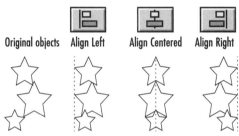

Original objects Align Left Align Centered Align Right

⑤⑨ *The effects of the **vertical align commands.***

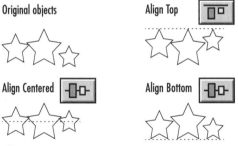

Original objects Align Top

Align Centered Align Bottom

⑥⓪ *The effects of the **horizontal align commands.***

Aligning Objects

The Align palette provides commands that align objects or distribute them evenly along a horizontal or vertical axis.

To work with the Align palette:

1. Choose **Window** > **Align.** This opens the Align palette ⑤⑧.

   or

   If the Align palette is behind other palettes, click the Align palette tab.

2. Choose Show Options from the Align palette submenu to see all the commands in the palette.

To align objects:

1. Select two or more objects.

2. Click an alignment icon as follows:
   • Click a vertical alignment icon to move the objects into left, centered, or right alignment ⑤⑨.
   • Click a horizontal alignment icon to move the objects into top, centered, or bottom alignment ⑥⓪.

TIP The align commands move objects based on the best representative of the controls. For instance, the Align Left command uses the left-most object; Align Top uses the top-most object, and so on. *(See the sidebar on page 87.)*

Aligning Objects

You can also move objects so the spaces between certain points of the objects are equal. This is called distributing objects.

To distribute objects:

1. Select three or more objects.

2. Click a distribute icon as follows:
   - Click a vertical distribute icon to move the objects so that their tops, centers, or bottoms are equally distributed ❻❶.
   - Click a horizontal distribute icon to move the objects so that their left edges, centers, or right edges are equally distributed ❻❷.

You can also distribute objects based on their size. This ensures that the space between the objects is equal.

To distribute the space between objects:

1. Select three or more objects.

2. Click a distribute space icon as follows:
   - Click the vertical space icon to move objects so the vertical spaces between them are equal ❻❸.
   - Click the horizontal space icon to move objects so the horizontal spaces between them are equal ❻❹.

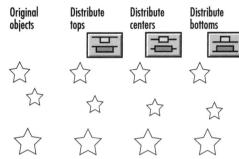

❻❶ *The effects of the* **vertical distribute** commands. *Notice that the middle object changes position to create an even distribution.*

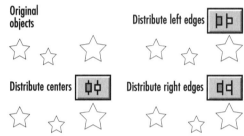

❻❷ *The effects of the* **horizontal distribute** commands. *Notice that the middle object changes position to create an even distribution.*

❻❸ *The effect of the* **vertical distribute space** command.

Original objects   Distribute horizontal space

❻❹ *The effects of the* **horizontal distribute** space commands.

65 *The* **Use Spacing option for Distribute Objects** *lets you set a specific distance between the tops, centers, bottoms, or sides of objects.*

66 *The* **Use Spacing option for Distribute Spacing** *lets you set a specific distance between objects.*

Can You Set an Anchor For Alignment or Distribution?

When you want to align or distribute objects, you may want to designate a specific object to be used as the alignment reference point.

Unfortunately, there is no way to designate a specific object to be used as part of the alignment and distribution commands.

InDesign aligns and distributes objects as follows:

- The left-align and -distribute commands use the left-most object as the anchor.

- The right-align and -distribute commands use the right-most object as the anchor.

- The top-align and -distribute commands use the top-most object as the anchor.

The Align palette also has controls to space objects numerically. You can apply a numerical distance between the tops, centers, bottoms, or sides of objects.

To use spacing to distribute objects:

1. Select two or more objects.

2. Check Use Spacing in the Distribute Objects section of the Align palette **65**.

3. Enter the numerical distance in the Use Spacing field.

4. Click one of the Distribute Objects icons. Now the objects are separated by inserting a specific space between the tops, centers, bottoms, or sides of the objects.

TIP If a positive number moves the objects in the wrong direction, use a negative number.

You can also set a specific numerical distance between the objects themselves. This is very useful when you want the same amount of space between objects, but the objects themselves have different sizes.

To set the spacing between objects:

1. Select two or more objects.

2. Check Use Spacing in the Distribute Objects section of the Align palette **66**.

3. Enter the numerical distance in the Use Spacing field.

4. Click one of the Distribute Spacing icons. Now a specific amount of space is added between the objects horizontally or vertically.

TIP If a positive number moves the objects in the wrong direction, use a negative number.

Grouping Objects

You can group objects so you can easily select and modify them as a unit.

To group objects:

1. Select the objects you want to group.

2. Choose **Object > Group.** A bounding box encloses all the objects ❻.

TIP The Selection tool selects all the objects in a group as a single unit.

Ungrouped items

Grouped items

❻ *When selected with the Selection tool, grouped items display a bounding box around the entire group.*

You can also create groups within groups. This is called *nesting*.

To nest groups:

1. Select the grouped objects.

2. Hold the Shift key and select another object or group.

3. Choose **Object > Group.**

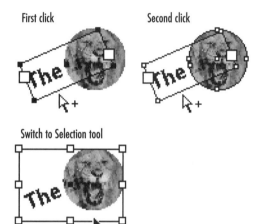

First click

Second click

Switch to Selection tool

❻ **Selecting nested groups** *with the Group Selection tool.*

Once you have grouped objects, you can select individual objects within the group.

To select objects within groups:

1. Choose the Direct Selection tool.

2. Click to select one object in the group.

3. Hold the Opt/Alt key and click the same object again ❻. This selects the entire group.

4. If the group is nested within other groups, click again on the same object to select the next level of the nest.

To ungroup objects:

1. Select the group.

2. Choose **Object > Ungroup.**

3. If you have nested groups, continue to ungroup the objects as necessary.

69 *The* **padlock icon** *indicates that the Lock Position command has been applied.*

How Safe Are Locked Objects?

I sincerely hope that you lock your front door more securely than the Lock Position command locks objects.

The Lock Position command only locks the position of the object. The object can still be selected using either the selection tools or the Select All command.

If there is text within the selected object, the text can be selected and otherwise modified.

If there is a placed image within the select object, the image can be replaced by choosing a new object with the Place command *(see page 149)*.

If you need more security for your objects—for instance, to avoid inadvertently changing the color of an object—then you should lock the object's layer *(see page 228)*.

Locking Objects

You can also lock objects so they cannot be moved or modified. This prevents people from inadvertently moving objects.

TIP Locking objects is not the same as locking the layers of a document. *(See Chapter 11, "Layers" for more information on working with layers.)*

To lock the position of an object:

1. Select the objects you want to lock.
2. Choose **Object** > **Lock Position.** A small padlock appears if you try to move or modify the object **69**.

TIP Locked objects can be selected, copied, pasted, and their colors and contents can be modified.

To unlock objects:

1. Select the objects you want to unlock.
2. Choose **Object** > **Unlock Position.**

Locking Objects

WORKING IN COLOR 5

My first computer was a Macintosh SE, which is currently serving as a bookend under my desk. It has a built-in screen that is even smaller than the pages of this book. The screen only displayed black-and-white images.

Still I used it to create all sorts of full-color illustrations, maps, and designs. I just defined all my colors using numerical values and exercised my vivid imagination to visualize what the job would actually look like when it was finally printed.

I doubt you're using anything as primitive as my old computer. Today it's hard to find anyone who doesn't have a full-color monitor measuring 17 inches or more. (If you don't have a large monitor, my condolences.)

Interestingly, though, there are very few differences in the principles of working in color from the old days to now. In fact, the basics of working in color aren't computer specific; they come from years and years of print shops printing color images in documents.

Working with Color Modes

There are three different models for defining colors: CMYK, RGB, and LAB. Each model is used for different purposes. You choose the color mode and mix colors in the Color palette. *(See Chapter 6, "Styling Objects" for how to apply colors to objects and text,)*

❶ *The* **Color palette** *with the options turned off shows only the spectrum or ramp for choosing colors.*

To work with the Color palette:

1. If the Color palette is not visible, choose **Window >Color** to open the palette ❶.

   or

   If the Color palette is behind other palettes, click the Color palette tab.

2. If the color sliders are not visible, click the palette tab or choose Show Options from the Color palette menu ❷.

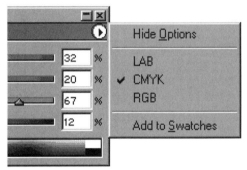

❷ *The* **Color palette menu** *lets you choose among the three color models.*

The CMYK color model is used primarily for print work. CMYK colors are mixed using percentages of the four inks used in process printing: cyan, magenta, yellow, and black.

To mix CMYK colors:

1. Choose CMYK from the Color palette menu. This opens the palette in the CMYK mode ❸.

2. Choose one of the following methods to define the amount of cyan, magenta, yellow, or black ink in the color:

   - Type a value from 0 to 100 percent in the four color fields.
   - Drag the sliders for each of the four color fields.
   - Click a color in the CMYK spectrum area.

   TIP Click the solid white or black rectangles to the right end of the spectrum to quickly get 100% black or white.

   TIP Hold the Shift key as you drag one slider to have the others move along with it.

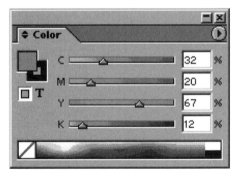

❸ *The Color palette with the CMYK (cyan, magenta, yellow, and black) print color controls.*

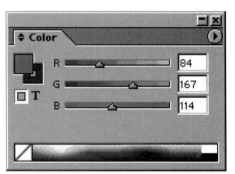

❹ *The Color palette set for mixing RGB (red, green blue) colors for onscreen display such as Web sites.*

Understanding CMYK Color

Each of the colors in CMYK corresponds to one of the inks used in typical four-color printing. Cyan is a shade of blue. Magenta is red. Yellow is … well, yellow. And black is black — I want my baby back.

If you are creating print documents, you will want to define your colors using CMYK colors. Not only is the CMYK system overwhelmingly used for print work, it is the system you are most familiar with, whether you're aware of it or not. Yellow and cyan make green; magenta and yellow make orange, and so on.

In theory, you shouldn't need more than three colors for printing. If you mix cyan, magenta, and yellow together, you should get a solid black color. In reality, however, those inks are not pure enough to create solid black; instead they create a dark brown.

That's why process printing uses four colors. In addition to cyan, magenta, and yellow, a fourth *key color*—black—is added to create the really black areas. That's where the term CMYK comes from.

The RGB color model is used primarily for onscreen work such as presentations and Web sites. The RGB colors — red, green, and blue — are mixed using representations of the three colors of light that blend together in television and computer monitor screens. You can create more vivid colors using RGB colors than with CMYK colors.

To mix RGB colors:

1. Choose RGB from the Color palette menu. This opens the palette in the RGB mode ❹.

2. Choose one of the following methods to define the amount of red, green, or blue in the color:
   - Type the value from 0 to 255 in the three color fields.
   - Drag the sliders for each of the three color fields.
   - Click a color in the RGB spectrum area.

Working with Color Modes

The LAB color model defines colors according to a *luminance* (lightness) component, and two color components, *a* and *b*. The *a* component defines the green to red values. The *b* component defines the blue to yellow values. LAB colors are designed to be device-independent so that the color does not change from one source to another.

TIP The proper name for LAB is L*a*b and is pronounced by spelling out the name (*el-ay-bee*), not by saying the word "lab".

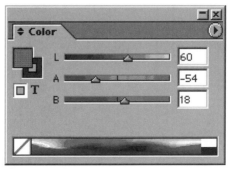

⑤ *The* **LAB Color palette** *mixes colors that look consistent no matter whether you print or display them onscreen.*

To mix LAB colors:

1. Choose LAB from the Color palette menu. This opens the palette in the LAB mode **⑤**.

2. Choose one of the following methods to define the three components of the color:
   - Type the value from 0 to 100 in the L field or type the value from -128 to 127 in the A or B fields.
   - Drag the sliders for each of the fields.
   - Click a color in the LAB spectrum area.

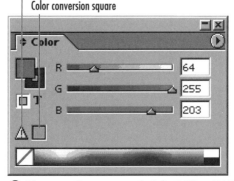

⑥ *The* **out-of-gamut symbol** *for RGB or LAB colors indicates that the color shown on screen will not print as seen using process color inks.*

The out-of-gamut symbol appears if you choose an RGB or LAB color that cannot be printed using process inks **⑥**.

To convert out-of-gamut colors:

- Click the small square next to the out-of-gamut symbol. This converts the color to the closest process color.

You can add colors from the Color palette to the Swatches palette. *(See the next section on for more techniques to store colors.)*

To transfer colors from the Color palette:

1. Define the color in the Color palette.

2. Choose Add to Swatches from the Color palette menu. The color appears as a new color swatch in the Swatches panel.

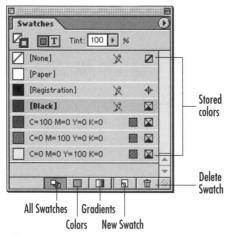

Stored colors

Delete Swatch

All Swatches | Gradients

Colors | New Swatch

❼ *The* **Swatches palette** *shows all the saved colors.*

Name

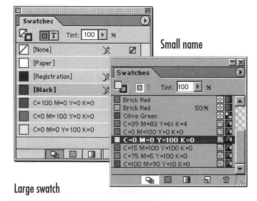

Small name

Large swatch

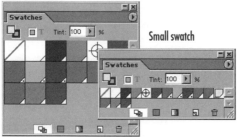

Small swatch

❽ *The four choices for the display of the Swatches palette.*

Defining and Storing Color Swatches

A color swatch is a color that has been defined and is stored in the Swatches palette.

To work with the Swatches palette:

1. If the Swatches palette is not visible, choose **Window** > **Swatches** to open the palette **❼**.

   or

   If the Swatches palette is behind other palettes, click the Swatches palette tab.

2. To see the different types of swatches, click the icons at the bottom of the palette as follows:

   - **Show All Swatches** displays both the color and gradient swatches in the palette.
   - **Show Color Swatches** displays only the color swatches in the palette.
   - **Show Gradient Swatches** displays only the gradient swatches in the palette. *(See page 106.)*

3. To change the display of the swatches in the palette, choose the following from the Swatches palette menu **❽**:

   - **Name** displays a list of the swatch names in a large typeface.
   - **Small Name** uses a more compact typeface to display the swatch names.
   - **Small Swatch** displays only the square of the swatch color or gradient.
   - **Large Swatch** displays a larger square of the swatch color or gradient.

   TIP Each icon for the types of swatches has its own display setting. So the color swatches can be displayed in the Small Name setting while the gradients are shown in the Large Swatch display.

Although you can apply colors to objects and text directly from the Color palette, this is not considered a good production workflow. Instead, use the Swatches palette to add the color currently defined in the Color palette.

TIP If you apply colors from the Color palette, they are called unnamed colors. Unnamed colors can cause production problems later on and should be avoided. *(See "Avoiding Unnamed Colors" on page 105.)*

To add a color to the Swatches palette:

1. Use the Color palette to define a color *(see page 92).*

2. Click the New Swatch icon at the bottom of the palette. The new color is automatically added to the Swatches palette.

InDesign also lets you drag colors from the Color palette into the Swatches palette.

To drag colors into the Swatches palette:

1. Create the color in the Color palette.

2. Drag the color from the Color palette fill or stroke box to the bottom of or between two colors in the Swatches palette.

3. Release the mouse when a black line appears ❾. The new color is added and takes its name from the color values.

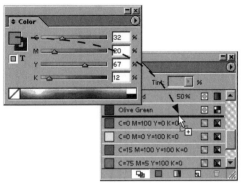

❾ *You can drag colors from the Color palette into the Swatches palette.*

The Color "Paper"

The swatch labeled [Paper] in the Swatches palette allows you to change the background color of the pages in your document. This can be helpful if your document will be printed on colored paper, specialty paper, or even newsprint that is not completely white. You can modify the paper color to help judge how your images will look when printed.

The Registration Color

"Registration" is a color that is set to print on all plates of a document. For instance, if your document will be printed using process colors, you might want to create a note or mark that should be seen on all four plates. Rather than make the note in a combination of cyan, magenta, yellow, and black, you can apply the color Registration to the text for the note. This prints the note as a combination of all four inks.

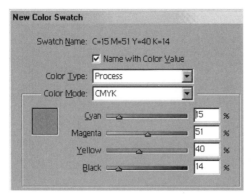

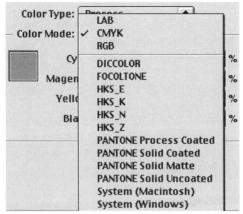

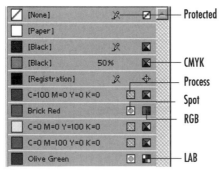

⑩ *Use the* **New Color Swatch dialog box** *to define colors to be added to the Swatches palette.*

⑪ *The* **Color Mode menu** *in the New Swatch dialog box.*

⑫ *The* **icons in the Swatches palette** *identify the different types of colors and color modes.*

Rather than use two palettes to define and store colors, you can define and add new colors to your document using only the Swatches palette.

To define a new color swatch:

1. Choose New Color Swatch from the Swatches palette menu. This opens the New Color Swatch dialog box **⑩**.

   or

   Opt/Alt-click the Add Swatch icon at the bottom of the Swatches palette.

2. To name the color swatch yourself, deselect the checkbox for Name with Color Value.

   or

   Leave the setting checked to name the color swatch using the values used to define the color.

3. Choose Process or Spot from the Color Type pop-up list. *(See the sidebar "Process or Spot?" on the next page for an explanation of the difference between process and spot color.)*

4. Choose one of the modes from the Color Mode menu **⑪**. *(See Working with Color Modes on page 92 for a description of the three color modes.)*

   or

   Choose one of the Swatch Libraries at the bottom of the Color Mode menu **⑪**. *(See Using Swatch Libraries on page 102 for more details on these types of colors.)*

5. Use the sliders to change the values from the ones originally defined.

6. Click OK. This adds the color to the Swatches palette **⑫**.

Defining and Storing Color Swatches

Of course, once you have defined a color swatch, you can modify its color definition. This changes the appearance of all text and objects that use that color.

To modify a color swatch:

1. Select the swatch and choose Swatch Options from the Swatches palette menu. This opens the Swatch Options dialog box **⑬**.

    or

    Double-click the swatch in the palette.

2. Make changes to the color.

    TIP The Swatch Options dialog box adds a Preview checkbox. Use it to see how the changes affect the colors applied to objects in the document.

3. Click OK to apply the changes.

Once you create color swatches, you can apply them via the Fill and Stroke controls in the Toolbox or Color palette.

To apply a swatch color:

1. Create the object or text that you want to color.

2. Select either the Fill or Stroke icons in the Color palette or Toolbox. *(See Chapter 6 "Styling Objects" for more information on the Fill or Stroke icons.)*

3. In the Swatches palette, click the color you want. This applies the swatch to the object.

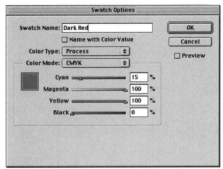

⑬ *Once you define a swatch, you modify it in the* **Swatch Options** *dialog box.*

Process or Spot?

Process colors are those printed using small dots of the four process inks, cyan, magenta, yellow, and black. Spot colors are printed using special inks.

For example, if you look at the process color green printed in a magazine, that color is actually a combination of cyan and yellow printed together in a series of dots. However, a spot color green is printed by using actual green ink.

One benefit of spot colors is that you can exactly match a special color or use specialty colors such as fluorescents or metallics that could never be created using process inks. You can also use a spot color together with black as a two-color job. This is cheaper than printing four-color process colors.

The benefit of process colors is that you use just four inks to create thousands of different color combinations.

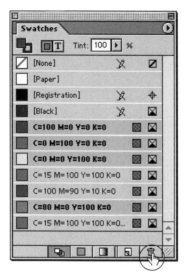

 *Click the* **Delete Swatch icon** *to delete the selected swatches.*

 *The* **Delete Swatch dialog box** *controls what happens to colors when they are deleted from a document.*

You can also delete colors from the Swatches palette.

To delete swatches:

1. Select the color you want to delete.

TIP To select a series of adjacent swatches, hold the Shift key and select the last swatch in the series. This highlights the first and last swatch and all the swatches in between.

TIP Hold the Command/Ctrl key to select non-adjacent swatches.

2. Click the Delete Swatch icon **14** or choose Delete Swatch from the Swatches menu.

3. If the swatch is used within the document, the Delete Swatch dialog box appears asking how you want to replace the deleted swatch **15**:

   • To swap the color with one from the Swatches palette, choose Defined Swatch and then pick a swatch from the pop-up list.
   • To leave the color as an unnamed color applied to the object, choose Unnamed Swatch. *(See page 105 for more information on unnamed colors.)*

TIP The default swatches None, Paper, Black, and Registration cannot be deleted.

If you have many colors in your document that you are not using, you may want to delete them to avoid confusion when the file is sent to a print shop.

To delete all unused swatches:

1. Choose Select All Unused in the Swatches palette menu.

2. Click the Delete Swatch icon or use the Delete Swatch command in the Swatches menu.

Defining and Storing Color Swatches

You can also select several swatches and merge them into one color.

TIP The Merge Swatches command makes it easy to globally replace all instances of one defined color with another. This is especially helpful for changing the colors of objects which aren't part of the Find/Change command.

⑯ *Drag a swatch to move it from one position to another.*

To merge swatches:

1. Click to select the first color. This is the final color that you want the other colors to change to.

2. Hold the Cmd/Ctrl key and click to select another swatch. This is the color that you want to delete.

   or

   Hold the Shift key and click to select a range of swatches. These are the swatches you want to delete.

4. Choose Merge Swatches from the Swatches palette menu. This deletes all the swatches except the swatch that was first selected. That swatch is applied to all text and objects that used the deleted swatches.

The position that swatches appear in the palette comes from the order that they were created. However, you can easily change the order of the swatches. This makes it possible to group colors according to their use or appearance.

To move swatches to new positions:

1. Select a swatch in the palette.

2. Drag the swatch to a new position. A black line indicates where the swatch will be located ⑯.

3. Release the mouse button.

The Cost of Colors

Why is it important to delete unused colors?

One reason is if you are going to send your documents to a service bureau or print shop for final output. It can be confusing to the people who are going to open your file if they see many colors in a document which is supposed to be printed in black and white.

At the very least, they're going to wonder if they've got the right instructions. At the worst, they delay printing the file until they talk to someone.

Also, it may seem like a little thing, but every color adds to the size of the file. Even in these days of huge hard drives, its always better to keep your files as lean as possible.

The Swatch Libraries

InDesign ships with a collection of third-party swatch libraries that contain the color definitions used by professional color systems. *(See the next page for working with swatch libraries.)*

Dicolor holds spot colors that can be matched in the DIC Color Guide.

Focoltone holds process colors. Color matching materials are available from Focoltone International, Ltd.

HKS is a system of spot colors used for industrial design and production in Europe.

Pantone Process Coated consists of process colors. **Pantone Solid Coated** contains spot colors. **Pantone Solid Uncoated** consists of the same spot colors as Coated, adjusted so they represent printing on uncoated paper. All Pantone colors can be matched to materials available from Pantone, Inc.

System (Macintosh) includes the colors of the Macintosh operating system.

System (Windows) includes the colors of the Windows operating system.

Toyo consists of spot colors. Color matching materials are available from the Toyo Ink Manufacturing Co., Ltd.

Trumatch provides process colors. Color matching materials are available from Trumatch, Inc.

Web consists of the 216 colors that are shared by both the Macintosh and Windows system colors.

You may find it easier to duplicate a swatch and then adjust it than to start from scratch.

To duplicate a swatch:

◆ Select the swatch and choose Duplicate Swatch from the Swatches palette menu.

or

Select the swatch and click the New Swatch icon.

or

Drag the swatch onto the New Swatch icon.

When you define and store colors with a specific document open, those colors are stored in the Swatches palette only for that document. However, you can create colors that are available as the default colors for all new documents.

To create default colors:

1. Close all documents but leave InDesign running.

2. Use any of the methods in this section, "Storing Colors" to define and store a color in the Swatches palette. The color will appear in the Swatches palette of all new InDesign documents.

Defining and Storing Color Swatches

Using Swatch Libraries

Rather than defining your own color mixtures, you can use the swatch libraries from professional color systems from companies such as Pantone or Trumatch. These color libraries usually have printed samples that you can refer to in order to see how the color will appear when printed.

To add colors from swatch libraries:

1. Open the New Swatch dialog box *(see page 97)* or the Swatch Options dialog box *(see page 98)*.

2. Choose one of the Swatch Libraries listed in the Color Mode list ⓱. This displays the colors in the library ⓲.

3. Scroll through the library to select the color you want to add to your document.

   or

   Instead of scrolling through a long list, type the name or number associated with the color in the Swatch Library field.

You can use the Swatch Libraries to open color palettes from other InDesign documents and Adobe Illustrator documents.

To import swatches from other documents:

1. Choose Other Library from the Color Mode list ⓱.

2. Navigate to select the InDesign or Illustrator document. The colors appear in the window.

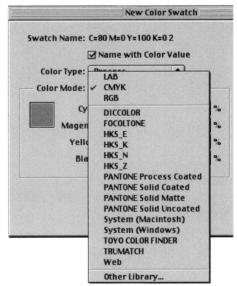

⓱ *The* **Swatch Libraries** *in the Color Mode list.*

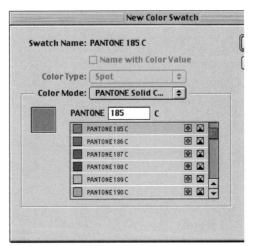

⓲ *An example of the window that displays a swatch library, such as the Pantone Solid Coated colors.*

Using Swatch Libraries

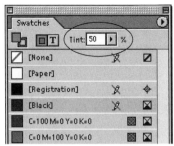

⑲ *Use the* **Tint field** *to create a screened version of a swatch color.*

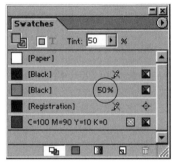

⑳ *A* **tint swatch** *is listed with the same name as the base color and the tint percentage.*

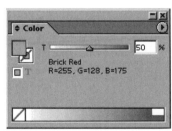

㉑ *The Color palette displays* **a slider and tint ramp** *when a base color is chosen.*

Creating Tints

Tints are screened or lighter versions of colors. Spot color tints create screens of the base color. Process color tints reduce the amounts of the process inks that define the color.

To create a tint swatch:

1. Select the *base color,* that is, the swatch color that you want to tint.

2. Use the Tint field in the Swatches palette to create a screen of the swatch color **⑲**.

3. Click the New Swatch icon to store the tint percentage as a swatch in the Swatches panel.

TIP The tint swatch appears in the Swatches palette with the same name as the base color but with the tint percentage listed **⑳**.

TIP The tint field percentage continues to tint other swatches in the palette until you reset the field to 100%.

As you select a color swatch as a base color, the Color palette displays a slider and spectrum of the color.

To tint a swatch using the Color palette:

1. Select the swatch color that you want to tint.

2. In the Color palette, use the slider or click in the ramp to create a percentage of the base color **㉑**.

3. Click the New Swatch icon to create a tint swatch of the percentage you defined.

You can also create a tint swatch using the Swatches palette menu.

To store a tint swatch of a color:

1. In the Swatches palette, select the *base color,* that is, the color you want to tint.

2. Choose New Tint Swatch from the Swatches palette menu. The New Tint Swatch dialog box appears **22**.

3. Adjust the tint slider to a percentage.

4. Click OK. The tint swatch appears in the Swatches palette with the same name as the base color but with the tint percentage listed.

Once you store a tint swatch, you can modify the tint percentage. This updates all the objects that use that tint swatch.

To modify tint swatches:

1. Double click the name of the tint swatch in the Swatches palette. This opens the Swatch Options dialog box for tints **23**.

2. To change the tint value, adjust the Tint slider at the bottom of the dialog box.

TIP You can also modify the sliders for the base color when you open the Swatch Options dialog box to modify a tint.

3. Click OK to apply the changes.

TIP Anytime you modify the swatch used as a base color, all tints of that color update automatically.

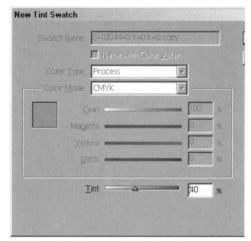

22 *The* **New Tint Swatch dialog box** *lets you set the percentage of a tint.*

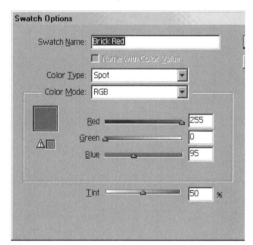

23 *The* **Swatch Options for a tint swatch** *let you change the tint percentage or modify the base color of the tint.*

Working with Unnamed Colors

Unnamed colors are colors that are applied to objects directly from the Color palette instead of through the Swatches palette.

To apply unnamed colors to a fill or stroke:

◆ With an object or text selected, use the Color palette to define a fill color. This applies the unnamed color to the fill of the object or text.

or

With an object or text selected, use the Color palette to define a stroke color. This applies the unnamed color to the stroke of the object or text.

You may find it difficult to modify unnamed colors if they are scattered through a document. Your service bureau or print shop may also have problems working with unnamed colors. Fortunately, you can easily convert unnamed colors into named colors.

To name unnamed colors:

◆ Choose Add Unnamed Colors from the Swatches palette menu. All unnamed colors are added to the palette named with their percentage values.

TIP Open the Swatch dialog box for each color to change its name *(see page 98)*.

Creating Gradient Swatches

Gradients are blends that change from one color into another. InDesign creates gradients as swatches that can then be applied to objects. *(See Chapter 6, "Styling Objects" for information on applying gradients to objects and text.)*

To define a gradient:

1. Choose New Gradient Swatch from the Swatches palette menu. The New Gradient Swatch dialog box appears **24**.

2. Enter a name for the gradient in the Swatch Name field.

3. Choose Linear or Radial in the Type field **25**.

4. Click a color stop on the Gradient Ramp to define a color in the gradient.

TIP You need to select a color stop in order to see the Stop Color list.

5. Choose the type of color for the selected stop from the Stop Color list as follows:
   • **Named Color** shows you the list of colors in the Swatches palette.
   • **LAB, CMYK, or RGB** displays the sliders that let you define the color using the Lab, CMYK, or RGB values.

6. Click the other gradient stop to define a color for it.

7. Adjust the midpoint control to change the position where the two colors blend equally.

8. Click OK to add the gradient to the Swatches palette **26**.

TIP If you don't see the gradient listed in the Swatches palette, click either the Show All Swatches or Show Gradient Swatches icon at the bottom of the Swatches palette.

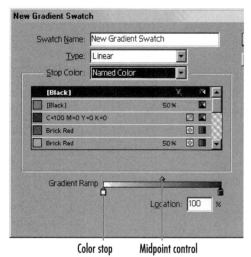

Color stop   Midpoint control

24 *Use the* **New Gradient Swatch dialog box** *to define a gradient of blended colors.*

Linear gradient

Radial gradient

25 *A* **linear gradient** *changes colors along a line. A* **radial gradient** *changes colors in a circular pattern.*

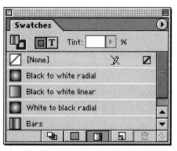

26 *Gradients are stored in the Swatches palette.*

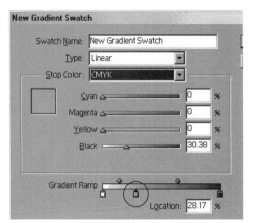

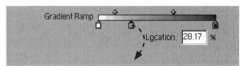

27 *Click under the Gradient Ramp to add a color stop to gradient.*

28 *Drag a color stop off the Gradient Ramp to delete that color from the gradient.*

The Gradient Dialog Boxes

What's the difference between the New Gradient Swatch dialog box and the Gradient Options dialog box? Not much, really.

When you create a gradient you get the *New* Gradient Swatch dialog box. That's because it's a *new* gradient. When you modify a gradient you get the Gradient *Options* dialog box. That's because you're creating *options* to an existing gradient.

The Gradient Options dialog box also has a preview checkbox because once you've create a gradient, you might want to preview what making changes does to the document.

All gradients must have at least two colors. However, you can easily add more colors to a gradient.

To add gradient color stops:

1. Open the New Gradient Swatch or Gradient Options dialog boxes. *(See the sidebar on this page for the difference between the two dialog boxes.)*

2. Click the area below the gradient ramp. This adds a color stop to the ramp area **27**.

3. Make whatever changes you want to the color stop.

4. If necessary, move the color stop to a new position.

5. Click OK to apply the changes to the gradient swatch.

To delete a gradient color stop:

◆ Drag the color stop away from the ramp area and release the mouse **28**. The gradient reblends according to the colors that remain.

TIP You cannot have fewer than two color stops in a gradient.

To modify a gradient swatch:

1. Select the gradient swatch and choose Swatch Options from the Swatches palette menu. This opens the Gradient Options dialog box.

   or

   Double-click the gradient in the palette.

   TIP Use the Preview checkbox to see how the changes affect the gradients applied to objects in the document.

2. Adjust the midpoint, stop colors, or gradient type.

3. Click OK to apply the changes.

Creating Gradient Swatches

Creating Unnamed Gradients

Just as you can create unnamed colors, you can also create unnamed gradients. These are gradients that are created only within the Gradient palette and are not stored in the Swatches palette.

TIP Like unnamed colors, I don't like working with unnamed gradients.

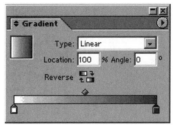

㉙ *Use the* **Gradient palette** *to create unnamed gradients.*

To work with the Gradient palette:

1. If the Gradient palette is not visible, choose **Window > Gradient** to open the palette **㉙**.

   or

   If the Gradient palette is behind other palettes, click the Gradient palette tab.

2. Choose Show Options from the Gradient palette menu to see all the controls in the palette.

TIP If the color stops are not visible, click the area under the ramp to display the color stops in the Gradient palette.

To create unnamed gradients:

1. Use the Type pop-up list to choose between Linear or Radial.

2. Select a color stop and adjust the sliders in the Color palette to define the color at that position.

   or

   Hold the Opt/Alt key and click the name of a swatch in the Swatches palette.

3. Select another color stop and use the sliders in the Color palette to define the color at that position. *(See the exercises on page 107 to add or delete color stops.)*

4. Set the Angle of the gradient in the Angle field.

5. Click the Reverse icon to reverse the positions of the color stops.

(see page 312).

Process and Spot Colors in Gradients

A gradient defined using process colors is separated onto CMYK plates.

A gradient that contains two tints of the same spot color will be separated onto the single spot color plate. If you want the gradient to fade to white, create a gradient between the spot color and a 0% tint of the spot color.

You can create a gradient between two spot colors. However, to avoid moire patterns in the gradient, you must assign different screen angles to those spot colors in the Inks dialog box *(see page 312).*

For instance, if you had a gradient of spot red to spot yellow, you would want to make sure each color had a screen angle that is 45° different from the other. Ask your print shop for details on setting the screen angles for spot colors.

You cannot create gradients as a combination of spot and process colors, because the spot color is automatically converted to a process color.

30 *The* **Eyedropper tool** *lets you sample colors from placed images.*

31 *The* **Eyedropper tool** *can sample colors from placed images.*

Once you have a defined gradient in the Gradient palette, you can store it as a swatch.

To store an unnamed gradient:

1. Create the gradient in the Gradient palette.

2. Click the New Swatch icon in the Swatches palette.

   or

   Drag the preview of the gradient from the Gradient palette into the Swatches palette.

Using the Eyedropper

You can also create colors by using the Eyedropper tool. The Eyedropper tool lets you sample colors from placed graphics. *(See Chapter 8, "Imported Graphics" for more information on placing graphics.)*

To sample and store colors from placed graphics:

1. Click the Eyedropper tool in the Toolbox **30**.

1. Move the eyedropper cursor over the color of a placed graphic **31**.

2. Click to sample the color.

   TIP If you have already used to Eyedropper to sample a color, hold the Opt/Alt key to have the Eyedropper sample a new color.

3. Click the New Swatch icon in the Swatches palette. The sampled color is stored as a color swatch.

   TIP The eyedropper samples the color in the same color mode as the placed graphic. So RGB images create RGB colors; CMYK images create CMYK colors.

   TIP The Eyedropper can also be used to sample and apply fills, strokes, and transparency attributes of objects and text formatting. *(See Chapter 6, "Styling Objects" and Chapter 14, "Automating Text.")*

Using the Eyedropper

Overprinting Colors

Overprinting is a technique that allows you to set the color of one object to mix with any colors underneath. For instance, without overprinting, a yellow object placed over a blue background will print as yellow. But with overprinting turned on, the yellow object mixes with the blue background to create green.

To set a fill or stroke to overprint:

1. Select the object.
2. If the Attributes palette is not visible, choose **Window > Attributes** to open the palette ㉜.

   or

   If the Attributes palette is behind other palettes, click the Attributes palette tab.
3. Check Overprint Fill to set the object's fill color to overprint.
4. Check Overprint Stroke to set the object's stroke color to overprint.

TIP Check Nonprinting in the Attributes palette to set an object not to print. This is helpful if you want to add comments for production use that aren't meant to be seen in the finished piece.

In the past, the only way to see the effects of setting an object to overprint was to wait until the object was separated and printed by a commercial printer. InDesign lets you see a simulation of overprinting onscreen.

To turn on the overprint preview:

◆ Choose **View > Overprint Preview**. InDesign shows the effects of those colors set to overprint ㉝.

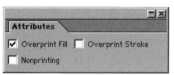

㉜ *Use the* **Attributes palette** *to set an object to overprint.*

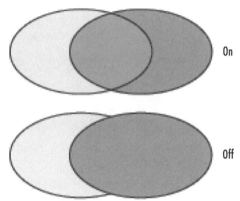

On

Off

㉝ *Turn on the* **Overprint Preview command** *to see the effects of overprinting onscreen.*

Rules of Overprinting

You may come across a situation where the overprint preview doesn't seem to work. Most likely there is nothing wrong with the preview—it's how the color values were defined.

The rules of overprinting state that a color only overprints if it *doesn't share a common plate* with the color below. So, 100% cyan will overprint with 100% yellow to form green; however as soon as you add any percentage of yellow to the cyan, then the top color no longer overprints the bottom.

Overprinting Colors

STYLING OBJECTS 6

Here's where you get a chance to express your creativity. Styling refers to applying fills, strokes, gradients, and effects to frames, lines, and text. If you're bored with plain black text on a white background, InDesign lets you change the text and background colors to almost anything you can imagine.

Most other programs let you style objects and text with fills, strokes, and gradients. InDesign certainly does also.

However, InDesign has broken new ground in offering sophisticated effects such as transparency, drop shadows, and glows. These are the types of effects that art directors and designers could only dream about creating with other page layout programs.

With InDesign, they can make those dreams a reality.

Applying Fills

Fills are the effects applied to inside frames or text. So you can apply one color fill to the text inside a frame and other color fill to the frame itself. (It will be very difficult to read the text if you apply the same color fill to both the text and the frame.) A fill can be a solid color or a gradient. *(See Chapter 5, "Working in Color" for more information on defining colors and gradients.)*

To apply a fill to an object:

1. Select an object.
2. Make sure the Container icon is chosen in the Toolbox or the Swatches or Color palette ❶. This indicates that the object will be modified.
3. Click the Fill icon in the Toolbox or the Swatches or Color palette ❷.
4. Choose a color or gradient in the Color, Gradient, or Swatches palettes.

You don't have to select an object to apply a fill. You can simply drag a swatch onto any object on the page.

To drag fill effects onto objects:

1. Drag a gradient or color swatch from the Toolbox or the Color, Gradient, or Swatches palettes onto the object ❸.
2. Release the mouse button when the swatch is inside the object. This fills the object with the color or gradient.
   TIP If you release the mouse button when the swatch is on the edge of the object, you will apply the effect to the object's stroke *(see page 116)*.

Toolbox

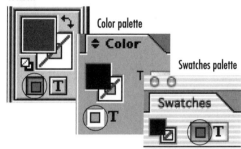

❶ *The* **Container icons** *(circled) indicate an effect will be applied to an object, not text.*

Toolbox

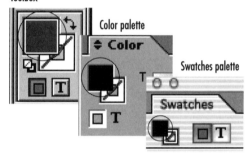

❷ *The* **Fill icons** *(circled) indicate an effect will be applied inside an object.*

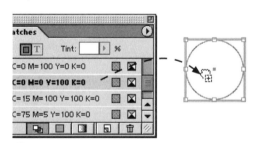

❸ *You can drag a swatch inside an object to apply a fill effect.*

Applying Fills

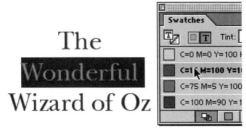

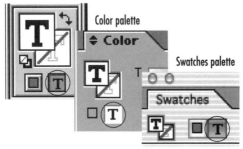

❹ *Choose a swatch to apply the color or gradient to selected text.*

Toolbox

❺ *The* **Text icons** *(circled) set an effect to be applied to all the text within a frame.*

❻ *The* **Gradient icon** *in the Toolbox indicates that a color or gradient will be applied.*

You can also apply fill colors to selected text in a text frame.

To apply a fill to selected text:

1. Use the Text tool to highlight the text.
2. Click the Fill icon in the Toolbox or the Swatches or Color palette.
3. Choose a swatch in the Color, Gradient, or Swatches palette **❹**.

TIP When text is highlighted, the color of the text is inverted. Deselect to see the actual text color.

You can also apply a fill to all the text in a frame with just the frame selected.

To apply a fill to all the text in a frame:

1. Select the text frame that contains the text to which you want to apply the fill.
2. Click the Fill icon in the Toolbox or the Swatches or Color palette.
3. Click the Text icon in the Toolbox or the Swatches or Color palette **❺**.

TIP The *T* inside the Fill icon indicates the text will be affected, not the frame.

4. Choose a swatch in the Color, Gradient, or Swatches palette.

You can also apply a gradient to text or objects.

To apply a gradient fill:

1. Click the Fill icon in the Toolbox or the Swatches or Color palette with the container or text icons selected.
2. Click the gradient icon in the Toolbox **❻**.

 or

 Click a gradient in the Swatches or Gradient palette.

Applying Fills

Once you have applied a gradient to an object or text, you can modify how the gradient is applied using the Gradient tool.

To adjust a gradient fill:

1. Select the object that contains the gradient you want to modify.

2. Choose the Gradient tool in the toolbox .

3. Drag the Gradient tool along the angle that the linear gradient should follow 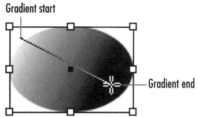.

   or

   Drag the Gradient tool to define the start and end points of a radial gradient **9**.

TIP The start of the drag positions the first color. The end of the drag positions the final color.

TIP You can create a 3D sphere effect by positioning the start of a radial gradient slightly off-center in an ellipse. If the center color is lighter than the outside color, the sphere appears to bulge toward the viewer. If the center color is darker than the outside color, the sphere appears to bulge away from the viewer.

7 *The* **Gradient tool** *in the Toolbox lets you modify the appearance of gradients.*

Gradient start

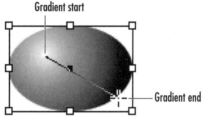

Gradient end

8 *Drag the Gradient tool to set the the start and end points and the angle of a linear gradient.*

Gradient start

Gradient end

9 *Drag with the Gradient tool to set the start and end points of a radial gradient.*

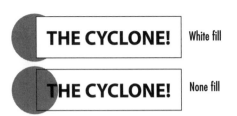

White fill

None fill

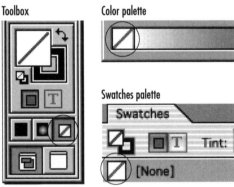

⑩ *The difference between a text frame with a white fill and a none fill.*

Toolbox   Color palette

Swatches palette

⑪ *The* **None** *icons (circled) indicate the background of an object will be transparent.*

⑫ *An example of how a compound path creates a hole in an object.*

You can also apply a fill of None to an object. This makes the background of the object transparent **⑩**.

To apply a fill of None:

1. Select the object.
2. Click the None icon in the Toolbox or the Swatches or Color palette **⑪**.

TIP If the object is not in front of others, you may not see a difference between a white and none fill. Check the icon to be sure.

Another way to style objects is to create a compound path. A compound path allows one path to punch a hole in another. This makes the inside path transparent while the outside path is solid **⑫**.

To create a compound path:

1. Select two paths.
2. Choose **Object** > **Compound Paths** > **Make.**

TIP If the second object is not completely contained inside the first, the hole will appear where the objects overlap.

TIP Compound paths must contain the same fill and stroke effects.

You can release a compound path back to separate objects to restore the inside path to a solid color.

To release a compound path:

1. Select compound path.
2. Choose **Object** > **Compound Paths** > **Release.**

Applying Stroke Effects

Strokes are the effects applied to the edge of objects and text, or along lines. *(See pages 119–122 for other ways to style strokes.)*

TIP In QuarkXPress, stroke effects are called frames or line effects.

To apply a stroke to an object:

1. Select the object.

2. Make sure the Container icon is chosen in the Toolbox or the Swatches or Color palette ❶. This indicates that the object will be modified.

3. Click the Stroke icon in the Toolbox or the Swatches or Color palette ⓭.

4. Choose a swatch in the Color, Gradient, or Swatches palette.

You can also apply a stroke by dragging a swatch onto any object on the page.

To drag stroke effects onto objects:

1. Drag a gradient or color swatch from the Toolbox or the Color, Gradient, or Swatches palette onto the edge of the object.

2. Release the mouse button ⓮. This applies the color or gradient as a stroke.

TIP If you release the mouse button when the swatch is inside the object, you will apply the effect to the object's fill *(see page 112)*.

InDesign makes it easy to swap the fill and stroke settings for an object.

To swap the fill and stroke settings:

♦ Click the double-headed arrow in the Toolbox ⓯. This switches the fill and stroke of a selected object.

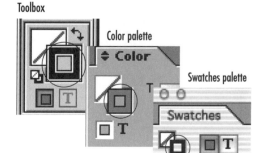

Toolbox

Color palette

Swatches palette

⓭ *The Stroke icons* (circled) *set an effect to be applied to the outside of an object or text.*

⓮ *Drag a swatch onto the edge to apply a stroke effect to an object.*

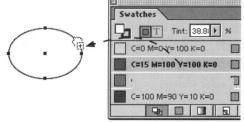

⓯ *Click the Swap Fill and Stroke icon in the Toolbox to switch the settings.*

Dorothy
Dorothy

16 *A stroke effect applied to text.*

| Solid fill | Linear gradient fill | Radial gradient fill |

17 *The effect of a linear gradient applied as a stroke with three different types of fills.*

Permission to Stroke Text

If you have worked with other desktop publishing programs, you may have found that strokes applied to text deform the shape of the characters. This happens because the stroke is applied on both the outside and the inside of the text. As a result, most teachers like me warned our students never to stroke text—not in headlines and not in body copy.

InDesign, however, only places strokes on the outside of text. This means that it does not distort the characters. So you have complete permission to stroke text in InDesign.

You can also stroke the outside edges of text with a color or gradient **16**.

To apply a stroke to selected text:
1. Use the Text tool to highlight the text.
2. Click the Stroke icon in the Toolbox or Color palette.
3. Choose a swatch in the Color, Gradient, or Swatches palette.

To apply a stroke to all the text in a frame:
1. Select the text frame that contains the text to which you want to apply the stroke.
2. Click the Text button in the Toolbox or Color palette.
3. Click the Stroke icon in the Toolbox or Color palette.
4. Choose a swatch in the Color, Gradient, or Swatches palette.

You can also apply a gradient as a stroke to text or objects.

To apply a gradient stroke:
1. Click the Stroke icon in the Toolbox or the Swatches or Color palette.
2. Click the Gradient icon in the Toolbox or the Swatches or Gradient palette.
3. Use the Gradient tool to modify the angle or length of the gradient applied to a stroke *(see page 117)*.
- **TIP** A linear gradient applied as a stroke creates a beveled effect. This may be combined with a solid or gradient fills for 3-dimensional effects **17**.

Color is only one aspect of a stroke effect. The Stroke palette controls the rest of the stroke attributes.

To work with the Stroke palette:

◆ If the Stroke palette is not visible, choose **Window > Stroke** to view it .

   or

   If the Stroke palette is behind other palettes, click the Stroke palette tab.

⓲ *The Stroke palette with all its options displayed.*

One of the most important attributes of a stroke is its thickness. This is controlled by changing the stroke weight ⓳.

To set the stroke weight (thickness):

1. Select the object.
2. Use the weight field controls to set the thickness of the stroke ⓴.

TIP To prevent you from modifying the inside of an object when you add a stroke, choose Weight Changes Bounding Box from the Stroke palette submenu ㉑. This is helpful if the object contains a placed image (*see Chapter 8, "Imported Graphics"*).

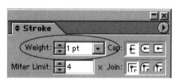
⓳ *Different stroke weights.*

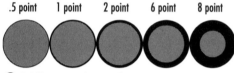
⓴ *The* **Weight controls** *let you change the stroke thickness.*

Warning: Watch Out When You Scale or Shear Stroked Objects!

Be careful if you use any of the Scale or Shear tools or the commands in the Transform palette with stroked objects.

InDesign scales the stroke weight as well as the object. So a stroke weight that is displayed as 1 point may actually be thinner or thicker after scaling. The shear tool can also distort the appearance of the stroke.

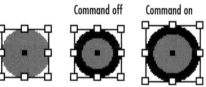
㉑ *With the* **Weight Changes Bounding Box** *command on, adding a stroke increases the size of the object.*

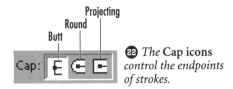

22 *The* **Cap** *icons control the endpoints of strokes.*

Butt
Round
Projecting

23 *The three Cap settings applied to strokes.*

24 *The* **Join** *buttons control how the corners of strokes are displayed.*

Miter   Round   Bevel

25 *The three Join settings applied to strokes.*

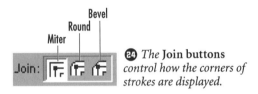

26 *The* **Miter Limit** *field controls how long a miter point may extend.*

Miter limit 7   Miter limit 6

27 *Lowering the miter limit changes the display of the miter to a bevel join.*

A stroke's style is also controlled by the end caps and joins, which form point and corners.

To set the caps and joins:

1. Select an object that has a stroke applied to it.

2. In the Stroke palette, use the Cap icons **22** to change the way the ends of open paths are treated **23**:
    *   **Butt** ends the stroke in a square.
    *   **Round** ends the stroke in a semi-circle.
    *   **Projecting** ends the stroke in a square that extends our from the end point.
    TIP The Cap settings have no effect on closed paths such as rectangles, ellipses, and polygons.

3. Use the Join buttons **24** to change the way two segments of a path meet at corners **25**:
    *   **Miter** joins the segments at an angle.
    *   **Round** joins the segments with a curve.
    *   **Bevel** joins the segments with a line between the segments.
    TIP The join commands affect only corner points. *(See Chapter 7, "Pen and Beziers" for information on the types of points.)*

Sometimes a mitered join becomes too long and pointed. Fortunately you can control its length.

To set the miter limit:

1. Select an object with a mitered join.

2. In the Stroke palette, increase the amount in the Miter Limit field to control the size of the angle between the segments **26**.

TIP If the size of the angle exceeds the miter limit, a bevel is substituted **27**.

The default setting for strokes displays them as a solid line. However, you can modify strokes so they are displayed as stripes ㉘.

To apply stripe styles to strokes:

1. Apply a stroke to an object.
2. Choose one of the seven stripe styles from the Stroke Type menu ㉙.

TIP Use the Stroke Weight field to increase or decrease the size of the stripe.

TIP The gap between the stripes is always clear, not white.

InDesign also gives you three pre-set dash styles and one custom style. These pre-set styles let you quickly apply two different dash looks ㉚.

To apply the pre-set dashed styles:

1. Apply a stroke to an object.
2. Choose one of the two pre-set dashes from the Stroke Type menu:
   - **Dash (3 and 2)** creates a dash that is 3 times the stroke weight with a gap between the dashes that is 2 times the stroke weight.
   - **Dash (4 and 4)** creates dashes and gaps that are 4 times the stroke weight.

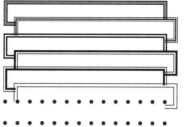

㉘ *The **seven stripe styles** for strokes.*

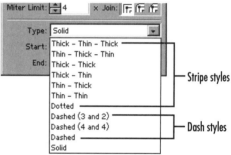

㉙ *The **Type menu** in the Stroke palette lets you apply stripes or dashes to strokes.*

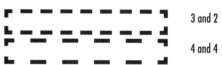

3 and 2

4 and 4

㉚ *The effects of the two pre-set dash styles on 3-point strokes.*

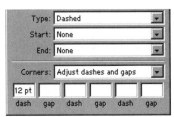

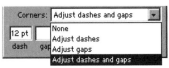

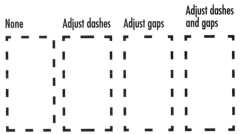

❸❶ *The* **Dashed settings** *at the bottom of the Stroke palette.*

❸❷ *Use the* **Corners** *list to make adjustments in how dashes and gaps are distributed on a stroke.*

❸❸ *Examples of how the Corners settings affect the appearance of a dashed stroke.*

InDesign also lets you customize the size of the dashes and the gaps between them.

To create custom dashed strokes:

1. Apply a stroke to an object.

2. Choose Dashed from the Stroke Type pop-up menu. The dashed settings appear at the bottom of the Stroke palette **❸❶**.

3. Enter an amount in the first dash field for the length of all of the dashes in the line.

4. Enter an amount in the first gap field for the size of the space between all of the dashes.

5. To create a series of dashes and gaps with irregular lengths, enter other values in the rest of the dash and gap fields.

TIP Apply round caps to add round ends to the dashes.

6. If necessary, use the Corners list **❸❷** to adjust the distribution of the dashes and gaps along the stroke **❸❸**:

   - **None** leaves the dashes and gaps as they are. This can cause unequal dashes at the corners.
   - **Adjust dashes** changes the stroke so that the corner dashes are equal.
   - **Adjust gaps** changes the stroke so that the gap lengths are equal.
   - **Adjust dashes and gaps** changes the stroke to make the best fit so that both the corner dashes and gaps are equal.

Applying Stroke Effects

You can add arrowheads and other end shapes to the ends of lines and to open paths 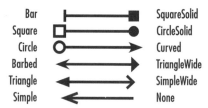.

To add arrowheads and end shapes:

1. Select an object with open ends.
2. Add a graphic to the beginning of the object, by choosing a shape from the Start menu in the Stroke palette .
3. Add a graphic to the end of the object, by choosing a shape from the End menu.

Adding Corner Effects

InDesign can modify the shape of objects by adding special corner effects. You can apply these effects to any object that has corner points.

TIP You can change a star's points to round by applying a rounded corner effect.

To apply corner effects:

1. Select an object with corner points.
2. Choose **Object > Corner Effects.** The Corner Effects dialog box appears .
3. Choose one of the effects from the Effect menu.
4. Set the size of the effect.

TIP Check Preview so you can see how the settings look.

5. Click OK to apply the settings 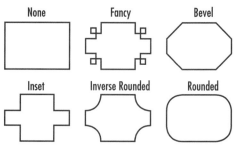.

TIP You can change corner effects later by selecting the object and reopening the dialog box. However, the individual points within the effect cannot be manipulated.

The twelve different types of **arrowhead styles** *for paths.*

Choose an arrowhead style from the **Start or End menus** *in the Stroke palette.*

The **Corner Effects dialog box** *lets you apply different corners to objects.*

An example of applying the special corner effects applied to rectangles.

38 *The* **Transparency palette** *controls the object's opacity and its interaction with other objects.*

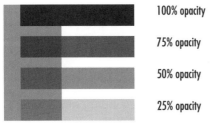

100% opacity

75% opacity

50% opacity

25% opacity

39 *An example of how different opacity settings change the display of an object filled with black.*

40 *The* **Opacity slider** *in the Transparency palette lowers the visibility of objects.*

41 *An example of how a white frame set to 50 percent opacity creates a ghost area in the image.*

Applying Transparency

The command center of all the transparency controls in InDesign is located in the Transparency palette.

To open the Transparency palette:

◆ Choose **Window** > **Transparency** to open the palette **38**.

or

If the Transparency palette is behind other palettes, click the Transparency palette tab.

Ever since desktop publishing began, designers have requested some way to see through one object to the others behind it. One way to do this is to reduce the opacity, or increase the translucence, in an object **39**.

To reduce an object's opacity:

1. Select the object that you want to see through.

2. Use the Opacity slider in the Transparency palette to reduce the visibility of the object **40**.

TIP Once you have activated the Opacity field or slider, you can use the up and down arrow keys on the keyboard to increase or decrease the amount of opacity.

TIP Place a white frame at a reduced opacity over an image to "ghost" that area in the image **41**. You can then add a text frame over the ghosted area.

If you have used Adobe Photoshop, you should be familiar with the Blend Mode menu. This allows the colors and shades in one object to interact with the objects below.

To add a blend mode to objects:

1. Select the object that you want to interact with the objects below it.

2. Choose a blend mode from the list in the Transparency palette ❷. *(See the opposite page for a description and display of the blend modes.)*

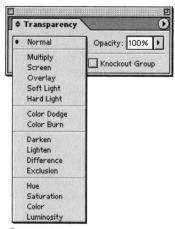

❷ *The Blend mode menu lets you change the interaction between objects.*

As you apply a blend mode or an opacity setting, you may need to control how the transparency is applied. One such control is called a *knockout group*. Objects in a knockout group display their blend modes or opacity settings on other objects, but not with each other ❸.

To create a knockout group:

1. Apply a blend mode or opacity setting to an object.

2. Repeat for any additional objects.

TIP Each object can have its own blend mode or opacity setting, or they all can have the same settings.

3. Use the Selection tool and select the objects that have the blend mode or opacity settings applied. These are the objects you *don't* want to interact with each other.

4. Choose **Object > Group**.

5. With the group selected, click the Knockout Group checkbox in the Transparency palette ❹.

TIP If the Knockout Group checkbox is not visible, click the palette tab or choose Show Transparency Options from the Transparency palette menu.

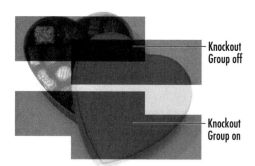

Knockout Group off

Knockout Group on

❸ *With the Knockout Group turned on, blended objects do not interact with each other.*

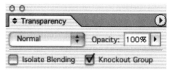

❹ *The Knockout Group checkbox in the Transparency palette changes the interaction of grouped objects between each other.*

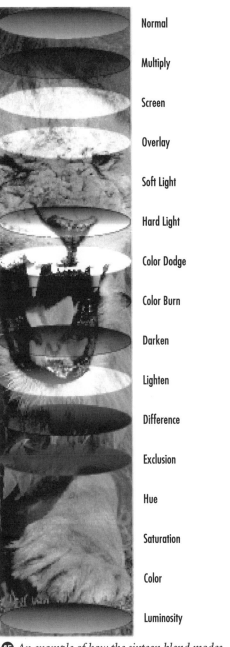

Normal

Multiply

Screen

Overlay

Soft Light

Hard Light

Color Dodge

Color Burn

Darken

Lighten

Difference

Exclusion

Hue

Saturation

Color

Luminosity

45 *An example of how the sixteen blend modes interact when placed over an image.*

Understanding the Blend Modes

The best way to understand the blend modes is to experiment and explore. Here's a quick rundown of how they work **45**.

- **Multiply** multiplies the bottom color with the top color.

- **Screen** is the inverse of Multiply.

- **Overlay** preserves the highlights and shadows of the base color while mixing in the top color.

- **Soft Light** is similar to shining a diffused spotlight on the artwork.

- **Hard Light** is similar to shining a harsh spotlight on the artwork.

- **Color Dodge** lightens the bottom color to reflect the top color.

- **Color Burn** darkens the bottom color to reflect the top color.

- **Darken** displays either the bottom or topcolor—whichever is darker.

- **Lighten** selects the bottom or top color—whichever is lighter.

- **Difference** subtracts one color from another depending on which has the greater brightness.

- **Exclusion** is similar to Difference but is lower in contrast.

- **Hue** replaces the hue of the bottom object with the top hue.

- **Saturation** replaces the saturation of the bottom object with the top.

- **Color** colorizes the bottom object with the top color.

- **Luminosity** changes the bottom object's luminence with the top.

Difference, Exclusion, Hue, Saturation, Color, and Luminosity modes do not blend spot colors, only process colors.

For the opposite effect of a Knockout group you use the Isolate Blending command. With this command, the objects in the group display their blend modes with each other, but not with objects outside the group 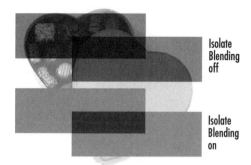.

TIP The Isolate Blending command only affects the blend mode settings, not any opacity settings.

To isolate the blending in objects:

1. Apply a blend mode to an object.

2. Repeat for any additional objects.

TIP Each object can have its own blend mode, or all objects can have the same settings.

3. Use the Selection tool and select the objects that have the blend mode. These are the object that you *don't* want to interact with the other objects.

4. Choose **Object > Group**.

5. Keep the group selected, click the Isolate Blending checkbox in the Transparency palette **47**. The objects in the group interact with each other, but not with other objects on the page.

46 *With the* **Isolate Blending** *turned on, blended objects only interact with each other, not the objects below.*

47 *The* **Isolate Blending checkbox** *in the Transparency palette limits grouped objects to interact only with each other.*

DOROTHY

48 *An example of a drop shadow applied to text.*

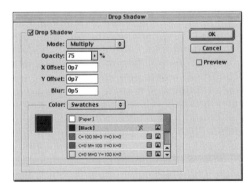

49 *An example of a drop shadow applied to text and positioned over a placed image.*

50 *An example of a drop shadow applied to a placed image.*

Drop Shadow
☑ Drop Shadow
Mode: Multiply ◆
Opacity: 75 ▸ %
X Offset: 0p7
Y Offset: 0p7
Blur: 0p5
Color: Swatches ◆
☐ [Paper]
■ [Black]
☐ C=100 M=0 Y=0 K=0
☐ C=0 M=100 Y=0 K=0
☐ C=0 M=0 Y=100 K=0

OK / Cancel / ☐ Preview

51 *The* **Drop Shadow dialog box** *controls how shadows are applied to objects, text, and images.*

Adding Drop Shadows and Feathers

One of the most desired features in graphics programs is an automatic drop shadow that is cast behind objects, text, or images **48** – **50**. While it's been very easy to add drop shadows in Adobe Photoshop or Adobe Illustrator, it has not been easy to do so in page-layout programs—that is until InDesign.

To add a drop shadow to an object:

1. Select the object, text frame, or placed image you want to have a drop shadow.

2. Choose **Object** > **Drop Shadow**. This opens the Drop Shadow dialog box **51**.

3. Click the Drop Shadow checkbox. This displays the rest of the drop shadow controls.

TIP Click the Preview checkbox so you can see the effects as you change the settings.

4. Set the Mode list to choose the blend mode for the shadow.

TIP The Mode list settings are the same as the blend mode settings in the Transparency palette *(see pages 124 and 125)*.

5. Set the Opacity amount for how transparent the shadow should be.

6. Set the *X* Offset and *Y* Offset to create the distance between the shadow and the object.

7. Set the Blur amount for how soft the edges of the drop shadow should be.

8. Use the Color list to set a color for the shadow.

TIP You can use the Swatches list to choose named colors or switch to CMYK, RGB, or LAB colors.

9. Click OK to apply the shadow.

TIP You can't apply a shadow to just a portion of text. The effect is applied to all the text in the frame.

To remove a drop shadow from an object:

1. Select the object that has the drop shadow applied.

2. Choose **Object > Drop Shadow**. This opens the Drop Shadow dialog box.

3. Uncheck the Drop Shadow checkbox. This turns off the drop shadow effect.

🔼 *The Feather dialog box controls how soft edges are applied to objects, text, and images.*

InDesign lets you apply feather commands to objects. This softens the edges of the images.

To add a feathered edge to an object:

1. Select the object, text frame, or placed image you want to have a feathered edge.

2. Choose **Object > Feather**. This opens the Feather dialog box 🔼.

3. Click the Feather checkbox. This displays the rest of the feather controls.

🔳 Click the Preview checkbox so you can see the effects as you change the settings.

4. Use the Feather Width controls to set how thick the feather should appear.

5. Choose one of the settings in the Corners list as follows 🔼:

   • **Sharp** feathers by closely following the contours of the object.

   • **Round** feathers by rounding off any sharp corners in the image.

   • **Diffuse** makes the edges of the object fade from opaque to transparent.

🔳 Use Diffuse if you want to match the Feather command in Adobe Illustrator.

8. Click OK to apply the feather.

To remove a feather from an object:

1. Select the object that has the feather applied.

2. Choose **Object > Feather**. This opens the Feather dialog box.

3. Uncheck the Feather checkbox. This turns off the feather effect.

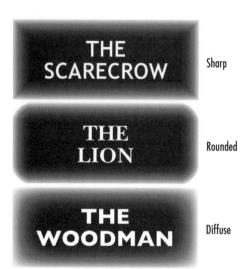

🔼 *The **three different corner settings** for applying a feather effect.*

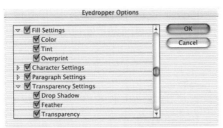

54 *The* **Eyedropper tool** *in the Toolbox lets you sample object attributes.*

55 *Use the Eyedropper Options dialog box to set which attributes the Eyedropper will sample and apply.*

56 *The* **white eyedropper** *lets you sample the object attributes.*

57 *The* **black eyedropper** *applies object attributes from one object to another.*

Using the Eyedropper

Imagine you've finished styling an object with exactly the right combination of fill, stroke, and transparency attributes. And now you'd like to apply those same settings to a different object. That's where the Eyedropper tool comes to the rescue. First you have to set which attributes the Eyedropper tool will sample.

To set the eyedropper options:

1. Double-click the Eyedropper tool in the Toolbox **54**. This opens the Eyedropper Options dialog box **55**.

2. Click the triangles to open each of the attribute categories

TIP The object categories are Fill, Stroke, and Transparency. *(See page 281 for working with the two text categories.)*

3. Use the checkboxes to choose which attributes you want the Eyedropper tool to sample.

4. Click OK to set the options.

Once you set the eyedropper options, you can sample and apply object attributes.

To sample and apply object attributes:

1. Choose the Eyedropper tool.

2. Click the white eyedropper cursor inside the object that you want to sample **56**. The cursor changes from white to black.

TIP If an object has a stroke, but no fill, click on the object's outline to sample its stroke.

3. Click the black eyedropper cursor inside the object that you want to change **57**. This changes the object's attributes.

4. Click the eyedropper inside any other objects that you want to change.

As you work with the Eyedropper tool, you may want to unload one set of attributes and sample new ones.

To sample new attributes:

1. Hold the Opt/Alt key. The eyedropper cursor changes to white.

2. Click the cursor inside a new object that you want to sample.

3. Release the Opt/Alt key to apply the new setting to objects.

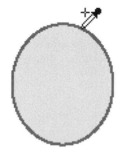

58 *The* **white precision eyedropper** *allows you to sample a specific color.*

You may not want to sample all the attributes in an object—just the fill or stroke. That's when you can use the Eyedropper tool in its precision mode. The precision mode allows you to sample and apply just the color to either a fill or stroke.

59 *The* **black precision eyedropper** *lets you apply a specific color to either the fill or stroke.*

To use the precision eyedropper:

1. Choose the Eyedropper tool. Hold the Shift key. A plus sign appears next to the white eyedropper cursor **58**. This indicates that the Eyedropper tool is in the precision mode.

2. Click the precision white eyedropper cursor on the fill or stroke color you wish to sample. The cursor turns into the precision black eyedropper **59**.

3. Click the precision eyedropper on either a fill or stroke of the object that you want to change. Only the fill or stroke is changed.

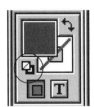

60 *Click the* **Default Fill and Stroke icon** *in the Toolbox to set the fill to none and stroke to black.*

Setting Object Defaults

You can make any of the object settings the default for any new objects you create. You can set the object defaults for the current document or globally for all new documents.

To set current document defaults:

1. With a document open, deselect any objects.

2. Make whatever changes you want in the Stroke palette or other palettes. This sets the defaults for the open document.

To set global defaults:

◆ With no document open, make whatever changes you want in the Stroke or other palettes. This sets the global defaults for all new documents.

InDesign also has its own default fill and stroke setting of a black stroke and no fill. This can be easily applied to objects.

To apply the InDesign fill and stroke defaults:

◆ Click the Default Fill and Stroke icon in the Toolbox **60**.

PEN AND BEZIERS 7

I remember the first time I tried to use the Pen tool in a computer graphics program. I clicked the tool and dragged across the screen in the way I thought would create a simple curve. Instead, I got a wild series of lines that shot out in different directions. When I tried to change the shape of the curves, things got even worse. I was so startled I immediately closed up the program and didn't use the Pen tool for a long, long time.

When I finally got up enough nerve to try the tool again, it took a lot of trial and error but eventually I was able to understand the Pen and Bezier controls. Once I got it, I realized the principles are simple. I just wish someone had written out easy to understand, step-by-step instructions. So think of this chapter as the instructions for the Pen tool that I wish I had back then.

This chapter gives you all the fundamentals to working with the Pen tool. However, if you would like to learn how to use the Pen tool through tutorial movies and audio narration, may I suggest you visit **www.zenofthepen.org.**

The site has an electronic tutorial you can purchase to help you learn the Pen tool in Adobe InDesign as well as other programs such as Adobe Illustrator and Adobe Photoshop.

Pen Points

One of the most important tools in any graphics program is the Pen tool. Fortunately InDesign has a Pen tool that lets you create much more sophisticated shapes in your layout than can be created with the basic shape tools. *(See Chapter 4, "Working with Objects" for more information on working with the basic shapes.)*

TIP If you are familiar with the Pen tool in Adobe Illustrator or Macromedia FreeHand, you will find it very easy to master the Pen in InDesign.

If you've never used a Pen tool in any graphics program, you will understand more if you first become familiar with the elements of paths.

Elements of Paths

- **Anchor points** define a path at points where the path changes **❶**.

- **Segments** are the paths that connect anchor points **❶**.

- **Control handles** extend out from anchor points; their length and direction control the shape of curves of the segments **❶**.

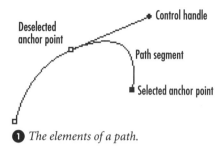

❶ *The elements of a path.*

The Father of Bezier Curves

Some people call the curves created by the Pen tool *Bezier curves*. This is in honor of Pierre Bezier (*Bay-zee-ay*), the French mathematician.

Monsieur Bezier created the system of mathematics that is used to define the relationship of the control handles to the shape of the curve.

Adobe Systems, Inc., adopted this mathematical system when it created the PostScript language which is used as the basis of graphics programs. InDesign, along with many other programs, uses Bezier curves as the mathematics behind each curve.

Drawing in a Page Layout Program?

You may be wondering why you would use the Pen tool in InDesign. After all, didn't I mention in Chapter 4 that you should use a dedicated illustration program such as Adobe Illustrator if you need artwork?

I limit using InDesign's Pen tool to simple things. If I need some sort of curved or wavy line, I use InDesign's Pen tool. For instance, all the curved arrows in this book were created with the Pen tool. However, if I want a perfect spiral, I would use Illustrator's Spiral tool. *(See Chapter 8, "Imported Graphics" for how to bring Illustrator paths into InDesign.)*

If I need to jazz up some text, I stay within InDesign. But if I need a complete map of New York State with highways, rivers, and scenic attractions, I work in Illustrator.

*Click the **Pen tool** in the Toolbox to create lines.*

 The start icon for the Pen tool.

 Click with the Pen tool to create a corner point, shown as a small square.

 Straight lines extend between the plain corner points.

The small circle next to the Pen cursor indicates that you will close the path.

Drawing Lines

Different types of anchor points create different line shapes. Straight lines are formed by creating *plain corner points.*

To create straight lines:

1. Click the Pen tool in the Toolbox ❷.
2. Position the cursor where the path should start. A small *X* appears next to the Pen which indicates that you are starting the path ❸.
3. Click. A plain corner point appears as a colored square. The Pen cursor is displayed without any symbol next to it ❹.
4. Position the cursor for the next point and click. This creates another plain corner point with a straight line that connects the first point to the second.

TIP Hold the Shift key to constrain the straight lines to 45-degree angles.

5. Continue clicking until you have created all the straight-line sides of the object ❺.

TIP If you have not closed the path (*see the next exercise*), hold the Cmd/Ctrl key and click with the Selection tool. This deselects the path and allows you to start a new one.

To close a path with a straight line:

1. Move the Pen over the first point. A small circle appears next to the Pen ❻. This indicates that you can close the path.
2. Click. This closes the path with a plain corner point and allows you to start a new path.

Drawing Lines

Drawing Curves

Smooth curve points create curves like the track a roller coaster follows. There are no abrupt changes from one curve to another.

To create smooth curves:

1. Drag the Pen tool where you want to start the curve. Handles extend out from the point.

TIP The length and angle of the handle controls the curve's height and direction.

2. Release the mouse button.

TIP You do not see a curve until you create the next point of the path.

3. Move the cursor to where you want the next part of the curve. Drag to create the curved segment between the two smooth curve points **7**.

4. Continue to create curved segments by repeating steps 2 and 3 **8**.

To close a path with a smooth curve:

1. Move the Pen over the first point. A small circle appears indicating that you can close the path.

2. Drag backwards to close the path **9**.

A corner curve point creates curves with an abrupt change in direction. The path of a bouncing ball illustrates a corner curve.

To create a corner curve:

1. With the Pen tool active, drag to create an anchor point with control handles.

2. Without releasing the mouse button, hold the Opt/Alt key and then drag to pivot the second handle **10**.

3. Release the mouse button when the second handle is the correct length and direction.

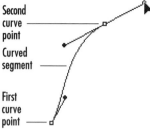

Second curve point
Curved segment
First curve point

7 *Drag with the Pen tool to create smooth curves.*

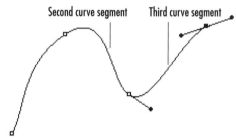

Second curve segment   Third curve segment

8 *A path with a series of curved segments.*

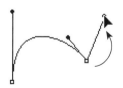

Second drag
First drag
Final drag
Third drag

9 *Dragging backwards closes a path with a smooth curve.*

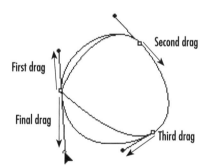

10 *Hold the Opt/Alt key to pivot the handles, which creates a corner curve.*

Drawing Curves

⓫ *Move the cursor back over a point and click to retract a handle along a curve.*

⓬ *Drag with the Pen tool over an existing anchor point to extend a handle out from the point.*

General Pen Rules

As you work with the Pen tool, there are some rules you should follow:

Use the fewest number of points to define a path. Too many points add to the size of the file and make it difficult to edit the path later.

Try to limit the length of the control handles to one-third the length of the curve. This is sometimes called the *One-Third Rule*. The One-Third Rule makes it easier to edit and control the shape of curves.

Changing Curves and Corner Points

If you retract the handle that extends out from a curve point, the next segment becomes a straight line.

To retract a handle:

1. Drag to create a smooth curve point.

2. Move the Pen cursor back over the anchor point. A small angle symbol appears next to the cursor.

3. Click. The handle retracts back into the anchor point. The point is now a corner point with only one handle.

4. Continue the path with either a straight line or a curved line.

TIP Click to make the next path segment straight. Drag to make the next path segment curved.

If you create a corner point with no control handles, you can extend a single handle out from that anchor point.

To extend a handle from a point:

1. Click to create a corner point with no handles.

2. Move the Pen cursor back over the anchor point you just created. A small angle symbol appears next to the cursor ⓫.

3. Drag to pull a single handle out from the anchor point ⓬.

4. Continue the path with a curved line.

Modifying Paths

Once you create a path, you can still change its shape and the position of the points. You can also split a path into two separate segments or join two segments together. When you move points, you use the Direct Selection tool.

To move individual points:

1. Click the Direct Selection tool in the Toolbox .

2. Position the tool over the point you want to move.

3. Drag the point to the new position.

To select and move multiple points:

1. Click the Direct Selection tool in the Toolbox.

2. Drag to create a rectangular marquee around the points you want to select 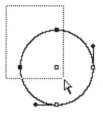. The selected points appear solid. The unselected points appear hollow.

   or

   Hold the Shift key as you click to select the points.

   TIP You can select points in one path or multiple paths.

3. Drag the point to the new position.

The Direct Selection tool also lets you change the length and direction of the control handles.

To move control handles:

1. Click the Direct Selection tool.

2. Click a point on the path. This displays the control handles for that point.

3. Position the Direct Selection tool over the end point of the handle.

4. Drag the handle to the new position 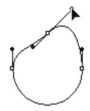.

⑬ *The* **Direct Selection tool** *in the Toolbox; use it to move points.*

⑭ *Drag a marquee to select multiple points. The center point does not turn black.*

⑮ *The Direct Selection tool changes the length and position of a control handle.*

16 *The **Scissors tool** in the Toolbox allows you to snip paths in two.*

17 *The Scissors tool splits a path into two points, one on top of the other.*

18 *The results of applying the Reverse Path command to a path with an arrowhead.*

You may want to separate one path into two parts—for instance, to separate two halves of a circle. The Scissors tool makes it easy to split or break a path into segments.

To split paths:

1. Select the path.

2. Click the Scissors tool in the Toolbox **16**.

3. Position the cursor where you want to split the path.

4. Click to split the path at that point.

TIP The Scissors tool splits the path by creating two points, one on top of the other. Use the Direct Selection tool to move one point away from the other **17**.

TIP Paths that contain text cannot be split into two distinct segments.

The direction of a path comes from the order in which you draw the path. You can change the direction of the path.

To change the path direction:

1. Use the Direct Selection tool to select the path.

2. Choose **Object > Reverse Path.** This switches the start and end points of the path **18**.

Modifying Points

So what happens if you create the wrong point with the Pen tool? Are you stuck? Does it mean you have to redraw the entire path? Thankfully, no—there are many ways to change the paths made with the Pen tool, as well as paths made with other tools. *(See Chapter 4, "Working with Objects" for more information on working with the basic shapes.)*

A simple way to change a path is to add a point. This helps you turn one shape into another.

19 *The* **Add Anchor Point** **tool** *in the Toolbox.*

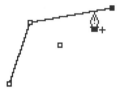

20 *The Add Anchor Point tool over a path segment.*

To add points to a path:

1. Select the path.

2. Choose the Add Anchor Point tool in the Toolbox **19**.

3. Click the path where you want to add the point.

TIP The Pen tool automatically changes to the Add Anchor Point tool when positioned over a path segment **20**.

21 *The* **Delete Anchor Point** **tool** *in the Toolbox.*

You can delete points from a path without causing a break in the path.

To delete points from a path:

1. Select the path.

2. Choose the Delete Anchor Point tool in the Toolbox **21**.

3. Click to delete the point of the path.

TIP The Pen tool also changes to the Delete Anchor Point tool when positioned over a point on a path **22**.

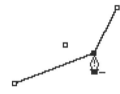

22 *The Delete Anchor Point tool over a point.*

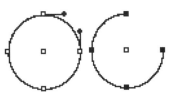

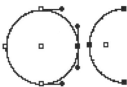

23 *When you select and* **delete a segment**, *you keep the points on either side of the segment.*

24 *When you select and* **delete a point**, *you delete both segments that were attached to the point.*

25 *The* **Convert Direction Point tool** *in the Toolbox.*

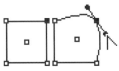

26 *Drag with the Convert Direction Point tool to change a corner point into a smooth curve point.*

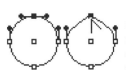

27 *Click with the Convert Direction Point tool to change a smooth curve point into a corner point.*

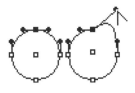

28 *Drag a handle with the Convert Direction Point tool to change a smooth curve point into a corner curve point.*

You may also want to create an open path by deleting a segment or the point between two segments.

To delete a segment in a path:

1. Use the Direct Selection tool to select the segment that you want to delete.
2. Press the Delete key choose **Edit** > **Clear**. This deletes the segments and opens the path **23**.

TIP If you select a point with the Direct Selection tool, the two segments on either side of the point can be deleted **24**.

You can also change the control handles around an anchor point. This changes the shape of the segments controlled by that anchor point.

To modify an anchor point:

1. Select the path.
2. Choose the Convert Direction Point tool in the Toolbox **25**.
3. Use the tool as follows to change the anchor points:
   - Press and drag a corner point to create a smooth curve point with two handles **26**.
   - Click a smooth curve point to create a corner point with no handles **27**.
   - Drag one of the handles of a smooth curve point to create a corner curve point **28**.

Modifying Points

Using the Pencil Tool

You may find it difficult to use the Pen to draw paths—especially positioning anchor points and Bezier handles. Fortunately the Pencil tool is much easier to use.

TIP If you are familiar with the Pencil tool in Adobe Illustrator, you will find it easy to work with InDesign's Pencil tool.

To draw with the Pencil tool:

1. Click the Pencil tool in the Toolbox **29**. A small *X* next to the Pencil cursor indicates you are about to start the path **30**.

2. Press and drag with the Pencil **31**.

3. To close the path, hold the Opt/Alt key **32**. A small *O* next to the cursor indicates the path will be closed.

4. Release the mouse to create the path.

The Pencil tool can also be used to edit existing paths and reshape paths.

To edit paths with the Pencil tool:

1. Select the path that you want to reshape.

TIP The Pencil tool can edit paths created by tools such as the Pen or the frame tools.

2. Move the Pencil tool near the selected path. The *X* next to the cursor disappears. This indicates that you are about to edit the path.

3. Drag along the path. When you release the mouse button, the path is reshaped **33**.

TIP If you don't get the results you expect, drag the Pencil tool in the opposite direction.

 29 *The* **Pencil tool** *in the Toolbox.*

 **30** *The X next to the Pencil cursor indicates you are about to start a new path.*

31 *Press and drag to create a path with the Pencil tool.*

 **32** *The circle next to the Pencil cursor indicates the Opt/Alt key will close the path.*

33 *Drag the Pencil tool next to a selected path to reshape the path.*

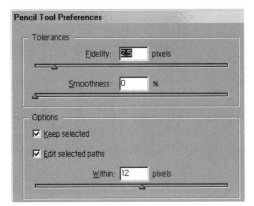

❸❹ *The* **Pencil Tool Preferences dialog box** *allows you to control the appearance of the path.*

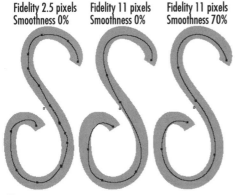

Fidelity 2.5 pixels   Fidelity 11 pixels   Fidelity 11 pixels
Smoothness 0%   Smoothness 0%   Smoothness 70%

❸❺ *The Pencil tool fidelity and smoothness settings change the appearance of the path.*

You can change how the Pencil tool responds to the movements of the mouse as you drag. The preferences also control how the Pencil tool edits paths.

To set the preferences for the Pencil tool:

1. Double click the Pencil tool in the Toolbox. This opens the Pencil Tool Preferences dialog box **❸❹**.

2. Set the amount of Fidelity using the slider or field. The lower the amount of Fidelity, the more the path will follow the motions of the mouse **❸❺**.

3. Set the amount of Smoothness using the slider or field. The higher the setting for Smoothness, the more the path will follow curved shapes **❸❺**.

4. Check Keep Selected to keep the path selected after you have drawn it. This makes it easier to reshape the path.

5. Check Edit Selected paths to turn on the reshape option.

6. If the Edit Selected Paths option is turned on, use the slider or field to set how close the Pencil tool must come, in pixels, to the path you want to reshape.

Using the Smooth Tool

Once you have created a path, you may want to delete extra points so that the path is smoother.

TIP If you are familiar with Illustrator's Smooth tool, you will find it easy to use the Smooth tool in InDesign.

To smooth paths with the Smooth tool:

1. Select the path that you want to smooth.
2. Click the Smooth tool in the Toolbox **36**.
3. Press and drag the Smooth tool along the path.
4. Release the mouse. The path is redrawn with fewer points **37**.

You can change how the Smooth tool responds to the movements of the mouse as you drag.

To set the preferences for the Smooth tool:

1. Double click the Smooth tool in the Toolbox to open the Smooth Tool Preferences dialog box **38**.
2. Use the slider or field to set the Fidelity amount **39**. The lower the amount, the more the new path will follow the original path.
3. Use the slider or field to set the Smoothness amount **39**. The higher the setting, the more curved the path.
4. Check Keep Selected to keep the path selected after you have smoothed it. This makes it easier to increase the smoothness of the path.

36 *The* **Smooth tool** *in the Toolbox.*

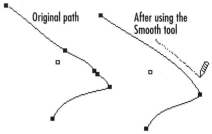

37 *Drag the Smooth tool along a path to remove points and eliminate small bumps and curves.*

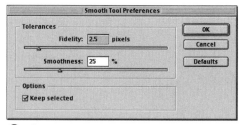

38 *The* **Smooth Tool Preferences** *allow you to control how much the Smooth tool affects the appearance of paths.*

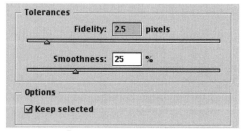

39 *Adjust the sliders for the Fidelity and Smoothness to control how the Smooth tool affects the appearance of paths.*

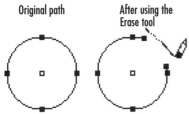

40 *The* **Erase tool** *in the Toolbox.*

Original path   After using the Erase tool

41 *The Erase tool deletes points as you drag it along a path.*

Using the Erase tool

You may want to delete parts of paths. Rather than selecting and deleting individual points, you can use the Erase tool to drag to delete parts of a path.

TIP If you are familiar with the Erase tool in Adobe Illustrator, you will find it easy to use the Erase tool in InDesign.

To delete paths with the Erase tool:

1. Select the path that you want to delete parts of.

2. Choose the Erase tool in the Toolbox **40**.

3. Press and drag the Erase tool along the path.

4. Release the mouse to display the new path **41**.

TIP The Erase tool will always open a closed path.

TIP If you drag the Erase tool over the middle of an open path, you create two separate open paths. Both open paths will be selected.

Deleting or Removing Points: Which tools or commands do what?

You may find yourself confused by all the different tools and commands for deleting or removing points and segments. Here's a review of which tool does what:

Add and Delete Anchor Points: These two tools always add or delete anchor points without creating any breaks in the path.

Erase: This tool will always create a break in the path.

Scissors: When applied to a point or segment, this tool creates two endpoints at that position.

Delete command: The Delete command always removes points or segments that were selected with the Direct Selection tool. If applied to selections in the middle of a path, the command will break the path in two.

IMPORTED GRAPHICS 8

One reason desktop publishing became so popular is how easy it made combining graphics such as photographs and illustrations with type for layouts.

In the years before personal computers, specialized workers, toiling under the exotic name *strippers*, manually trimmed away the blank areas around graphics so that text could be placed around the image. (The name stripper is derived from combining strips of film together.)

Even more complicated was placing text over an illustration. The image and text had to be combined by photography and then stripped into the layout.

With page layout programs such as InDesign it takes a few clicks of a mouse to combine type and artwork together. It's enough to make old-time strippers hang up their tassels!

Placing Artwork

Most artwork for InDesign comes from other sources. You can use scanners or digital cameras to make graphics. Or the artwork can be created in the computer using programs such as Adobe Photoshop, Adobe Illustrator, Macromedia FreeHand, or Adobe Acrobat. The easiest way to place artwork is to create the frame automatically when you import the artwork.

To place artwork in an automatic frame:

1. Choose **File > Place.** This opens the Place dialog box ❶.

2. Navigate to find the file you want to import. *(See "File Formats" on the next page for a list of the types of files you can place in InDesign.)*

3. Check Show Import Options to open the Import Options dialog box before you place the file ❷. *(See page 153 for more information on working with Import Options.)*

4. Click Choose to load the graphic into an image cursor ❸.

TIP Hold the Shift key as you click Choose to open the Import Options dialog box, even if the option is not checked.

5. Click the cursor to place the graphic in a rectangular frame the same size as the artwork.

   or

   Drag the image cursor to define the size of the rectangular frame.

TIP Only the frame is sized when you drag the image cursor. The artwork stays at its actual size. *(See page 156 for how to change the size of an image inside a frame.)*

❶ *Use the* **Place dialog box** *to open a file you wish to place. Check Show Import Options to make refinements to the imported file.*

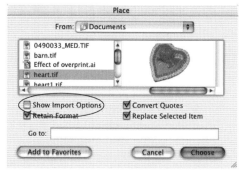

❷ *The* **Image Import Options dialog box** *for TIFF and Photoshop images.*

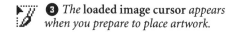

❸ *The* **loaded image cursor** *appears when you prepare to place artwork.*

File Formats

A wide variety of graphic formats can be added to InDesign documents. These formats are recommended for professional printing:

Adobe Illustrator (AI)

Adobe Photoshop (PSD)

Encapsulated PostScript (EPS)

Desktop Color Separation (DCS)

Joint Photographer's Expert Group (JPEG)

Portable Document Format (PDF)

Portable Network Graphics (PNG)

PostScript (PS)

Scitex Continuous Tone (SCT)

Tagged Image File Format (TIFF)

Although the following formats can be inserted into InDesign documents, they are not recommended for use in commercially printed documents. They are acceptable for low-resolution or non-PostScript printers:

Macintosh Picture (PICT)

Graphics Interchange Format (GIF)

PC Paintbrush (PCX)

Windows Bitmap (BMP)

Windows Metafile (WMF)

You can also place artwork into an existing frame. This is handy if you have set up empty frames as placeholders for graphics.

To place artwork into an existing frame:

1. Use one of the tools to create a rectangular, elliptical, or polygonal frame.

TIP You can use either the frame tools that create graphic frames or the tools that create unassigned frames *(see page 67)*.

2. Use either the Selection or Direct Selection tool to select the frame.

3. Choose **File** > **Place** and navigate to find the image you wish to place.

4. Click Choose in the Place dialog box. The file automatically is inserted within the frame.

TIP You can also use the Pen tool to create frame shapes *(see Chapter 7, "Pen and Beziers")*.

To replace the artwork in an existing frame:

1. Select the frame that contains the artwork you want to replace.

2. Choose **File** > **Place** and navigate to find the image you wish to place.

3. Click Replace Selected Item in the Place dialog box ❶.

4. Click Choose in the Place dialog box. The new image automatically replaces the contents of the frame.

To move or copy artwork betweem frames:

1. Use the Direct Selection tool to select the artwork you want to replace.

2. Choose **Edit** > **Cut** or **Edit** > **Copy**. This places the artwork on the clipboard.

3. Select the frame that you want to move the artwork into.

4. Choose **Edit** > **Paste Into**. The contents of the clipboard are pasted into the frame.

Placing Artwork

Specialty Frames

Frames don't have to be singular items. You can make multiple frames act as a single item by converting them to a compound shape. Frames combined into a compound shape display a single image across all the items in the compound.

To create a compound shape:

1. Select the frames you want to combine into a compound shape.

TIP If the frames overlap, InDesign displays a transparent area *(see page 115)*.

2. Choose **Object** > **Compound Paths** > **Make**. If the frame is a graphic frame, the diagonal lines cross through all the frames in the compound ❹.

To add an image to a compound shape:

1. Select the compound shape.

2. Use any of the techniques described on the previous pages to add the image to the selected frame. The image crosses through the spaces between the elements of the compound shape ❺.

To split a compound shape:

1. Select the compound shape.

2. Choose **Object** > **Compound Paths** > **Release**.

❹ *Individual frames display diagonal lines within each object (top). A* **compound shape** *displays the diagonal lines within the entire compound (bottom).*

❺ *A placed image is seen across all the items in a compound shape.*

CYCLONE **Frame**

CYCLONE **Paths**

❻ *The* **Create Outlines command** *converts text into paths that can then be modified.*

❼ *Text converted to paths can also hold imported graphics.*

You can also create special frame shapes by converting text to frames.

TIP If you can't draw for beans, you can convert the characters in dingbat fonts into shapes such as hearts, arrows, snowflakes, and so on.

To convert text to frames:

1. Use the Selection tool to select the frame that contains the text.

   or

   Highlight the selected text within the frame.

2. Choose **Type** > **Create Outlines.** Each character of text is converted to paths that can be modified **❻**.

TIP You can also place images into the converted text paths as with compound shapes **❼**.

TIP The converted paths are created as compound paths. Release the compound shape to color each individual frame or place different images in each frame.

TIP If you select only a portion of the text within the frame, the highlighted text is converted to inline graphics within the frame. *(See page 161 for more information on working with inline graphics.)*

Specialty Frames

If you work with a vector-drawing program such as Adobe Illustrator or Macromedia FreeHand, you can also convert the paths in those programs to InDesign frames.

TIP This technique can be used with any program that copies paths using the AICB (Adobe Illustrator Clipboard).

To import paths as frames:

1. Position the windows in the vector program and InDesign so they are both visible on screen.

2. Select the paths in the vector-drawing program.

3. Drag the paths from the vector-drawing program onto the window of the InDesign document.

4. When a black line appears around the perimeter of the InDesign window, release the mouse button. The paths are converted to InDesign unassigned frames **8**.

TIP If you don't have the screen space to see both windows at once, you can also copy the paths from the vector program and paste them in InDesign.

TIP Once the graphic has been converted to an InDesign frame, it can be used to hold an image or text **9**.

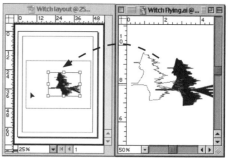

8 *Artwork can be* **dragged from a vector program** *and converted into InDesign frames.*

9 *Graphics converted to frames can hold images or text.*

Dragging from Illustrator 10

If you want to import paths from Illustrator 10, you need to change the default preferences.

Choose Files & Clipboard in the Preferences dialog box. Under the Clipboard section, check the AICB (no transparency setting) setting. Then click the Preserve Paths button.

If this is not done, the Illustrator paths will not be converted to frames.

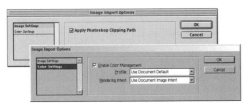

⑩ *The two parts of the* **Image Import Options** **dialog box** *lets you control pixel images such as TIFF and Photoshop files.*

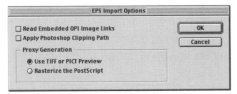

⑪ *The* **EPS Import Options dialog box** *lets you control imported EPS files.*

Setting Image Import Options

When you import a graphic, you have some choices as to how that image is placed. The dialog box options change, depending on whether you import a pixel-based image, an EPS, or a PDF.

To set the import options for pixel images:

1. In the Place dialog box check Import Options.

2. Choose a pixel-based image. This opens the Image Import Options dialog box for pixel-based images **⑩**.

3. Select Image Settings. If the image has a clipping path, you can choose Apply Photoshop Clipping path *(see page 168)*.

4. Select Color Settings. If the image has a color profile, you can turn on the color management *(see page 300)*.

5. Click OK to place the image.

To set the import options for EPS images:

1. In the Place dialog box check Import Options.

2. Choose an EPS file. This opens the EPS Import Options dialog box **⑪**.

3. Check Read Embedded OPI Image Links only if your service bureau has instructed you to have InDesign read the OPI links and perform the image swapping.

4. Check Create Frame From Clipping Path to convert the embedded path to a frame.

5. Set the options in the Proxy Generation to control the preview of the image:

   • **Use TIFF or PICT Preview** uses the preview that was created with the file.

   • **Rasterize the PostScript** displays the actual PostScript data as a preview. This lets you see custom PostScript code such as is found in FreeHand.

6. Click OK to place the image.

Setting Image Import Options

InDesign also lets you place PDF files as graphics. The import options for PDF files are different than those for the other types of graphics.

TIP Native Illustrator 10 files are also placed using the PDF import options.

To import PDF files:

1. In the Place dialog box check Import Options.

2. Choose a PDF file. This opens the Place PDF dialog box **⑫**.

4. Use the page selectors to select the page you want to place.

5. Use the Crop To pop-up list to determine how the PDF should be cropped within the frame **⑬**. Choose one of the following crop options:

   - **Content** crops to the active elements of the page, which includes pagemarks.
   - **Art** crops to the area defined as placeable art.
   - **Crop** crops the area that is displayed or printed by Acrobat.
   - **Trim** crops to the area that is the final trim size.
   - **Bleed** crops to the area that is the total size of the image if a bleed area has been specified.
   - **Media** crops to the page size of the original document.

6. Choose Preserve Halftone Screens to use any halftone screens specified within the PDF document.

7. Choose Transparent Background to show only the elements of the page without the opaque background **⑭**.

TIP If you choose Transparent Background, you can make it opaque by adding a fill color to the frame that contains the PDF.

8. Click OK to place the image.

Page controls

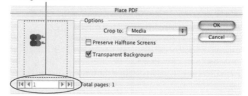

⑫ *The* **Place PDF dialog box** *controls how PDF files are placed.*

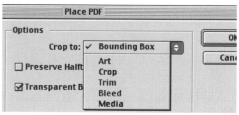

⑬ *The* **Crop to menu** *in the Place PDF dialog box controls the size of the placed artwork.*

Transparency off   Transparency on

⑭ *The effect of the* **Transparent Background** *on a placed PDF image.*

Frame and image   Image only   Frame only

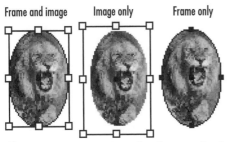

⓯ *The display of the bounding boxes and points indicate what items are selected.*

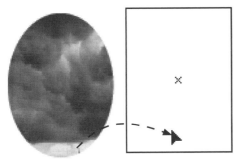

⓰ *If you move an object quickly, you only see a bounding box as the item is being moved.*

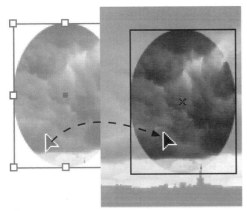

⓱ *If you press and pause before you move, you see preview of the image being moved.*

Modifying Placed Images

After you place an image, you may want to move or modify it. Which tool you use and where you click affects what will be selected.

To select and move both the frame and the image:

1. Use the Selection tool and click the frame holding the image. A bounding box appears that indicates that the frame and its content are selected **⓯**.

2. Press and drag the selection to move both the frame and the image.

TIP If you move quickly, you will see only a bounding box of the moved items **⓰**. If you press and pause for a moment, you will see a preview of the items being moved **⓱**.

To select the image within the frame.

1. Use the Direct Selection tool and click inside the frame where the image is visible. A bounding box for the image appears **⓯**.

TIP If the image is larger than the frame, this bounding box will appear outside the boundaries of the frame.

2. Press and drag the image to move it without disturbing the frame.

TIP As you press, the areas of the image that are outside the frame are displayed lighter than the area within the frame.

To select and move just the frame:

1. Use the Direct Selection tool and click the edge of the frame. The points on the frame appear **⓯**.

2. Hold the Opt/Alt key and click the frame again to select all the points.

3. Release the Opt/Alt key and drag the frame to move it to reveal a new part of the image.

When you apply transformations to frames that contain placed images, you have a choice as to which objects—the frame, the image, or both—are transformed. Here are some helpful guides.

TIP If you pause before you drag with any of the transform tools, you will see a preview of the image as you transform it.

To transform both the frame and the placed image:

1. Use the Selection tool to select both the frame and the placed image.

2. Make sure that Transform Content is chosen in the Transform palette menu.

3. Use any of the Transform palette fields or transform tools **18**.

To modify the frame only:

1. Turn off Transform Content and use the previous exercise to scale the object.

   or

   With Transform Content turned on, hold the Opt/Alt key as you use the Direct Selection tool to select the frame.

2. Use any of the Transform palette fields or transform tools to modify only the selected frame **19**.

To modify the placed graphic only:

1. Use the Direct Selection tool to select the artwork within the frame.

2. Use any of the Transform palette fields or transform tools to modify only the selected image **20**.

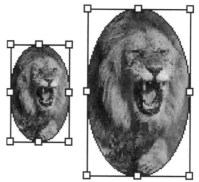

18 *The* **Transform Content** command *allows you to modify a frame and a placed image at the same time.*

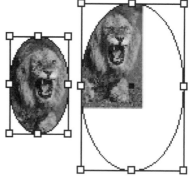

19 *With* **Transform Content** *turned off, the frame is modified but the image remains its original size.*

20 *With just the image selected, the transform tools and commands modify the image, but not the frame.*

㉑ *The effect of the* Fit Content to Frame command.

㉒ *The effect of the* Fit Content Proportionally command.

㉓ *The effect of the* Fit Frame to Content command.

㉔ *The effect of the* Center Content to Frame command.

Fitting Graphics in Frames

InDesign gives you several commands to quickly position and resize artwork within frames.

To resize the graphic to the frame size:

1. Use the Selection tool to select both the frame and the graphic.
2. Choose **Object > Fitting > Fit Content to Frame.** This changes the size of the graphic to fit completely within the area of the frame **㉑**.

TIP This command does not preserve the proportions of the artwork; the artwork may become distorted.

To proportionally resize to the frame size:

1. Use the Selection tool to select both the frame and the graphic.
2. Choose **Object > Fitting > Fit Content Proportionally.** This changes the size of the graphic to fit completely, and without distortion, within the frame **㉒**.

To resize the frame to the graphic size:

1. Use the Selection tool to select both the frame and the graphic.
2. Choose **Object > Fitting > Fit Frame to Content.** This changes the size of the frame so that the artwork fits completely within the area of the frame **㉓**.

To center the graphic within the frame:

1. Use the Selection tool to select both the frame and the graphic.
2. Choose **Object > Fitting > Center Content to Frame.** This repositions the graphic so it is centered within the frame without changing the size of either the graphic or the frame **㉔**.

In addition to the commands that position graphics, you can also position images numerically within frames using the X and Y coordinates in the Transform palette.

To numerically position graphics within frames:

1. Check Show Content Offset in the Transform palette menu ㉕.

2. Use the Direct Selection tool to select the graphic inside the frame.

3. Enter the X and Y coordinates in the Transform palette. The image moves to a new position relative to the frame ㉖. This is called the *content offset*.

TIP Small plus signs (+) next to the X and Y coordinates in the Transform palette indicate that Show Content Offset is turned on ㉗.

To numerically position graphics on the page:

1. Uncheck Show Content Offset from the Transform palette menu.

2. Use the Direct Selection tool to select the graphic inside the frame.

3. Set the X and Y coordinates in the Transform palette. The image moves to a new position relative to the page rulers ㉖. This is called the *absolute offset*.

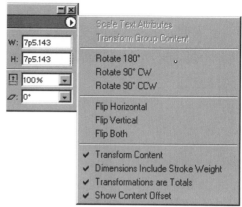

㉕ *The Transform palette menu lets you choose Show Content Offset.*

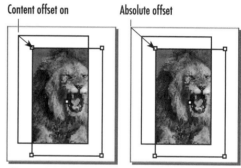

Content offset on   Absolute offset

㉖ *Content offset positions the graphic relative to the frame. Absolute offset positions the graphic relative to the page.*

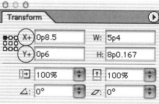

㉗ *The plus signs (+) next to the X and Y coordinates indicate that the position of the object is relative to the frame.*

28 *Before nesting, the circular frame with the placed image is a separate object.*

29 *After nesting, the circular frame is the content inside the rectangular frame.*

Nesting Elements

Once you have an image in a frame, you can then paste it into another frame. This technique is called *nesting elements* and it allows you to combine different types of images together.

TIP For instance, you can use nested elements to put a placed image inside a circular frame and then put that circular frame partially inside a rectangular frame. The top frame crops the side of the circular frame while the circular frame crops the placed image.

To create a nested frame:

1. Use the Selection tool to select the element to be nested inside the frame **28**.

TIP A nested element can be a graphic or text frame.

2. Cut or copy the element to the clipboard.

3. Select the frame that is to hold the nested element.

4. Choose **Edit > Paste Into**. This pastes the element inside the frame **29**.

TIP The Selection tool moves all the elements in the nest.

TIP Frames can hold multiple levels of nested frames. So you can have a frame within a frame within a frame, and so on.

TIP Use the Fit Content commands to automatically position the nested frame inside the parent frame *(see page 157)*.

Nesting Elements

A special set of steps is needed to select and move items that are part of nested elements.

TIP For instance, in the example given on the previous page, you might want to move the placed image and the circular frame without moving the rectangular frame that holds those elements.

To select and move nested elements:

1. Use the Direct Selection tool to select the nested element.

TIP If the item contains a placed image the image is selected and the hand cursor displayed **30**.

2. Hold the Opt/Alt + Shift keys. This changes the Direct Selection tool to the Group Selection tool.

TIP The plus (+) sign next to the white arrow indicates the Group Selection tool.

3. Click with the Group Selection tool to select the both the placed image and the frame **31**.

4. If you have many levels of nested elements, click with the Group Selection tool as many times as is necessary to select up through the nest levels.

5. Switch to the Selection tool when you have selected all the nested elements you want to move.

6. Drag the centerpoint of the selected nested elements. This allows you to move the selected nested elements together **32**.

TIP If you drag the bounding box handles instead of the centerpoint, you change the size of the nested element.

30 *The first click with the* **Direct Selection** *tool selects the placed image inside a nest.*

31 *The next click with the* **Group Selection** *tool selects both the frame and the placed image.*

32 *Use the* **Selection** *tool to drag the center-point of the selected frame to move the selected items of the nested elements.*

in case one of those great
whirlwinds arose,
mighty enough
to crush any building in
its path. It was reached by

③ *An* **inline graphic** *flows along with the text.*

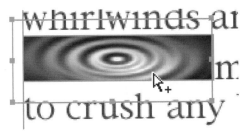

③ *The* **Group Selection tool** *allows you to select multiple items within nested elements.*

Uses for Inline Graphics

The biggest problem with inline graphics is that most people forget they are available.

Have you ever wanted to use a little picture instead of a plain bullet? Inline graphics make it easy.

You can also use an inline graphic to keep a picture of an author along with her biography.

Finally, paste a horizontal line as an inline graphic to make the fill-in-the-blank lines in a coupon.

Another type of nested elemented is called an *inline graphic*. An inline graphic is an object that is pasted as a character into the actual text story.

TIP For instance, you can use an inline graphic to make sure a placed image always stays near a certain area of text.

TIP An inline graphic can also be used to add images to a table *(see Chapter 13, "Tabs and Tables")*.

To create an inline graphic:

1. Select the element that you want positioned.

2. Cut or copy the element to the clipboard.

3. Click to place an insertion point where you want the inline graphic to be positioned.

4. Choose **Edit > Paste**. The element is pasted into the text and flows along with any changes to the text **③**.

TIP Use the Direct Selection tool to select the frame and placed image inside an inline graphics **③**.

TIP Use the Selection tool to select and move inline graphics up or down inside the text.

Nesting Elements

Styling Placed Images

Once you have placed a graphic within a frame, you can employ many techniques to stylize the frame or the image. For instance, you can change the color of the frame or the color of the image.

To color the frame fill or stroke:

1. Use the Selection tool to select the frame.

2. Click the Fill icon in the Toolbox or Color or Swatches palette.

    or

    Click the Stroke icon in the Toolbox or Color or Swatches palette.

3. Choose a color in the Swatches palette. If the Fill icon is chosen, the fill color is visible wherever the image does not fill the frame **35**.

If you import a grayscale image, you can change the color that is applied to the image.

To color a grayscale image:

1. Use the Direct Selection tool to select the grayscale image.

2. Choose the Fill icon in the Color palette or Toolbox.

    TIP The default fill color for grayscale images is black.

3. Change the tint value the lighten the image.

    or

    Choose a color in the Color or Swatches palette. The grayscale values change to a tint of the color chosen **36**.

4. Use the steps in the previous exercise to change the fill color of the frame. This colorizes the white areas of the image.

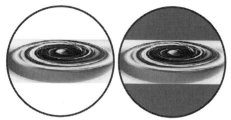

35 *When a frame is selected, choosing a fill color changes the background color of the frame.*

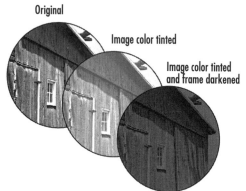

Original

Image color tinted

Image color tinted and frame darkened

36 *You can change the appearance of a grayscale image by changing the image color or the fill color of the frame.*

Colorizing Grayscale Images

Your service bureau may instruct you not to colorize grayscale images. Or you may get a warning from a pre-flight program.

In theory there is nothing wrong with colorizing grayscale images, but individual production workflows may not be able to handle the images.

If you get a warning about grayscale images, check with the service bureau as to whether or not it can handle them.

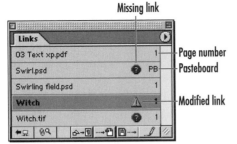

Missing link · Page number · Pasteboard · Modified link

37 *The* **Links palette** *lets you view and work with the linked images in a document.*

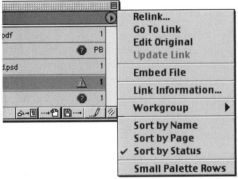

38 *The* **Links palette menu** *contains the commands for working with the Links palette.*

Linking Graphics

When you place an image, you do not actually place the image into the document. Only the screen preview of the image is incorporated as part of the file. In order to print the file, InDesign needs to access the original graphic. This is called a *link*.

TIP It is possible to link text files as well as graphics, but there are few practical advantages. *(See "Links for Text Files" on page 165 for a discussion on the merits of linking text files.)*

To examine the links in a document:

1. Choose **File > Links**. This opens the Links palette **37**. The Links palette shows all the linked images in the document with their page numbers. Special icons indicate the status of the image.
   - **Missing Link** indicates that InDesign can't find the original graphic.
   - **Modified Link** indicates that the graphic has a different date from when it was originally placed.

2. Use the Links palette menu to sort the list of graphics as follows **37**:
   - **Sort By Name** arranges the graphics in alphabetical order.
   - **Sort By Status** arranges the missing or modified graphics together.
   - **Sort By Page** arranges the graphics according to the page they are on.

The Missing or Modified Links notice appears when you open a file that has a missing or modified link 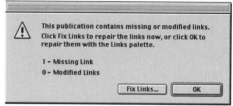.

To relink graphics when you open a document:

1. Click the Fix Links button in the Missing or Modified Links notice. All modified graphics are automatically updated.

2. If there are missing links, the operating system navigation dialog box opens. Use it to find each missing graphic.

TIP It is not necessary to find missing links as you work on a document. For instance, if you only need to work on text, you don't need to find missing graphics. However, you must fix all links before you send out a document to be printed.

If you open a document without choosing the Fix Links button, you can still use the Links palette to find missing graphics.

TIP Using the Links palette lets you carefully check each graphic to make sure it is the one you want to modify.

To relink a missing graphic:

1. Select the missing link in the Links palette.

2. Click the Relink button. This opens navigation dialog box where you can find the missing file.

   or

   Choose Relink from the Links palette menu.

3. Navigate to find the missing file.

4. Click OK to relink the graphic.

39 *The* **Missing or Modified Links** *notice appears when you open a file that has a missing link to a text or graphics file.*

Pixels or Vectors?

There are two main types of graphics in desktop publishing. Pixel-based images (sometimes called *bitmapped,* or *raster* images) display images as a arrangement of small rectangles. Scanners and digital cameras all capture images in pixels. Adobe Photoshop lets you paint or modify pixels.

Vector images display artwork according to paths filled with colors. They are the same as the vector shapes in InDesign. Programs such as Adobe Illustrator and Macromedia FreeHand create vector images.

Pixel-based images are usually used for photographs or images with blends. Vector images are usually used for more precise images such as maps or technical drawings.

One of the big benefits of working with vector images is that they can be scaled up or down without losing any details. Pixel-based images can lose detail if they are scaled up too high.

Links for Text Files

InDesign also lists the link information for placed text files. If you move or modify the original text file that was placed in the InDesign document, you will see a notice when you open the file that links are missing or modified.

It might seem like a good idea to use the Update Link command to update the text within the InDesign document. However, if you do, you will lose any formatting or changes you have applied within InDesign.

In most cases it is not necessary to keep the link for text files. You are probably better off embedding the text file within the document (*see page 167*).

However, if you are working with InCopy or some other sort of workgroup software, you may not be able to embed text files within the document. Check with your workgroup supervisor for the proper procedures.

If a graphic has been modified, you can use the Links palette to update the link.

To update modified links:

1. Select the modified link in the Links palette.
2. Click the Update Link icon.

   or

   Choose Update Link from the Links palette menu.

TIP You can select more than one link to update multiple graphics.

The Links palette also lets you move quickly to a specific graphic.

To jump to a linked graphic:

1. Select the link in the Links palette.
2. Click the Go To Link button.

   or

   Choose Go To Link from the Links palette menu.

The Links palette can also be used to open and edit a graphic.

To edit a linked graphic:

1. Select the graphic you want to place.
2. Choose Edit Original from the Links palette menu.

   or

   Click the Edit Original button in the Links palette. The graphic opens in the program that created it.

Linking Graphics

You may want to know a little bit about the image that is placed in a file. The Link Information dialog box gives you a cornucopia of information about the imported graphics.

To see the link information:

1. Select the linked graphic in the Links palette.

2. Choose Link Information from the Links palette menu. This opens the Link Information dialog box .

    -   **Name** shows the name of the file.
    -   **Date Modified** shows when the file was last saved.
    -   **Size** shows the size of the file.
    -   **Page** shows what page the file is on.
    -   **Link Needed** shows if the file will be embedded in the document.
    -   **Color Space** shows the type of color information in the file.
    -   **Profile** shows what type of color management profile has been applied to the file.
    -   **File Type** shows what program was used to save the file.
    -   **Content Status** shows if the item is missing, modified, or up to date.
    -   **Location** shows the complete path to find the file.

3. If necessary, use the Relink button to find missing graphics.

4. Use the Next or Previous buttons to move to other graphics in the Links palette.

5. Click the Done button when you are finished.

⑩ *The* **Link Information dialog box** *gives you information about a placed graphic.*

When to Embed Graphics

You may be tempted to embed many, if not all, of your graphics within the InDesign document. After all, it makes it much easier to send a file to the service bureau if you don't have to remember to send the graphics along with it. *(For more information on preparing files for printing, see Chapter 17, "Output.")*

Embedding graphics increases the size of the InDesign file. Just a few large graphics can make the InDesign file balloon in size. This means the file will take a long time to open or save.

You shouldn't have problems, though, if you embed small graphics, such as logos. Just remember that each time you embed a small graphic, it adds to the file size. Page after page of small graphics adds up.

My own feeling is to avoid embedding graphics. That way I don't have to worry about the file size.

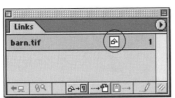

41 *The* **Embed icon** *in the Links palette indicates that all the information necessary to print the graphic is stored in the InDesign file.*

42 *The* **Unembed alert box** *lets you choose to link back to the original file or create a new file.*

Embedding Graphics

Usually, only the preview of a graphic is contained within an InDesign file. You can, however, embed a graphic within the InDesign file. This means that all the information necessary to print the file is contained within the InDesign document.

TIP Embedded graphics will increase the size of the InDesign file *(see "When to Embed Graphics" on the opposite page.)*

To embed placed images or text:

1. Select the placed image.

   or

   Select the frame that contains the imported text.

2. Choose Embed File from the Links palette menu. If you have selected a graphic, the embed icon appears next to the file name in the Links palette **41**.

   or

   If you have selected text, the file name disappears from the Links palette.

TIP Embedded text files do not add to the size of the InDesign file.

TIP Once you have embedded a graphic, InDesign no longer needs to find the original file on your hard disk.

To unembed images:

1. Select the embedded image.

2. Choose Unembed File from the Links palette menu. The Unembed alert box appears **42**.

3. Click Yes to link the embedded graphic back to the original file that was placed into InDesign.

   or

   Click No. A dialog box appears asking you to choose the destination for a new file.

Embedding Graphics

Using Clipping Paths

Raster images saved as TIFF or EPS files are always rectangular. If you want to see only part of the image you import, you can create a *clipping path* that surrounds the part of the image that you want to see. The rest of the image becomes transparent. One way to create a clipping path is to use Adobe Photoshop to create paths for the file.

To import a file with a clipping path:

1. In Photoshop, use the Path tools to create a path around the image 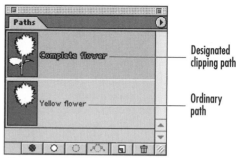.

TIP Although you will not see the clipping in Photoshop, the areas of the image inside the path will be visible. The areas outside the path will be invisible.

2. Use Photoshop's Path palette menu to designate the path as a clipping path.

3. Save the file as a TIFF, EPS, or Photoshop file.

TIP You can have many paths saved as part of a Photoshop file, but only one path can be designated as a clipping path.

4. In InDesign, choose **File > Place** and choose the file you have created.

5. In the Import Options, check Apply Photoshop Clipping Path . The image is automatically clipped so that only the areas inside the path are visible .

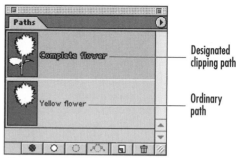

Designated clipping path

Ordinary path

43 Photoshop's Paths palette *shows the paths saved with the file. Clipping paths are shown in outlined type.*

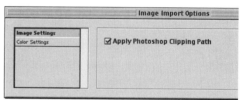

44 *The* Image Import Options dialog box *lets you choose to apply a clipping path to a file.*

45 *An example of how a* **clipping path** *allows an image to have a transparent background.*

Using Clipping Paths

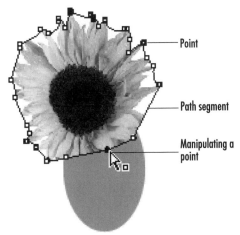

Point

Path segment

Manipulating a point

46 *Use the Direct Selection tool to manipulate the shape of a clipping path around an image.*

47 *The* **Image Import Options** *dialog box lets you choose the type of clipping path for a file.*

48 *The* **Image Import Options** *dialog box lets you select a clipping path to a file.*

Once you have a clipping path applied to a graphic, you can change the shape of the path to show or hide areas of the image.

To modify the shape of a clipping path:

1. Use the Direct Selection tool to select the placed image. If the image has a clipping path, the path will appear as a series of points and path segments **46**.

2. Use any of the path techniques to change the shape of the clipping path. *(See Chapter 7, "Pen and Beziers" for information on working with paths.)*

You don't have to designate a clipping path in Photoshop. InDesign lets you select any path, saved with the image file, as a clipping path.

To choose a path as an InDesign clipping path:

1. Select the placed image.

2. Choose **Object > Clipping Path**. The Clipping Path dialog box appears.

3. Use the Type menu in the Clipping Path dialog box to select Photoshop path **47**.

4. Use the Path menu to select which path should be used as a clipping path **48**.

5. Click the Preview button to see the effects of choosing a path.

6. Click OK to apply the path.

What happens, though, if an image doesn't contain a clipping path? Fortunately, InDesign can create a clipping path from the edges—or the differences between the dark and light colors of the image.

To create a clipping path from an image:

1. In the Clipping Path dialog box, choose Detect Edges from the Type menu 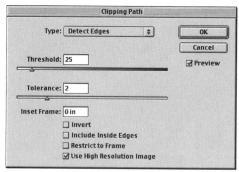.

2. Adjust the Threshold slider to define the color that is used as the area outside the clipping path 🗐. *0* is pure white.

3. Adjust the Tolerance slider to allow a slight variation in the Threshold color 🗐. A high tolerance often smooths out small bumps in the path.

🗐 *The* **Clipping Path** *dialog box gives you special controls for creating a clipping path based on the appearance of the image.*

You can also use an alpha channel, saved with the file, as a clipping path.

TIP Alpha channels are grayscale images that are saved along with the color or black channels of an image.

To choose an alpha channel as a clipping path:

1. Use the Type menu in the Clipping Path dialog box to select Alpha Channel.

2. Use the Alpha menu to select which channel should be used as a clipping path.

3. Because alpha channels can contain shades of gray, adjust the Threshold slider to define the color that is used as the area outside the clipping path. *0* is pure white.

4. Adjust the Tolerance slider to allow a slight variation in the Threshold color. A high tolerance often smooths out small bumps in the path.

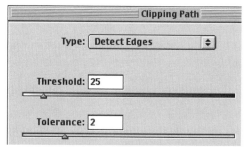

🗐 *The* **Threshold** *and* **Tolerance** *sliders let you control the shape of clipping paths created by the Detect Edges and Alpha Channel commands.*

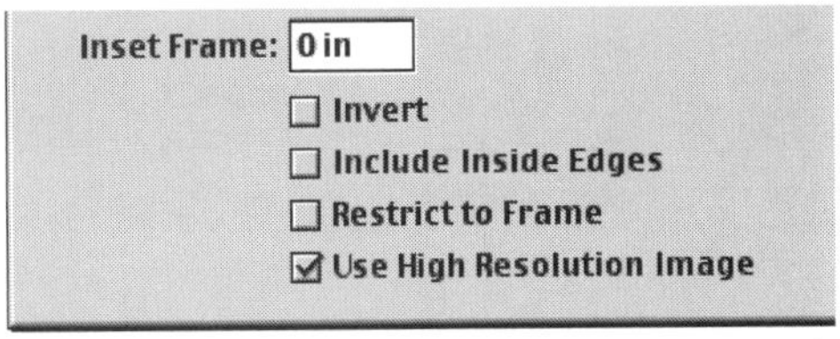

Inset Frame: 0 in

☐ Invert
☐ Include Inside Edges
☐ Restrict to Frame
☑ Use High Resolution Image

�*The **clipping path controls** at the bottom of the Clipping Path dialog box give you control over the shape and appearance of a clipping path.*

🔷*The* **Include Inside Edges** *in a clipping path creates transparent areas within the image such as the circled area next to the stem.*

The End of the Clipping Path?

Clipping paths are nasty, ugly things. They aren't easy to work with and they can't be made semi-transparent. They're often the cause of printing errors.

However, clipping paths are not suitable for many types of images. A clipping path acts like a knife that cuts out the background of an image. However, soft, curly hair may need variations in transparency that a clipping path can't provide.

Fortunately InDesign lets you use the transparency in Photoshop files to make parts of an image transparent *(see the next page)*.

All clipping paths can be further modified by using the controls at the bottom of the Clipping Path dialog box 🔷.

To modify the effects of a clipping path:

1. Type a positive value in the Inset Frame field to shrink the entire path into the image.

   or

   Type a negative value to expand the path outside the image.

   🔳 A small inset value may help a clipping path follow the contours of the image better.

2. If necessary, check Invert to switch which areas the path makes visible and which areas are left invisible.

3. Check Include Inside Edges to add areas that are enclosed by the foreground image to the clipping path 🔷.

4. Check Use High Resolution Image to create the path from the high resolution version of the file rather than the preview. This is a slower but more accurate way of calculating the path.

5. Check Restrict To Frame to prevent the clipping path frame from displaying any part of the image that is outside the frame that holds the image.

To delete the clipping path around an image:

1. Select the placed image.

2. Choose **Object** > **Clipping Path**. The Clipping Path dialog box appears.

3. Choose None from the Type pop-up list.

Using Clipping Paths

Importing Transparent Images

InDesign offers you a special advantage when you place native Photoshop (PSD) files. If there is any transparency in the placed image, InDesign displays the image with the same transparency as in the Photoshop file.

To use the transparency in a Photoshop file:

1. In Photoshop, use any of the tools to silhouette or fade the edges of the image. The Photoshop transparency grid indicates which parts of the image are opaque or transparent **53**.

2. Save the file as a Photoshop (PSD) file.

3. Import the file into the InDesign document. The areas that were tranparent in Photoshop will be transparent in InDesign **54**.

InDesign also knows how to read the transparency in placed Illustrator (AI) files.

To use the transparency in an Illustrator file:

1. In Illustrator, use any of the commands to apply transparency to the artwork.

2. Save the file as an Illustrator (AI) file.

3. Make sure that the PDF Compatibility option is checked in the Save dialog box.

4. Import the file into the InDesign document. The areas that were transparent in Illustrator will be transparent in InDesign **55**.

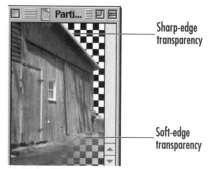

Sharp-edge transparency

Soft-edge transparency

53 **Photoshop's transparency grid** *indicates which areas will be transparent.*

54 *A transparent Photoshop file lets you see through to the black frame behind the image.*

55 *Transparency in an Illustrator image is maintained when placed over the text or other objects in InDesign.*

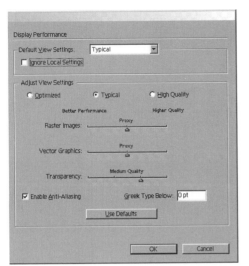

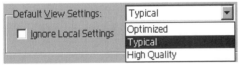

56 *The* **Display Performance dialog box** *controls how images and transparency effects are displayed.*

57 *The* **Default View Settings menu** *lets you choose which display performance setup is applied to images.*

Viewing Images

You can set placed images to display in different ways on the page. This lets you set how detailed the image appears or turn off the display entirely to speed the redraw of the page.

To set the default appearance of previews:

1. Choose **Edit** > **Preferences** > **Display Performance** (Mac OS 9 and Windows).

   or

   Choose **InDesign** > **Preferences** > **Display Performance** (Mac OS X). This opens the Display Performance Preferences dialog box **56**.

2. Choose one of the three options from the Default View Settings menu **57**.

   - **Optimized** is used when you want the fast screen redraw and best performance.
   - **Typical** is used when you want a better representation of the images.
   - **High Quality** is used when you want to see as much detail as possible onscreen. This option may cause InDesign to work slower than the other choices.

   TIP Each of the menu choices corresponds to one of the radio buttons in the Adjust View Settings controls.

3. Check Ignore Local Display Settings to override any display settings that have been applied to individual images *(see the next page)*.

As you work, you can switch between the menu commands without having to open the Display Performance Preferences dialog box.

To switch the default view setting:

1. With no object selected, Right-mouse click (Win) or Control-Click (Mac). This opens a contextual menu 🔂.

2. Choose one of the view settings from the Display Performance submenu.

3. Choose Ignore Local Display Settings to override any individual image previews *(see the next exercise)*. This does not delete those individual settings, it only overrides them.

4. Choose Clear Local Display Settings to delete any individual image previews.

TIP You can also use the View menu to choose the view settings or to override any individual image previews.

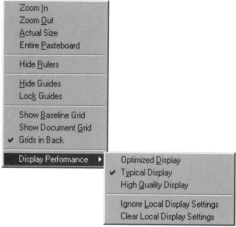

🔂 *The* Display Performance contextual menu *settings let you quickly switch from one display performance to another.*

You can also set each individual image to its own display setting. This lets you set one large image to faster screen redraw while showing more detail in other objects.

To set individual image previews:

1. Select the image.

2. Right-mouse click (Win) or Control-click (Mac). This opens the contextual menu for the display of that object 🔂.

3. Choose one of the options from the Display submenu of the contextual menu.

TIP The Use View Setting command sets the object back to whatever is the current View Setting is the Display Performance Preferences.

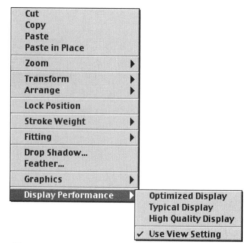

🔂 *The* Display Performance contextual menu *for an object lets you change the display performance for that object.*

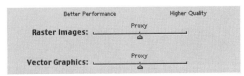

60 *The* **Adjust View Settings radio buttons** *give you three different display settings to apply to a document or individual images.*

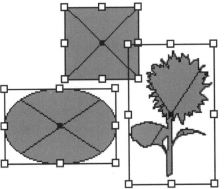

62 *An example of the* **Gray Out** *view setting.*

63 *The difference between the Proxy setting (top) and the High Resolution setting (bottom).*

The labels Optimized, Typical, and High Quality are merely guides. You can change the specific displays for raster images, vector art, and transparency effects in the Adjust View Settings area of the Display Performance Preferences.

To set the raster and vector displays:

1. Choose **Edit > Preferences > Display Performance** (Mac OS 9 or Win).

   or

   Choose **InDesign > Preferences > Display Performance** (Mac OS X).

2. Choose one of the radio button settings in the Adjust View Settings area **60**.

3. Drag the slider for the Raster Images or Vector Graphics as follows **61**:
   - **Gray Out** (far left) displays a gray background instead of the image **62**. This is the fastest performance.
   - **Proxy** (middle) displays a 72 ppi screen preview of the image **63**. This is the best performance that still shows what the image looks like.
   - **High Resolution** (far right) displays the maximum resolution in the image **63**.

4. Repeat the process for each of the other radio button settings.

TIP Raster Images and Vector Graphics settings don't have to be set for the same resolution. This allows you to have a faster redraw for large raster files, and more details in the lines of vector graphics.

Viewing Images

You can also set the display for the transparency effects as well as the drop shadows and feather effects.

To set the transparency effects displays:

1. Choose one of the radio button settings in the Adjust View Settings area.

2. Drag the Transparency slider as follows 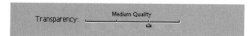:

   - **Off** (far left) displays no transparency effects. This is the fastest performance.
   - **Low Quality** (second from left) displays basic opacity and blend modes. Drop shadows and feathers are displayed in low resolution only. Some blend modes may change in the final output.
   - **Medium Quality** (second from right) displays drop shadows and feathers in low resolution.
   - **High Quality** displays higher resolution drop shadows and feathers. Blend modes appear in their correct CMYK color display.

3. Repeat the process for each of the other radio button settings.

Applying Effects to Images

When you have an imported image, there is a difference in how drop shadows and feathers are applied to either the frame or the image.

To apply effects to imported images:

- Select the object with the Selection tool to apply the effect to the frame that contains the image .

   or

   Select the image with the Direct Selection tool to apply the effect to the image within the frame .

- **TIP** If you apply a drop shadow to an image, you may need to enlarge the size of the frame in order to see the shadow.

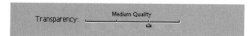

🟤 *The* **Transparency slider** *lets you control the display of drop shadows, feathers, and transparency effects.*

Image Selected   Frame Selected

🟤 *The difference between applying a drop shadow to an image versus a frame.*

TEXT EFFECTS 9

Go back and look at the advertisements they did back in the 1800s. (Yes, that was *before* I worked in advertising.) In those ads, the text marches along in a straight line without swearving toward or moving around the images.

Back in those days, it was extremely difficult to wrap text around an image. Each line of text would have had to be cut and pasted around the edges of an image.

The paste-up artists never dreamed of setting text along a path so that it follows the shape of a rollercoaster—that would have been far too much work!

Adding short horizontal rules to divide one paragraph from another was another tedious task. In fact, if you look closely at some old advertisements, you can see that the rule isn't perfectly centered in the column.

Fortunately, today's electronic page-layout programs make it easy to do all these special text effects with incredible precision.

Wrapping Text

One of my favorite effects to apply to text is to arrange it to flow around images and other objects. This is called the *text wrap*. InDesign gives you many different options for running text around native InDesign objects or imported graphics.

To apply a text wrap:

1. Select the object that you want the text to wrap around. This can be an imported graphic, a text frame, or an unassigned frame.

2. Choose **Window > Text Wrap**. This opens the Text Wrap palette ❶.

3. Choose one of the following options for how the text should flow around the object ❷.
   - **No wrap** lets the text flow above or below the object.
   - **Bounding Box** flows the text around the bounding box for the object.
   - **Object Shape** flows the text around the shape of the frame.
   - **Jump Object** flows the text to the next available space under the object.
   - **Jump to Next Column** flows the text to the next column or text frame.

4. Check Invert to force the text to flow inside the offset path ❸.

5. Enter an amount in the offset fields to contol the distance between the text and the object ❹.

TIP The number of available offset fields depends on the type of text wrap you choose.

❶ *The* **Text Wrap palette** *controls all the settings for how text flows around an object.*

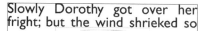

❷ *The five different* **text wrap buttons** *let you choose how the text wraps around objects.*

Slowly Dorothy got over her fright; but the wind shrieked so loudly all about her. At first she had wondered if she would be

Regular text wrap

Slowly Dorothy got over her fright; but the wind shrieked so loudly all about her. At first she had wondered if she would be dashed to pieces when the house fell again.

Invert text wrap

❸ *When the* **Invert command** *is turned on, the text wrap causes the text to flow inside, not outside, an object.*

❹ *The text wrap* **Offset controls** *allow you to set the distance between the text and a graphic.*

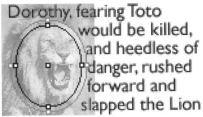

Dorothy, fearing Toto would be killed, and heedless of danger, rushed forward and slapped the Lion

⑤ *An example how an invisible object can be used to create a text wrap.*

A text wrap doesn't have to be around visible objects. You can use an object with no fill or stroke as the shape to wrap text around **⑤**.

To wrap text around an invisible object:

1. Draw an object with no fill or stroke.
2. Set the Text Wrap to Object Shape.

Once you set a text wrap, you can still manipulate it so that the text reads more legibly or fits more attractively into the contour of the object. This is called a *custom text wrap*.

To create a custom text wrap:

1. Select the object that has the text wrap applied to it.
2. Use the Direct Selection tool to manipulate the points on the text wrap path **⑥**.
3. Click the Pen tool between points on the text wrap path to add a new point to the path **⑦**.
4. Click the Pen tool on a point on the text wrap path to delete the point from the path **⑧**.

TIP Hold the Cmd/Ctrl key to access the Direct Selection tool while using the Pen tool.

⑥ *Use the Direct Selection tool to* **change the shape** *of a text wrap path.*

⑦ *Position the Pen tool over a path and click to* **add** *points to a text wrap path.*

⑧ *Position the Pen tool over a point and click to* **delete** *points from a text wrap path.*

When you choose Object Shape for the text wrap, InDesign lets you set the contour options for that shape. This gives you more control over the shape of the text wrap.

To set the text wrap contour options:

1. Use the Direct Selection tool to select the image.

2. Click the Object Shape icon in the Text Wrap palette.

3. Choose Show Options from the Text Wrap palette menu to display the Contour Options at the bottom of the Text Wrap palette ❾.

4. Use the Type pop-up list to choose the type of element that should be used to create the text wrap ❿:
   - **Bounding Box** uses the rectangle that contains the image.
   - **Detect Edges** uses the differences between the pixels of the image and its background.
   - **Alpha Channel** lets you choose an embedded alpha channel.
   - **Photoshop Path** lets you choose an embedded path.
   - **Graphic Frame** uses the shape of the frame that contains the image.
   - **Same As Clipping** uses whatever shape has been designated as the clipping path for the image (see page 168).

5. If you choose Alpha Channel or Photoshop Path, use the second pop-up menu to choose a specific channel or path.

6. Check Include Inside Edges to make the text wrap inside any holes in the image, path, or alpha channel.

❾ The **Contour Options** for a text wrap are available when Object Shape is chosen.

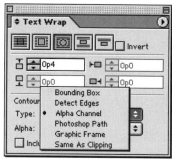

❿ The **Contour Options Type** menu lets you choose what object controls the shape of the text wrap.

> The Great
> State of Kansas

There was no garret at all, and no cellar — except a small hole dug in the ground, called a cyclone cellar, where the family could go in case one of those great whirlwinds arose, mighty enough to

⓫ An example of how **Ignore Text Wrap** keeps the map title from being affected by the text wrap applied to the outline of the state.

Text Frame Options

Columns
Number: 1
Gutter: 1p0
Width: 13p9
☐ Fixed Column Width

Inset Spacing
Top: 0p0
Left: 0p0
Bottom: 0p0
Right: 0p0

First Baseline
Offset: Ascent
Min: 0p0

Vertical Justification
Align: Top
Paragraph Spacing Limit: 0p0

☑ Ignore Text Wrap

⓬ The **Ignore Text Wrap checkbox** in the Text Frame Options dialog box prevents text from being affected by any text wrap settings.

You may find that you don't want some text to be affected by a text wrap. For instance, you might want to have some text run around an image but other text appear over the image **⓫**. That's when you need to direct the text frame to ignore a nearby text wrap.

TIP InDesign's text wrap works differently from QuarkXPress. In that program, only the objects above the text will create a text wrap. InDesign's text wrap affects text both above or below the object.

To ignore the text wrap:

1. Select the text frame that contains the text that you don't want affected by the text wrap command.

2. Choose **Object > Text Frame Options**. This opens the Text Frame Options dialog box **⓬**.

3. Check Ignore Text Wrap. The text in that frame is unaffected by any objects that have a text wrap applied.

TIP Text wrap applied to objects works across layers. Turning off the visibility of a layer does not change the effect of the text wrap *(see Chapter 11, "Layers" for more information on working with layers)*.

Wrapping Text

Text on a Path

When you create an object such as a text frame, the outside shape of the frame is called the object's path. Not only can InDesign fit text inside a text frame, it also lets you position text so that it runs along the outside of the frame.

To run text on the outside of a path:

1. Choose the Path Type tool in the Toolbox .

2. Move the tool so that it is near the path. A small plus sign appears next to the tool cursor ⓮.

3. Click with the Path Type tool. A blinking insertion point appears on the path.

4. Type the text. Use any of the text controls to select or modify the text.

TIP Use the Direct Selection tool to select the path and change its fill or stroke to none to make the path invisible. *(See Chapter 7, "Pen and Beziers" for more information on modifying paths.)*

Once you apply text to a path, you can drag to position the text.

To position text on a path:

♦ Drag the indicator at the start or end of the text on a path to change the start or end point of the text ⓯.

   or

   Drag the small indicator within the text to change the center point of the text. ⓰.

TIP You can also drag the center point indicator to the other side of the path to flip the text to the other side of the path.

TIP You can use the Paragraph palette *(see page 52)* to change the alignment of the text between the start and end indicators.

⓭ The **Path Type tool** *in the Toolbox is used to add text to a path.*

⓮ *The plus sign next to the Path Type cursor indicates you can click to add text to a path.*

⓯ *Drag the indicator line to move the text along a path.*

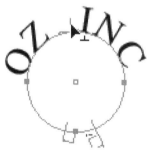

⓰ *The* **center point indicator** *allows you to move text or flip it from one side of the path to another.*

Text on a Path

⓱ *The* **Path Type Options dialog box** *allows you to control how text is applied to a path.*

⓲ *The* **Effect choices** *control the appearance of the text on the path.*

Wizardry — Rainbow

Wizardry — Skew

Wizardry — 3D Ribbon

Wizardry — Stair Step

Gravity

⓳ *The* **five effect settings** *applied to text on a path.*

To apply effects to text on a path:

1. Choose **Object > Path Type > Options**. This opens the Path Type Options dialog box **⓱**.

2. Use the Effect menu **⓲** to control how the text is positioned in relationship to the path **⓳**.

   - **Rainbow** positions the text in an arc along any curves in the path.
   - **Skew** distorts the text vertically as it is positioned along curves in the path.
   - **3D Ribbon** distorts the text horizontally as it is positioned along curves in the path.
   - **Stair Step** aligns the individual baselines of each letter so that the text stays vertical as it is positioned along curves in the path.
   - **Gravity** uses the distortion of the path to distort the text as it is positioned along curves in the path.

3. Click the Flip checkbox to position the text on the other side of the path.

4. If the spacing of the text is uneven, use the spacing control to tighten the character spacing around sharp turns and acute angles on the path.

TIP Higher values remove more space from between the characters.

TIP You can also drag the center point indicator to the other side of the path to move the text to the opposite side of the path.

Text on a Path

You can also control where the letters are positioned vertically on the path.

To set the vertical alignment of text on a path:

1. Use the Align menu to control how the text is positioned in relationship to the path 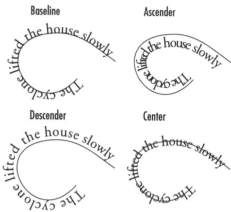.

   - **Ascender** positions the text so that the tops of the tallest letters touch the path.
   - **Descender** positions the text so that the bottoms of the lowest letters touch the path.
   - **Center** positions the text so that the middle of the text touches the path.
   - **Baseline** positions the text so that the baseline of the text touches the path.

2. Use the To Path menu to position the vertical alignment in one of the following positions :

   - **Top** positions the text relative to the top of the path's stroke weight.
   - **Center** positions the text in the middle os the path's stroke weight.
   - **Bottom** positions the text relative to the bottom of the stroke weight.

TIP You can also use the Baseline Shift controls *(see page 49)* to move the text up or down relative to the path.

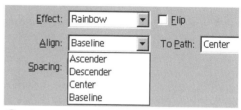

20 *The* **Align menu** *controls how the text is positioned in relationship to the path.*

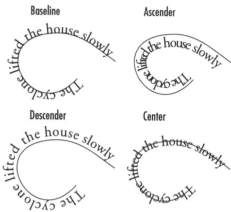

21 *The* **Align choices** *applied to text on a path.*

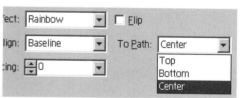

22 *The* **To Path menu** *positions the vertical alignment of the text on the path.*

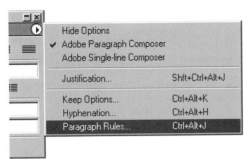

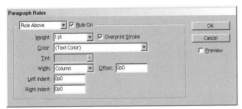

㉓ *The* **Paragraph palette menu** *contains the command to open the Paragraph Rules.*

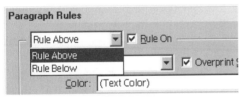

㉔ *The* **Paragraph Rules dialog box** *controls the settings for paragraph rules.*

Paragraph Rules

Rule Above ☑ Rule On

Rule Above
Rule Below

Color: (Text Color)

㉕ *Choose* **Rule Above** *or* **Rule Below** *to position the rule above or below a paragraph.*

㉖ *The controls to set the weight, color, and tint for paragraph rules.*

Working with Paragraph Rules

If you want a line (technically called a *rule*) to appear above or below a paragraph, you might draw a line using the Pen or the Line tool. Unfortunately if the text reflows, that line does not travel with the text. You could also paste the line into the text as an inline graphic *(see page 161),* but you would not have much control over that line.

The correct way to create a line above or below a paragraph is with paragraph rules. These are lines that travel with the paragraph and that can be applied as part of style sheets *(see page 278).*

To apply paragraph rules:

1. Select the paragraphs to which you want to apply the rule.

2. Choose Paragraph Rules from the Paragraph palette menu **㉓**. This opens the Paragraph Rules dialog box **㉔**.

3. Choose Rule Above or Rule Below to specify whether the rule appears before or after the selected paragraph **㉕**.

4. Check Rule On to activate the rule.

TIP If you want rules both above and below the paragraph, repeat steps 3 and 4.

5. Set an amount for the weight (or thickness) of the rule **㉖**.

6. Check Overprint Stroke to set the ink to overprint *(see page 110 for setting overprints)* **㉖**.

7. Use the Color pop-up list to apply a color to the rule **㉖**.

TIP The Text Color listing automatically changes the rule if the text color changes.

8. If you have chosen a color, use the Tint controls to create a shade of the color.

TIP Rules can be colored only with named colors from the Swatches palette.

The length of a rule (called its width) varies. The rule can be set to cover the width of the column or the width of the text. The rule can also be set to be indented from the column or text margins.

To control the width of a rule:

1. Choose from the Width list in the Paragraph Rules dialog box as follows **㉗**:
   - **Column** creates a rule that is the same width as the column that holds the text.
   - **Text** creates a rule that is the same width of the closest line of text **㉘**.

   TIP If you set a rule below a paragraph that ends in a short line, the rule will be the same length as the last line.

2. Set the Left Indent to the amount that the rule should be indented from the left side of the column or text **㉙**.

3. Set the Right Indent to the amount that the rule should be indented from the right side of the column or text **㉙**.

   TIP Use positive numbers to move the rule in from the margin **㉚**. Use negative numbers to move the rule outside the margin. The rule can extend outside the text frame.

By default the paragraph rule is positioned on the baseline of the text. You can control the position above or below the baseline **㉛**. This is called the *offset* of the rule.

To control the offset of a rule:

◆ In the Paragraph Rules dialog box, enter a value in the Offset field.
   - For a Rule Above, positive numbers raise the rule above the baseline.
   - For a Rule Below, positive numbers lower the rule below the baseline.

   TIP Negative numbers move rules in the opposite direction.

㉗ *The* **Width list** *lets you choose the length of paragraph rules.*

"From the Land of Oz," said Dorothy gravely. "And here is Toto, too. And oh, Aunt Em! I'm so glad to be at home again!" — **Column**

"From the Land of Oz," said Dorothy gravely. "And here is Toto, too. And oh, Aunt Em! I'm so glad to be at home again!" — **Text**

㉘ **Column width** *fits the rule to the width of the column.* **Text width** *fits the rule to the neighboring text.*

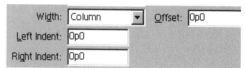

㉙ *The* **Left Indent and Right Indent fields** *let you modify the length of a rule.*

"From the Land of Oz," said Dorothy gravely. "And here is Toto, too. And oh, Aunt Em! I'm so glad to be at home again!" — **No indent**

"From the Land of Oz," said Dorothy gravely. "And here is Toto, too. And oh, Aunt Em! I'm so glad to be at home again!" — **Left and right indents**

㉚ *How changing the* **Left and Right Indent** *settings changes the look of rules.*

"From the Land of Oz," said Dorothy gravely. "And here is Toto, too. And oh, Aunt Em! I'm so glad to be at home again!" — **No offset**

"From the Land of Oz," said Dorothy gravely. "And here is Toto, too. And oh, Aunt Em! I'm so glad to be at home again!" — **0p8 offset**

㉛ *Change the* **Offset amount** *to move a rule up or down relative to the text.*

The Guardian of the Gate

It was some time before the Cowardly Lion awakened, for he had lain among the poppies a long while.

32 *A paragraph rule can create the effect of reversed text.*

Paragraph Rule

Rule Below ▲▼	☑ Rule On
Weight: 18 pt ▼	☐ Overprint Str
Color: [Black]	
Tint: 100% ▼	
Width: Column ▲▼	Offset: -1p3
Left Indent: 0p0	
Right Indent: 0p0	

33 *A dialog box showing the sample settings for a paragraph rule that create the effect of reversed text.*

True Story

When I first started learning page layout software, I used the art director's computer at the advertising agency where I worked. I stayed after hours to explore the programs and create my own documents.

When I saw the command "Rules" in the menu, I figured that was where they kept the laws governing the program. Since I didn't want to mess up the art director's machine, I never chose the command.

It was several years later (and several horrible jobs without any paragraph rules) that I discovered what the "Rules" were.

You can create many special effects with paragraph rules. One of the most common is to superimpose text inside paragraph rules to create the effect of reversed text. Most reversed text is white type inside a black background. However, any light color can be used inside any dark background **32**.

To reverse text using rules:

1. Apply a light color to a line of type.
2. Open the Paragraph Rules dialog box.
3. Create a Rule Below.
4. Set the weight of the rule to a point size large enough to enclose the text. For instance, if the text is 12 points, the rule should be at least 12 points.

TIP If you have more than one line of text, you need to calculate the size of the leading times the number of lines.

5. Set a negative number for the offset value.

TIP The offset amount should be slightly less than the weight of the rule. For instance a rule of 14 points might take an offset of − 11 points.

6. Check Preview so you can see the effect of the weight and offset settings you choose.
7. Adjust the weight and offset, if necessary.
8. Click OK to apply the rule **33**.

Working with Paragraph Rules

PAGES AND BOOKS 10

Most people who lay out documents work on projects that have more than one page—booklets, brochures, newsletters, menus, proposals, magazines, books, and so on. Even a lowly business card has two pages if you design a front and back.

Many techniques can be applied when working with multi-page documents. You need to add pages, flow text, apply page numbers, and force text to move to certain pages.

If you are working on very complex documents, you need to make sure all the pages have the same structure.

If you are working on a book, you will want to join individual chapters together. You may also want to automate the process of creating a table of contents or index.

Adding Blank Pages

InDesign gives you several ways to add pages to your document. The simplest way is to specify a certain number of pages before you start your document *(see page 16)*. You may, however, need to add pages after you have already started work on a document.

To add blank pages, you need to have the Pages palette visible.

To open the Pages palette:

♦ If the Pages palette is not visible, choose **Window > Pages** to open the palette ❶.

  or

  If the Pages palette is behind other palettes, click the Pages palette tab.

TIP A grid over the page display in the Pages palette indicates that a special effect such as a transparency, drop shadow, feather, or Photoshop transparency has been applied on that page ❷.

If you need to add just a few pages, you can add them manually.

To manually add pages:

1. Click the New Page icon in the Pages palette to add a single page.

  or

  Drag a master page or a non-master page from the master page area to the document area of the palette ❸. *(See pages 201–204 for how to work with master pages.)*

2. Repeat as many times as necessary until you have added all the pages you need.

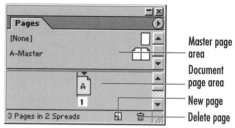

❶ *The* **Pages palette** *is the command center for multi-page documents.*

Master page area
Document page area
New page
Delete page

❷ *The* **grid over a page** *indicates that an effect such as transparency or drop shadow has been applied to that page.*

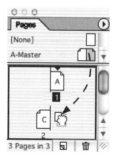

❸ *Drag a master page from the master page area of the Pages palette to the document area to add pages to a document.*

Adding Blank Pages

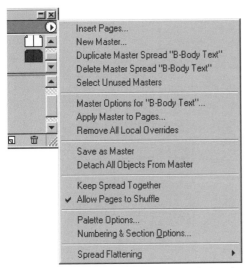

④ *The* **Pages palette menu** *gives you choices for working with pages in a document.*

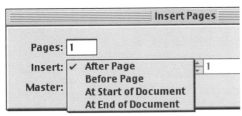

⑤ *The* **Insert Pages dialog box** *lets you add many pages at once to a document.*

⑥ *The* **Insert menu** *gives you specific choices as to where to insert pages.*

If you need to add many pages, you can add them automatically.

To automatically add pages:

1. Choose Insert Pages from the Pages palette menu **④**. The Insert Pages dialog box appears **⑤**.

2. Type the number of pages you want to insert in the Pages field.

3. Choose where to add the pages within the document from the Insert list as follows **⑥**:
   - **Before Page** lets you insert new pages before a specific page.
   - **After Page** lets you insert new pages after a specific page.
   - **At Start of Document** inserts new pages at the beginning of the document.
   - **At End of Document** inserts new pages at the end of the document.

4. Use the Master menu to choose the master page that the new pages should be based on.

   or

   Choose None from the Master menu to have no master page applied to the new pages.

5. Click OK. The new pages appear in the Pages palette.

Adding Blank Pages

Working with Pages

When your document has many pages, you can navigate from one page to another. InDesign has several different ways to move from page to page.

To move to a specific page:

◆ Double-click the page in the Pages palette that you want to move to. The page is centered within the document window.

or

Double-click the name of the spread to fit both pages in the document window.

TIP The selected page or spread is highlighted in the pages palette ❼.

TIP You can also scroll or use the Hand tool to move through the document.

To navigate using the window page controls:

◆ Click a page number in the window page controls list to navigate through the document ❽.

or

Enter a number in the Page field to move to a specific page.

To navigate using the Layout menu:

◆ Choose one of the following from the Layout menu:

- **First Page** moves to the first page of the document.
- **Previous Page** moves to the previous page.
- **Next Page** moves to the next page.
- **Last Page** moves to the last page of the document.
- **Go Back** moves to the page that was previously active.
- **Go Forward** moves to the page that was active before the Go Back command was applied.

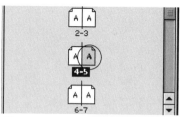

❼ *The selected page is highlighted in the Pages palette.*

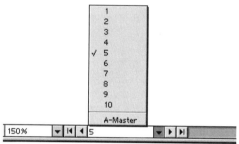

❽ *The* **window page controls** *at the bottom of the document let you navigate through the document.*

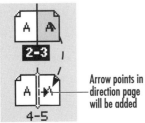

Arrow points in direction page will be added

⑨ *Pages can be moved by dragging their icons in the Pages palette.*

Before page drag   After page drag

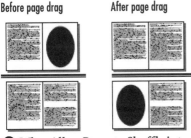

⑩ *When* **Allow Shuffling is turned off,** *a page moved between other pages is inserted between the pages, without moving the original pages.*

Before page drag   After page drag

⑪ *When* **Allow Pages to Shuffle is turned on,** *a page moved between two other pages forces one of the pages to the next spread.*

You can also duplicate and delete pages.

To duplicate pages:

1. Select the page or spreads you want to duplicate.
2. Drag the pages onto the New Page icon.

   or

   Choose Duplicate Spread from the Pages palette menu.

To delete pages:

1. Use the Pages palette to select the pages.

   TIP Hold the Shift key to select contiguous pages. Hold the Cmd/Ctrl key to select non-contiguous pages.

2. Choose Delete Pages from the Pages palette menu **③**.

   or

   Click the Delete Page icon at the bottom of the Pages palette.

3. When the confirmation dialog box appears, click OK to confirm your choice.

   TIP Hold the Opt/Alt key to bypass the confirmation dialog box.

You can control how pages are rearranged.

To rearrange pages in a document:

1. Choose Allow Shuffling from the Pages palette menu.
2. Drag a page next to or between the pages of a spread as follows **⑨**:
   - With Allow Pages to Shuffle turned on, the new page forces other pages to a new spread **⑩**.
   - With Allow Pages to Shuffle turned off, the new page is added to the existing spread without moving the other pages **⑪**.

   TIP The arrow cursor indicates which side of a gutter the new page is inserted.

Working with Pages

Creating Island Spreads

Most documents are either single-page or facing-page documents *(see page 17)*. However, you can create spreads with more than one or two pages. These are *island spreads* like the fold-outs found in special issues of magazines.

To add pages to a spread:

1. Choose the page or pages in the document area that you want to designate as the island spread.

2. Choose Keep Spread Together from the Pages palette menu.

TIP Brackets appear around the page numbers. This indicates that additional pages can be added to the spread .

3. Move a page in the document area next to the spread.

4. Release the mouse when the vertical line appears next to the spread ⓭. This adds the page to the island spread.

To dismantle an island spread:

1. Drag each page outside the spread.

   or

   Deselect Keep Spread Together from the Pages palette menu.

2. Choose Allow Pages to Shuffle from the Pages palette menu. A dialog box asks if you want to maintain the current number of pages in the spread ⓮.

3. Click the No button. This dismantles the island spread into the default number of pages per spread in the document.

⓬ *An example of an* island spread *in the Pages palette.*

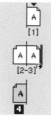

⓭ *The* thick black vertical line *indicates that the new page will be added to the island spread.*

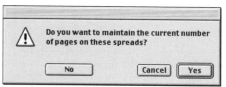

⓮ *You can dismantle an island spread by changing the number of pages in the spread.*

☑ Show Import Options ☑ Convert Quotes
☑ Retain Format ☑ Replace Selected Item

⑮ *The* **Import options** *in the Place dialog box.*

⑯ *The* **loaded text cursor** *indicates that you can place the imported text.*

Importing Text Files

InDesign lets you import text files saved from Microsoft Word 98 or higher *(see the next page)*. You simply save the file and import it into InDesign.

If you have an earlier version of Word, you should save the text in the RTF (rich text format). RTF files retain most of their original formatting and can be imported by InDesign.

InDesign can also import ASCII text—the most primitive computer text format. For example, when text is saved in the ASCII format any italic or bold formatting is lost.

Although ASCII text is stripped down, it is useful for importing text from databases or internet sites. However, you do have to reformat any text imported in the ASCII format.

Importing Text

If you have a short amount of text, you can easily type it directly in InDesign's text frames. However, if you are working with long amounts of text, you most likely will want to import the text from a word processing program.

To import text:

1. Choose **File** > **Place**. The options for placing images are at the bottom of the Place dialog box **⑮**.

2. Navigate to find the file you want to import.

3. Click Show Import Options to open the specific import options for that type of text file. *(See the next two exercises for specifics on importing Microsoft Word and Microsoft Excel files.)*

4. Click Retain Format to keep any formatting applied to the text.

5. Click Convert Quotes to replace "dumb" (straight) quotes with "smart" (curly) ones.

6. Click Replace Selected Item to replace the contents of a selected text frame with the new text.

7. Click Choose to load the text into a text cursor **⑯**. *(See page 197–199 for working with the text cursors.)*

TIP If you hold the Shift key as you click Choose, you open the Import Options dialog box even if the option is not checked.

TIP If the text file uses fonts not installed on your computer, an alert box informs you that the fonts are missing.

Importing Text

Setting the Import Options

The options for importing text change depending on which type of text file you choose to import.

To set the options for Microsoft Word files:

1. Choose Import Options to open the Microsoft Word® Import Options **17**.

2. Choose which parts of the document to include such as the table of contents, index, or footnotes and endnotes.

3. Choose how to convert manual page breaks that were inserted in the text.

TIP The import options for RTF files contain the same options as the Microsoft Word Import Choices.

To set the options for Microsoft Excel files:

1. Choose Import Options to open the Microsoft Excel® Import Options **18**.

2. Choose which parts of the spread sheet and cells you want to import.

3. Choose what formatting should be imported along with the cells.

TIP Excel files are imported as InDesign tables *(see Chapter 13, "Tabs and Tables").*

To set the options for ASCII files:

1. Choose Import Options to open the Text Import Options **19**.

2. Choose the character set, platform, and language to ensure that special characters are imported correctly.

3. Choose how to handle extra carriage (paragraph) returns at the end of lines and paragraphs.

4. Choose how to delete extra spaces inserted into the text.

TIP Most of the extra carriage returns and spaces are created when text is imported from Web pages.

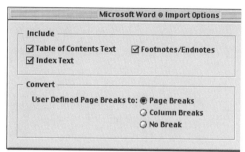

17 *The Microsoft Word® Import Options dialog box is used to import Word files.*

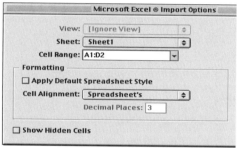

18 *The Microsoft Excel® Import Options dialog box is used to import Excel tables.*

19 *The Text Import Options is used to import raw ASCII text files.*

The **straight lines around the loaded text cursor** *indicates that the text will be placed into a new text frame.*

 The **curved lines around the loaded text cursor** *indicates that the text will be placed into an existing text frame.*

Lore dionsectet, velit num nit prat verosto eu facin ullan ex ex ero enis at. Duisismod lesequamet eum delisim nisl exeriureet acing ercilla alissed tat.

Lor ad te mincillan hendre feugiat praestio ea amet ip estrud dit in hendignis enim delenim ver sit velisi bla feugue delesequipit ulluptat alis nostrud doluptat. Ut prat luptat alit

22 *A sample of the* **placeholder text** *that is used to fill text frames.*

What Can You Do With a Loaded Cursor?

If you click with a loaded cursor in your hand, you flow the text onto the page. However, there are some things you can do without losing the text loaded into the cursor. You can:

Use any of the menu or Pages palette commands to add pages to the document.

Use the keyboard shortcuts to zoom in or out.

Use the scroll bars to move through the page or the document.

Move the onscreen elements, such as the palettes, to new positions.

Flowing Text

Once you have imported the text into the loaded text cursor *(see page 195)*, you have a choice as to how the text flows into the InDesign document.

To import text into a new frame:

1. Drag the loaded text cursor to create a text frame that contains the text **20**.

   or

   Click the loaded text cursor on the page. InDesign automatically creates a text frame the width of the margins of the page.

TIP To unload the text from the cursor, click any tool in the Toolbox.

To import text into an existing frame:

1. Move the loaded text cursor inside an existing frame.

TIP The parentheses around the cursor indicate that the text will flow into that frame **21**.

2. Click the loaded text cursor inside the frame. The text flows into the existing frame.

TIP To unload the text cursor, choose any tool in the toolbox.

You can fill a frame with dummy text instead of importing real text.

To add placeholder text:

1. Click inside a frame.

2. Choose **Type > Fill with Placeholder Text**. The dummy text fills the frame **22**.

TIP Use placeholder text instead of real text to avoid missing or modified text files in the Links palette *(see the sidebar on page 165)*.

Flowing Text

If the text that you import is too long to fit in the frame, the overflow symbol appears *(see page 41)*. Rather than manually load the overflow text into a new frame you can use the semi-autoflow command to easily load the cursor to create new text boxes that display the text.

To semi-autoflow text:

1. Import the text so that you have a loaded cursor .

2. Hold the Opt/Alt key to display the semi-autoflow cursor .

TIP The cursor displays curved lines if you place it inside an existing frame.

3. Click inside an existing frame or drag to create a text frame. The semi-autoflow cursor automatically loads any overflow text into a new cursor which is available to be placed into a new frame .

4. Hold the Opt/Alt key and click or drag to create another text box linked to the first.

5. Repeat step 4 as many times as necessary to place all the text in the story .

  *The semi-autoflow cursors let you flow text page by page.*

 The semi-autoflow cursor indicates that the text will automatically load any overflow into the text cursor.

 *After clicking with the semi-autoflow cursor the text is automatically loaded into a new cursor.*

 Each click with the semi-autoflow cursor loads the text onto new pages.

㉗ *Use the* **autoflow cursors** *to create all the pages necessary to hold the imported text.*

㉘ *The* **autoflow cursor** *indicates that new pages will be created as the text is imported.*

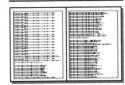

㉙ *After clicking with the autoflow cursor new pages are created that hold the text.*

| Number of Pages: 1 | ☑ Facing Pages |
| | ☑ Master Text Frame |

㉚ *Check Master Text Frame to create an automatic text frame on the master pages.*

㉛ *The* **link cursor** *indicates that the text will be inserted into a master text frame.*

The semi-autoflow command may not be practical for flowing more than a few pages of text. If you have many pages of text, you can automatically flow the text and create new pages at the same time using the autoflow feature.

To autoflow pages with text:

1. Use the Place command *(see page 195)* to load the text in the cursor.

2. Hold the Shift key. This cursor changes to the autoflow text cursor **㉗**.

3. Click anywhere inside the margins of the page **㉘**. This creates a text frame that automatically stretches between the width of the column. Additional text frames are created on new pages **㉙**.

TIP Hold the Opt/Alt+Shift key to create a special autoflow cursor. This automatically flows the text onto all the existing pages of the document, but does not generate any new pages.

InDesign also lets you flow text into the frames that are on master pages. Importing text into those frames means that if you change the master page, the text frames adjust accordingly. *(See page 201–204 for working with master pages.)*

To flow text into master page frames:

1. Click Master Text Frame in the New Document dialog box **㉚**. This creates an empty frame on each page of the document.

2. Use the Place command to load the text cursor.

3. Click inside the margins to flow text inside the master text frame on a page **㉛**.

TIP Use the semi-autoflow or autoflow commands to control how the text flows.

Flowing Text

Creating Text Breaks

As you flow text, you may want the text to jump or *break* to the next column, frame, or page. InDesign has special characters that force the text to break to a position.

To insert break characters:

1. Place the insertion point by the text that you want to have jump to the next location

2. Choose **Type** > **Insert Break Character**.

   or

   Control-click (Mac) or right-mouse click (Win) to choose Insert Break Character from the contextual menu.

3. Choose one of the following from the Insert Break Character menu:

   - **Column break** jumps text to the next column ❷.

   TIP If there is no column in the frame, the column break character forces the text to the next page.

   - **Frame break** jumps text to the next frame ❸.
   - **Page break** jumps text to the next page ❹.
   - **Odd page break** jumps text to the next odd page ❺.
   - **Even page break** jumps text to the next even page ❻.

   TIP To see a representation of the break characters, choose **Type** > **Show Hidden Characters**.

❷ *A column break character* forces text to the next column or page.

❸ *A frame break character* forces text to the next text frame.

❹ *A page break character* forces text to the next page.

❺ *An* odd page break character *forces text to the next odd-numbered page.*

❻ *An* even page break character *forces text to the next even-numbered page.*

Insert Break Character Shortcuts

You can also use the following shortcuts to insert break characters:

Enter inserts a column break.

Shift-Enter inserts a frame break.

Cmd-Enter (Mac) or **Ctrl-Enter** (Win) inserts a page break.

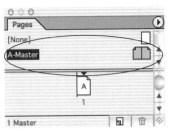

③ *Double-click a master page in the Pages palette to view that* **master page in the document window.**

Uses for Master Pages

Master pages allow you to automate page layout changes. For instance, if you have a hundred-page book, you wouldn't want to have to draw a text frame on every page and type the name of the chapter or book title.

Master pages allow you to place an object on the master page and have that object appear on all the document pages.

If you place an object on the master page, it will always be positioned in exactly the same spot on every page that has that master applied.

You can also use master pages to store design alternatives such as different column layouts or margin settings.

Think of master pages as the style sheets for pages.

Working with Master Pages

Every new document includes a master page. When you add objects to the master page, they appear on all the document pages based on that master page.

To add objects to a master page:

1. In the Pages palette, double-click the name of the master page **③**. This opens the master page in the document window.

2. Add text boxes, graphics, or any other elements you want on the master page.

TIP If the document has been set for facing pages, there are two sides to the master page, left-hand and right-hand. The left-hand master page governs the left-hand document pages. Similarly the right-hand master page governs the right-hand document pages.

3. Double-click the name of the document page to make it the active page. Any items placed on the master page now appear on the document page.

TIP Reopen the master page to make any changes to the master-page elements. Those changes appear on the document pages.

You can have many master pages in a document. The allows you to have different layouts for different parts of your document.

To create new master pages:

1. Choose New Master from the Pages palette menu. This opens the New Master dialog box .

2. Choose a letter for the prefix for the master page.

TIP The prefix is the letter that appears inside the pages that have that master page applied to them.

3. Enter a name for the master page.

4. Use the pop-up menu to set which master page, if any, the new master page should be based on.

TIP Basing one master page on another allows you to make changes on one master page that are applied to the other.

5. Enter the number of pages for the master. This allows you to create spreads that serve as master pages.

TIP To create a new master page without opening the New Master dialog box, hold the Cmd/Ctrl key and click the New Page icon at the bottom of the Pages palette.

As you work, you might want to convert a document page into a master page. InDesign makes it easy to turn a document page into a master page.

To convert a document page to a master page:

1. Select the page or pages.

2. Drag the page or pages from the document area to the master page area 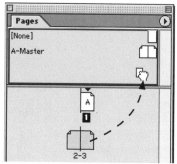.

   or

   Choose Save as Master from the Pages palette menu.

38 *The* **New Master dialog box** *allows you to set the attributes for the master page.*

39 *Drag a document page into the master page area to convert the document page to a master.*

Strategies For Basing Master Pages On Each Other

I have three master page spreads for this book. One master—the main master—holds only the guides and page numbers for the book. The master for ordinary pages is based on that main master. The master for the chapter opener is also based on that main master.

That way, if I need to move the page numbers I only need to change the page number on the main master. The other masters update automatically.

 40 *The* **Apply Master dialog box** *allows you to change the master that governs pages.*

 41 *The* **rectangle around the single page** *indicates that the master will be applied to that page only.*

 42 *The* **rectangle around the spread** *indicates that the master will be applied to the spread.*

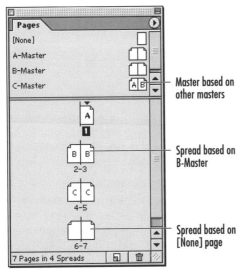

Master based on other masters

Spread based on B-Master

Spread based on [None] page

43 *The letters inside the page icons indicate what masters are applied to pages or other masters.*

The new pages you add to a document are based on the master page applied to the last page of the document. You can easily change the master page that governs pages.

To apply a new master to a page:

1. Select the page or pages.
2. Choose Apply Master to Pages from the Pages palette. This opens the Apply Master dialog box **40**.
3. Use the Apply Master pop-up list to apply a master to the pages.
4. Use the To Pages field to change the selected pages.

TIP The None page makes document pages that have no master page applied.

To apply masters with the Pages palette:

1. Drag the master page onto the document pages as follows:
   - To apply to a single page, drag onto the page. A rectangle appears around the page **41**.
   - To apply to a spread, drag the master onto the spread. A rectangle appears around the spread **42**.
2. Release the mouse button to apply the master to the page.

You can also base one master page on another using the Pages palette.

To base masters on existing masters:

1. Drag one master page onto another.
   - To base the spread on the master, drag the master onto the spread.
   - To base one page on the master, drag the master onto a single page.
2. Release the mouse button. The prefix of the master appears inside the second master page **43**. The prefix indicates that the master page governs the other master page.

Ordinarily you modify the elements of a master page only on the master page itself. However, you can create local overrides by changing the master-page elements on the document pages.

To modify master elements on document pages:

1. Hold Cmd/Ctrl-Shift and click the element you want to modify. This selects the element.

2. Make any local override changes to the element.

TIP An object can still have some links to the master page even if local overrides have been applied *(see "Overriding Master-Page Elements" on this page)*.

You might want to modify all the master elements on a page. Rather than release each item one by one, InDesign lets you do it with a single command.

To release all the master items on a spread:

◆ Choose Detach All Objects From Master in the Pages palette menu.

You can also hide master page items on document pages so they do not print.

To change the display of master page items:

◆ Choose View > Display Master Items. This unchecks the command.

TIP When the command is unchecked the master page items are hidden.

InDesign also lets you reattach items to the master page.

To reapply detached items to the master:

◆ Choose Remove All Local Overrides in the Pages palette menu.

Overriding Master-Page Elements

If you modify a master-page element on a document page, the local override loses its link to the master-page element. However, the element may have partial links to the master-page element.

Let's say you add a stroke to an object on the document page. From that point on, the stroke of the element is removed from the control of the element on the master page.

But, the element on the document page is allowed to move if you move the element on the master page. Also, the fill color of the elements changes if you change the master-page element. Only the formatting for stroke is separated from the master-page element.

How Many Master Pages?

While it may seem like a lot of work to set up master pages, the more masters you have the easier it is to lay out complicated documents.

A weekly magazine can easily have fifty or more master pages—some for special editorial spreads and others for different types of advertising spaces.

Some publishers insist that every page be based on a master and do not allow any modifications of the master-page elements. Others let the designers override the master pages.

You decide which way suits your work habits and the project.

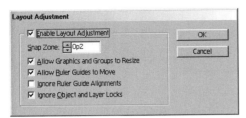

44 The **Layout Adjustment dialog box** *controls which elements change if you change document attributes such as the page size or margins.*

45 *The effect of changing the margins and page size when* **Enable Layout Adjustment** *is turned on.*

Adjusting Layouts

You certainly are not expected to set layouts perfectly the first time, every time. Fortunately, InDesign has a powerful layout adjustment feature that moves and resizes objects as you change the page size or margins.

Once layout adjustment is turned on, any changes to the layout will alter the position of the elements on both the master pages and document pages.

To set the layout adjustment options:

1. Choose **Layout > Layout Adjustment**. This opens the Layout Adjustment dialog box **44**.

2. Check Enable Layout Adjustment so that elements change when page size, orientation, margins, or columns are changed **45**.

3. Set a value for the Snap Zone to specify how close an object must be before it will align and move to a margin or column guide, or page edge.

4. Check Allow Graphics and Groups to Resize so that elements change size as well as move during the adjustment.

5. Check Allow Ruler Guides to Move to have ruler guides move as part of the layout adjustment.

6. Check Ignore Ruler Guide Alignments to keep objects from moving along with ruler guides.

7. Check Ignore Object and Layer Locks to move objects that are locked or on locked layers.

8. Click OK to set the options. The document changes according to the new settings when the document setup or margins are changed.

Working with Page Numbers

The most common element that is added to a master page is the page-number character.

To add automatic page numbering:

1. Draw a text frame on the master page where you want the page number to appear.

2. Choose **Type** > **Insert Special Character** > **Auto Page Number**. This inserts a special character in the text frame .

TIP The auto page number character is the prefix for the master page *(see page 202)*.

3. If the master page is a facing-page master, repeat step 3 for the other side.

You may want to change how page numbers are displayed or the number they start from. You do that by creating a new *section*.

To create a document section:

1. Move to the page where you want the section to start.

2. Choose Section Options from the Pages palette menu. The New Section dialog box appears .

3. Check Start Section to open the options.

4. Type the label (up to five characters) for the section in the Section Prefix field.

5. Use the Style pop-up list to set the format for the numbering 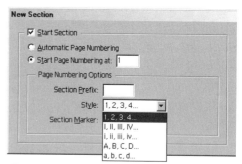.

6. Choose the Page Numbering options:
   - **Automatic Page Numbering** continues the count from the previous pages.
   - **Start Page Numbering At** lets you enter a number to start from a specific number.

7. Enter a label for the Section Marker 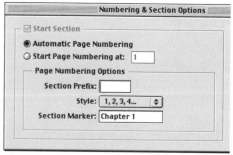. *(See the steps on the next page for how to work with the Section Marker.)*

46 The **auto page number character** appears as a letter on master pages but as a number on document pages.

47 The **New Section dialog box** lets you change the formatting and numbering of pages.

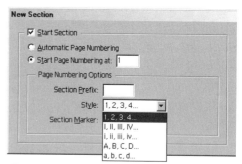

48 *The* **Style menu** *allows you to choose different formats for page numbering of a section.*

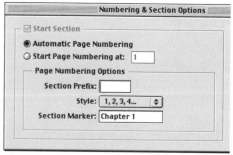

49 *The entry in the* **Section Marker field** *allows you to create custom labels for pages.*

50 The **section marker character** appears as the word Section on master pages but as the label on document pages.

Duis etummolore facilla faci bla consenit, consed sequissequis nulputpat. Duisim in velit vullum du: adigna conulla feuguer accumsan vulla faccumsan commodolore magna faciliquisi tat. Ut autatue dol

Continued on page 3

51 *The* **Next Page Number character** *shows the page number that the story is continued on.*

Continued from page 2

irit lutpatie vent nim irilit vullandreetumsan hendr feugait lobor sum ipis aliquisl dolore dunt dit vel e eugait lut delessi tat, si.

52 *The* **Previous Page Number character** *shows the page number that the story comes from.*

Once you have created a label for the Section Marker (see previous page) you need to insert a section marker character to see the label on pages.

To add a section marker character:

1. Open the master page for the pages.

2. Place the insertion point in a text frame where you want the section marker to appear.

3. Choose **Type > Insert Special Character** and then choose Section Name from the menu. This adds the word Section inside the text frame on the master page.

4. Move to the document page to see the custom label in the text frame **50**.

You can also insert special characters that create jump lines that show the page where the text flow continues to or from.

To create a continued to/from page number:

1. Place the insertion point in a text frame that touches the frame that holds the story.

2. Choose **Type > Insert Special Character** and then choose one of the following:

   • **Next Page Number** inserts the page number that the text jumps to or continues on **51**.

   • **Previous Page Number** inserts the page number that the text continued from **52**.

   TIP The continued to/from character needs a separate text frame so that if the text reflows, the continued to/from character doesn't move along with the text.

Changing the Pages Palette

You can also change how the Pages palette displays the layout of master pages and document pages.

To control the display of the Pages palette:

1. Choose Palette options from the Pages palette menu. This opens the Pages Palette Options dialog box ⓼.

2. Use the Pages Icon Size menu to change the size of the document pages icons.

3. Use the Masters Icon Size menu to change the size of the master page icons.

4. Uncheck Show Vertically to display the pages horizontally in the palette ⓼.

5. Choose Pages on Top to have the document pages shown at the top of the Pages palette.

6. Choose Masters on Top to have the master pages shown at the top of the Pages palette ⓼.

7. Use the Resize list to control how the master page and document page areas are affected when you change the size of the Pages palette.

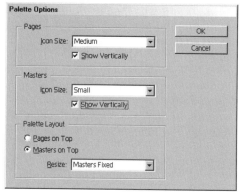

⓼ *The* **Pages Palette Options dialog box** *lets you control the appearance of the Pages palette.*

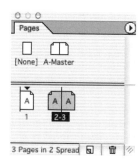

⓼ *The Pages palette when* **Show Vertically** *is turned off.*

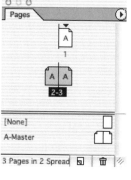

⓼ *An example of choosing* **Pages on Top.**

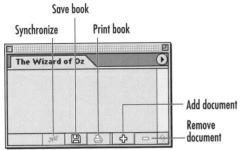

⑤⑥ *A book document has its own document icon.*

⑤⑦ *An empty* **Book palette** *displays the name of the book.*

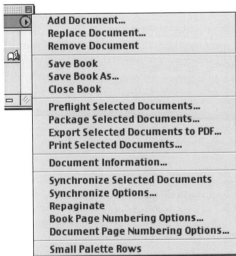

⑤⑧ *The* **Book palette menu** *contains commands for working with books and book documents.*

Making Books

Most people who create long documents, such as books, organize them so that each chapter or section is contained in its own document. An InDesign *book* is an electronic file that keeps track of all those documents.

To create an electronic book file:

1. Choose File > New > Book.
2. Use the dialog box to name the book document and save it in a location **⑤⑥**. The Book palette appears **⑤⑦**.

TIP The tab for the Book palette contains the name of the book.

Once you have created the electronic book file, you can then add the documents that make up the book.

TIP You don't have to create the book file first. For instance, I created these chapters before I added them to a book document.

To add documents to a book:

1. Click the Add document button at the bottom of the Book palette.

   or

   Choose Add Document from the Book palette menu **⑤⑧**.
2. Use the dialog box to find the document you want to add to the book. The name of the chapter appears in the Book palette.
3. Repeat steps 1 and 2 to add other documents to the book.

To remove documents from a book:

◆ Click the Remove document button at the bottom of the Book palette.

   or

   Choose Remove Document from the Book palette menu.

You can use the Book palette and Book palette menu to work with the various documents that make up the book.

To open documents in a book:

♦ Double-click the name of a document in the Book palette. The open book symbol next to the name indicates that the document is open 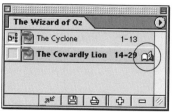.

59 *The* **open book icon** *indicates that document of the book is open.*

The order that documents are listed in the Book palette determines the page numbers of the book.

To change the order of the documents in a book:

♦ Drag the name of a document in the Book palette to a new position in the palette **60**.

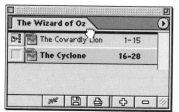

60 *Drag a listing in the Book palette to change the order the document appears in the book.*

One of the benefits of creating a book document is that you can have one file control the style sheets *(see page 278)* and colors *(see Chapter 5, "Working in Color")* for the other documents in the book. This way you only need to make changes to that style source file and all the other files synchronize to that file.

To set the style source for a book document:

♦ Click the Style Source box next to the name of the file that you want to control the rest of the documents in the book **61**.

To synchronize files to the style source:

♦ Click the Synchronize button in the Book palette.

   or

   Choose Synchronize Book in the Book palette menu.

TIP The menu command says Synchronize Selected Files if only some of the files in the book are selected.

Style source file   Synchronize button

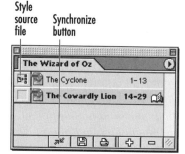

61 *The* **style source file** *is used to synchronize the style sheets and colors for the other documents in the book.*

Making Books

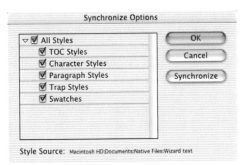

62 *Use the* **Synchronize Options** *dialog box to set which attributes of the style source file will be applied to the files in the book.*

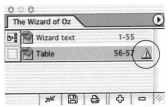

63 *The* **alert icon** *in the Book palette indicates that the file has been modified.*

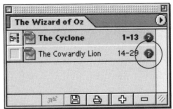

64 *The* **missing icon** *in the Book palette indicates that the file has been moved after it was imported into the book.*

To set the synchronizing options:

1. Choose Synchronize Options from the Book palette menu. The Synchronize Options dialog box opens **62**.

2. Choose the options that you want to apply from the style source document.

If you modify the individual files in a book document you need to update them in the Book palette.

To update files in a book:

1. Choose **File** > **Open** and then navigate to the book document you want to work on.

2. Use the Book palette to open, then modify any files in the book document. An alert icon appears next to the modified files **63**.

   or

   Use the Open command in the File menu to open, then modify any files in the book document.

3. Synchronize the files to the style source document *(see previous exercise)*.

You can also replace missing files in a book or swap one file for another.

To replace a file in a book:

1. Select the file in the Book palette that you want to replace.

   TIP A missing icon indicates that the file has been moved after being added to the book **64**. The Replace command lets you relink the missing file to the Book palette.

2. Choose Replace Document from the Book palette menu.

3. Navigate to find the file you want to replace or relink.

4. If necessary, synchronize the files.

Making Books

Files in a book automatically run in consecutive numbers. As you add or delete pages in one document, the page numbers in the rest of the book adjust. You control how the page numbers are adjusted.

To set how page numbers are adjusted:

1. Choose Book Page Numbering Options from the Book palette menu to open the dialog box **64**.

2. Choose the Page Order options as follows:
   - **Continue from previous document** starts new pages sequentially from the end of the previous listing.
   - **Continue on next odd page** always starts new pages on an odd number.
   - **Continue on next even page** always starts new pages on an even number.

3. If using the odd or even options results in a skipped page, check Insert Blank Page to insert a page.

4. Deselect Automatic Pagination to stop InDesign from automatically numbering the files in a book.

To set the numbers for each document in a book:

1. Choose Document Page Numbering Options from the Book palette menu to open the dialog box **65**.

2. Choose Automatic Page Numbering to number pages as they appear in the Book palette.

   or

   Choose Start Page Numbering At to set a specific page number to start that document on.

4. Set the rest of the options as described on page 206.

To force the pagination in a book:

- Choose Repaginate from the Book palette menu.

64 *Use the* **Book Page Numbering Options dialog box** *to set how pages shall be numbered in a book.*

65 *Use the* **Document Page Numbering Options dialog box** *to set how an individual document is numbered in a book.*

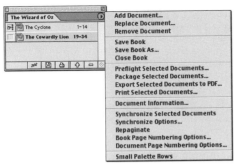

66 *If you select individual files in the Book palette list, the Book palette commands are applied to only the selected files.*

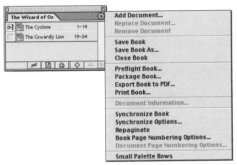

67 *With no document files selected, the Book palette commands are applied to all the book files.*

The Book palette also lets you apply printing and output commands to all the files in a book.

To print a book:

◆ Choose Print Book from the Book palette menu. *(See Chapter 17, "Output" for more information on printing files.)*

or

Click the Print icon in the Book palette.

To preflight a book:

◆ Choose Preflight Book from the Book palette menu. *(See page 321 for more information on the preflight command.)*

To package a book:

◆ Choose Package Book from the Book palette menu. *(See page 324 for more information on the package command.)*

To export the book files as a PDF:

◆ Choose Export Book to PDF from the Book palette menu. *(See page 329 for more information on the exporting as a PDF.)*

The Book palette menu commands change depending on which files are selected in the Book palette **66**.

To control what parts of a book are changed:

◆ Select the files in the book as follows:
  • Hold the Shift key and click to select contiguous files.
  • Hold the Cmd/Ctrl key and click to select non-contiguous files.
  • Click the area below the files to deselect the file. This applies commands to all the files in the book **67**.

Creating a Table of Contents

InDesign creates a table of contents by look-ing at the paragraph style sheets applied to paragraphs and then listing the text and the page numbers for those paragraphs. For instance, the table of contents for this book lists the entries for the chapter names and the A Heads for each section 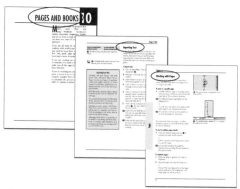.

To prepare a document for a table of contents:

1. Add the page or pages that will hold the table of contents.

TIP If the document is part of a book, make sure the book's pagination is current.

2. Apply paragraph styles to the paragraphs that you want to appear in the table of contents. *(See page 272 for more information on paragraph style sheets.)*

To define the styles for TOC entries:

1. Choose **Layout** > **Table of Contents** to open the Table of Contents dialog box 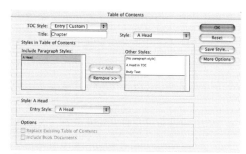.

2. Set each of the controls as described in the following exercises.

3. Click Save Style. This opens the Save Style dialog box .

4. Name the style and click Save.

To generate the table of contents:

1. Choose **Layout** > **Table of Contents** to open the Table of Contents dialog box.

2. Set each of the controls as described in the following exercises.

3. Click OK. This closes the dialog box and creates a loaded text cursor that contains the table of contents.

4. Click or drag the loaded cursor to apply the table of contents text where you want it to appear in the document.

68 *The paragraph styles applied to chapter titles and section heads in this book can be used to create a table of contents.*

69 *The* Table of Contents dialog box *lets you select and format listings for a table of contents.*

70 *The* Save Style dialog box *lets you save the settings from the Table of Contents dialog box.*

71 *Use the* **Title field in the Table of Contents dialog box** *to enter the text you want to appear before the listings.*

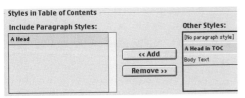

72 *Move styles from the Other Styles list to the Include Paragraph Styles list to determine which paragraphs are added to the table of contents.*

73 *Use the* **Entry Style menu** *to choose a style sheet that you have created to format the listing as it should appear in the table of contents.*

Other Uses for a Table of Contents

You're not limited to using the Table of Contents commands just for listings of chapters and section heads.

If you have a sales catalog you can use the commands to create a list of all the items that can be used as a price list.

I could generate a separate file for this book that lists all the titles for sidebars such as this.

In a book of illustrations, you can use it to create a list of names of all the artists for each illustration.

The only thing you need to remember is to assign a style sheet to each item that you want to appear in the table of contents.

The title is the label that is applied before each entry in the table of contents. You can set the type for the title as well as the paragraph style that formats the title.

To enter the title of the table of contents:

1. Type the text for the title in the Title field **71**.

2. Use the Style menu to the right of the Title field to choose which paragraph style is applied to format the title.

You choose the entries for a table of contents by selecting the paragraph style sheets that were applied to those sections of your documents.

To choose the listings for the table of contents:

1. Select a paragraph style listed in the Other Styles area of the Table of Contents dialog box **72**.

2. Click the Add button. This moves the style to the Include Paragraph Styles list.

3. Repeat steps 1 and 2 for any additional styles.

Most likely you will want to format the entries in a table of contents with a different format than the one they have within the document.

To format the entries in the table of contents:

1. Select the entry listing in the Include Paragraph Styles area.

2. Choose a paragraph style sheet from the Entry Style menu under the Style: [Name] in the Table of Contents dialog box **73**.

3. Repeat steps 1 and 2 for any additional styles.

Creating a Table of Contents

The Table of Contents dialog box has additional controls for more advanced options such as formatting the page numbers for each entry.

To open the additional table of contents controls:

◆ Click the More Options button in the Table of Contents dialog box 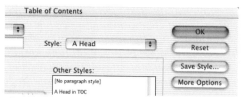. This opens the advanced options at the bottom of the dialog box.

TIP If the button says Fewer Options, then the dialog box already shows the advanced options.

74 Click the **More Options** button *to expand the controls in the Table of Contents dialog box.*

With the advanced options open, you can control the formatting and positioning of the page numbers 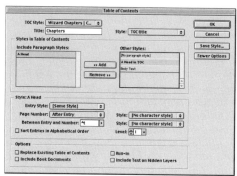.

To position and format the page numbers:

1. Use the Page Number menu to choose a position for the entry's page number :
   • **After Entry** positions the number after the entry.
   • **Before Entry** positions the number before the entry.
   • **No Page Number** lists the entry without any page number.
2. If desired, choose a character style from the Style list to the right of the Page Number menu.

TIP The character style lets you apply a special formatting such as a different typeface or bold format to the page number for each entry. *(See page 274 for working with character style sheets.)*

75 *The* **Table of Contents dialog box** *with all the options available.*

76 *The* **Page Number menu** *controls where the page number will appear.*

77 *Check* **Sort Entries in Alphabetical Order** *to alphabetize the table of contents.*

A table of contents doesn't have to be in the order that the items appear.

To alphabetize the table of contents:

◆ Check Sort Entries in Alphabetical order from the advanced options area .

Creating a Table of Contents

78 *The* **Between Entry and Number menu** *lets you enter a specific character to separate the entry and the page number.*

79 *The* **Style menu** *for the character between the entry and the number.*

80 *The* **options for the Table of Contents** dialog box.

The advanced options also let you control the divider character that is between the entry and the page number.

To control the divider character:

1. Select one of the character options from the Between Entry and Number menu **78**. The character symbol appears in the field.

2. If you want, type additional text before or after the character symbol. This lets you add a label such as "Page" before the page number.

3. If desired, apply a style from the Style menu for the Between Entry and Number character **79**.

To indent the entries in a table of contents:

◆ Use the Level controls to indent each table of contents entry **75**.

There are also several options you can set for a table of contents **80**.

To set the table of contents options:

◆ Select each of the table of contents options at the bottom of the Table of Contents dialog box as follows:

- **Replace Existing Table of Contents** lets you update or change the table of contents that has already been placed in the document.

TIP This option is only available if a table of contents has already been generated.

- **Include Book Documents** lets you create a table of contents for all the documents in a book.
- **Run-in** creates a single paragraph table of contents with each entry divided by a semi-colon (;) and a space.
- **Include Text on Hidden Layers** uses text that is on layers that are not visible.

Creating an Index

There are different ways to create an index in
InDesign. The simplest way is to add index
references to the words or phrases you want
to appear in the index.

To apply an index reference to text:

1. Select the text that you want to be
   indexed.
2. Choose **Window** > **Index** to open the
   Index palette ⓫.
3. Click the Reference button at the top of
   the palette.
4. Click the New Index entry or choose
   New Page References in the Index palette
   menu. The New Page Reference dialog
   box appears ⓬.
5. Click the Add button to add just that
   instance of the text to the Index palette.

   or

   Click the Add All button to add all the
   instances of the text to the Index palette.
6. Click OK to return to the document. An
   index reference marker appears before the
   referenced text ⓭.
7. Repeat these steps for each entry that you
   want added to the Index palette.

TIP The Index palette shows referenced text
along with the page numbers that the text
appears on ⓮.

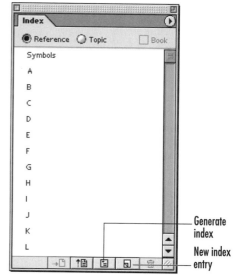

Generate
index

New index
entry

⓫ *The* **Index palette** *lets you define those items
that should be part of the index.*

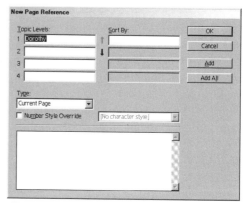

⓬ *Use the* **New Page Reference dialog box** *to
add specific index entries to the Index palette.*

⓭ *An* **index reference marker** *is visible in the
text when Show Hidden Characters is chosen.*

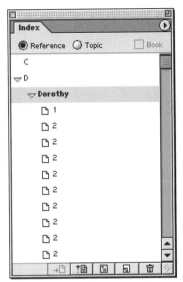

84 *The Index palette shows the pages that the each index entry appears on.*

85 *The* **Generate Index dialog box** *lets you create the index text file.*

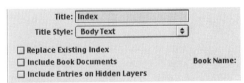

86 *The* **index options** *in the Generate Index dialog box.*

Once you have all the index references in the document, you can then generate the index text file.

To generate an index file:

1. Click the Generate Index button or choose Generate Index from the Index palette menu. The Generate Index dialog box appears **85**.

2. In the Title field, enter the text that you want for the title of index **86**.

3. Use the Title Style menu to choose a paragraph style for the formatting of the title of the index.

4. If you have already created an index, check the Replace Existing Index to replace the original index.

5. If the document is part of a book, check Include Book Documents to add those documents to the index.

6. Check Include Entries on Hidden Layers to include the text on hidden layers in the index.

7. Click OK. This closes the dialog box and creates a loaded text cursor that contains the index.

8. Click or drag to apply the index text where you want it to appear in the document.

Creating an Index

The Art of an Index

An index is much more than just a list of entries in a document. There is an art to creating a good index. You need to understand the meaning of the index entries and anticipate the items readers will want to search for.

Quite frankly, most designers are not prepared to create a truly elegant index. In fact, I hire a professional indexer who reads my books and creates an index for me.

Creating Hyperlinks

A hyperlink is an area of a page that can be clicked to send the reader to a new page, open a new document, move to a Web page, or even send a message in an e-mail program. InDesign lets you create those hyperlinks to add to your documents.

TIP Hyperlinks are only active when the file is exported as an Adobe PDF *(see page 329)* or an HTML document *(see page 341)*.

To open the Hyperlinks palette:

◆ Choose **Window > Hyperlinks**. This opens the Hyperlinks palette .

The first part to creating hyperlinks is to create a destination. A page destination specifies a page and the magnification for the link.

To create a page destination:

1. Choose New Hyperlink Destination in the Hyperlinks palette menu to open the New Hyperlink Destination dialog box .

2. Choose Page from the Type menu 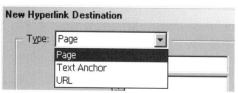.

3. Use the Page controls to enter the page number that you want to jump to.

4. If desired, use the Name field to enter a descriptive name for the page.

5. Choose the Zoom settings as follows :
   - **Fixed** displays the page as it was when the link was created.
   - **Fit View** displays the visible portion of the page.
   - **Fit in Window** displays the entire page in the document window.
   - **Fit Width** or **Fit Height** displays the width or height of the page.
   - **Fit Visible** displays the areas that contain text or graphics.
   - **Inherit Zoom** displays the same magnification that was active when the link was chosen.

6. Click OK to create the destination.

The **Hyperlinks** palette *is used to define both the destinations and the hyperlinks.*

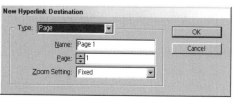

The **New Hyperlink Destination** *dialog box lets you set a page destination.*

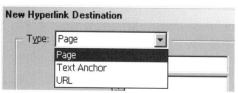

The **Type** menu *lets you choose the type of hyperlink destination.*

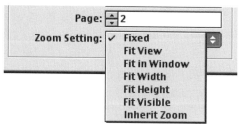

The **Zoom Setting** menu *controls the magnification of the destination page.*

(sidebar) Creating Hyperlinks

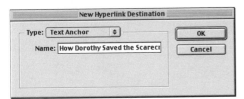

⑨ *The* **New Hyperlink Destination** *dialog* **box** *controls text anchor destinations.*

⑨② *The* **New Hyperlink Destination** *dialog* **box** *controls URL destinations.*

⑨③ *Use* **Hyperlink Destination Options** *dialog* **box** *to edit the destinations in a document.*

A text anchor destination displays specific text as the destination.

To create a text anchor destination:

1. Select the text that you want to be the destination.

2. Choose New Hyperlink Destination in the Hyperlinks palette menu to open the New Hyperlink Destination dialog box.

3. Choose Text Anchor from the Type menu **⑨**.

4. Enter a name for the destination.

A URL destination displays a uniform resource locator (URL) as a destination.

TIP URL destinations can be Web addresses or to any Internet resource protocol such as http://, ftp://, file://, or mailto://.

To create a URL destination:

1. Choose New Hyperlink Destination in the Hyperlinks palette menu to open the New Hyperlink Destination dialog box.

2. Choose URL from the Type menu **⑨②**.

3. Enter a name for the destination.

4. Enter the URL information.

You can edit the destinations that you create for the document.

To edit a destination:

1. Choose Hyperlink Destination Options in the Hyperlinks palette menu to open the dialog box.

2. Choose a previously defined destination from the Destination list.

3. Click the Edit button **⑨③**. The controls for the destination become active.

Creating Hyperlinks

Once you have set the destinations, you can then create the hyperlinks that are linked to those destinations.

To create a hyperlink:

1. Select the text or graphic that you want to be the hotspot or trigger area for the link.

2. Click the New Hyperlink button or choose New Hyperlink from the Hyperlinks palette menu. The New Hyperlink dialog box appears ⓐ.

3. Set the Destination as described in the next exercise.

4. Set the Appearance as described in the exercise on the following page.

5. Click OK to create the hyperlink. The link appears in the Hyperlinks palette ⓑ.

To choose the destination for a hyperlink:

1. Choose a previously defined destination from the Name list.

   or

   Choose Unnamed from the Name menu. This lets you create a destination using the New Hyperlink dialog box ⓒ.

2. Use the Document list to choose the destination document.

3. Choose the type of destination from the Type list.

4. Use the Page controls to set the page number.

5. Set the Zoom Setting as described on page 220.

To create a hyperlink from a URL in text:

1. Select the text that contains a complete URL such as http://www.vectorbabe.com.

2. Choose New Hyperlink from URL in the Hyperlinks palette menu.

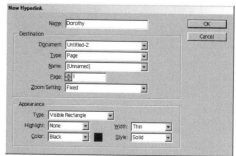

ⓐ *The* **New Hyperlink** *dialog box lets you create unnamed destinations as well as set the appearance of the hotspot area.*

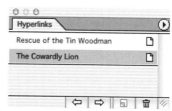

ⓑ *Two hyperlinks in the* **Hyperlinks** *palette.*

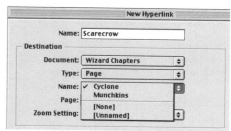

ⓒ *The* **Destination area** *of the New Hyperlink dialog box lets you create an unnamed destination or choose a previously defined destination.*

Creating Hyperlinks

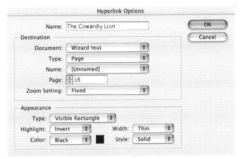

☞ *The* **Appearance area** *of the New Hyperlink dialog box lets you format how the hotspot area is displayed in the document.*

☞ *The* **Hyperlinks Options** *dialog box lets you edit exisitng hyperlinks.*

To choose the appearance of a hyperlink:

1. Use the Type menu to choose a setting for the visibility of the rectangle around the hotspot **☞**.

   - **Visible Rectangle** creates a rectangular area that can be seen.
   - **Invisible Rectangle** creates a hotspot area that is not shown.

2. Use the Highlight menu to choose the appearance of the hotspot area when clicked.

   - **None** makes no highlight on the area.
   - **Invert** creates the effect of inverting the colors of the hotspot area.
   - **Outline** creates an outline rectangle around the hotspot area.
   - **Inset** creates the effect of a 3D cutout in the hotspot area.

3. Use the Width menu to choose thickness of the visible rectangle.

   - **Thin** is the most tasteful setting.
   - **Medium** is a more obvious setting.
   - **Thick** is really too ugly to use.

4. Use the Style menu to choose the type of line for the visible rectangle.

   - **Solid** is the most tasteful setting.
   - **Dashed** doesn't look as nice.

5. Choose a color from the Color menu.

Once you have created hyperlinks, you can edit the hyperlinks later.

To edit hyperlinks:

1. Double click the hyperlinks entry in the Hyperlinks palette.

   or

   Choose Hyperlinks Options in the Hyperlinks palette menu.

2. Make changes in the Hyperlinks Options dialog box **☞**.

Creating Hyperlinks

You can use the Hyperlinks palette to move to either hyperlinks or their destinations.

To move to a hyperlink:

1. Select the hyperlink in the Hyperlinks palette.

2. Choose Go to Source from the Hyperlinks palette menu.

To move to a hyperlink destination:

1. In the Hyperlinks palette, select the hyperlink for the destination.

2. Choose Go to Destination from the Hyperlinks palette menu.

TIP If the destination is a URL, the default Web browser will be launched.

Creating Hyperlinks

LAYERS 11

When I was in advertising, we used to lay clear acetate sheets over our mechanical board as a way to create variations for our layouts. One acetate layer might have copy and prices for a test market newspaper ad. Another piece of acetate might have prices for a special Sunday-circular ad. Yet another might have copy without prices for the national magazine ads. The artwork and other graphics stayed on the bottom layer and was visible through the acetate layers.

When the mechanical was sent to be printed, the print shop workers flipped the different acetate sheets on or off the board to create the different types of ads. Because a new mechanical didn't have to be created for each variation, it saved us a lot of time and effort.

InDesign gives you the same sort of flexibility with electronic layers. You may have just two layers—one for text, the other for graphics. Or you can have a document with hundreds of different layers.

For instance, if you have English and French versions of a document, you can put the text for each language on its own layer. You can then display just one version at a time.

Creating and Deleting Layers

Every InDesign document opens with a default layer in the Layers palette. You don't have to do anything special to work with this default layer. It is instantly active and everything you do is automatically on that layer.

To open the Layers palette:

♦ If the Layers palette is not visible, choose **Window** > **Layers** to open the palette **①**.

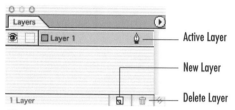

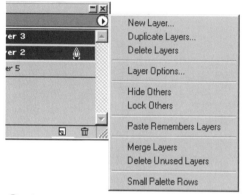

① *The* **Layers** palette *for all new documents contains one layer.*

As you work, you may want additional layers in your document.

To create new layers:

1. Choose New Layer from the Layers palette menu **②**. This opens the New Layer dialog box.

   or

   Click the New Layer icon. This creates a new layer without opening the New Layer dialog box.

3. Set the Layer Options as described in the next section.

4. Click OK to create the layer.

TIP You can open the Layer Options at any time by double clicking the name of the layer in the Layers pallete or by choosing Layer Options from the Layers palette menu.

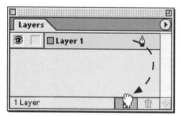

② *The* **Layers** palette menu *contains the commands for working with layers.*

It may be easier to create different versions of a document by duplicating a layer as well as the objects on that layer.

To duplicate a layer:

♦ Drag the layer onto the New Layer icon **③**. This creates a copy of the layer as well as all objects on that layer.

③ *You can duplicate a layer by dragging it onto the* **New Layer** *icon.*

Before paste

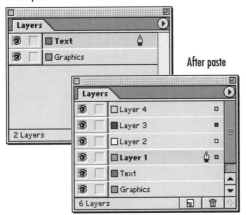

After paste

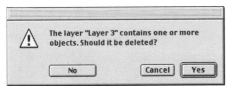

❹ *The* **Paste Remembers Layers command** *adds new layers when objects are pasted from one document to another.*

The layer "Layer 3" contains one or more objects. Should it be deleted?

| No | Cancel | Yes |

❺ *An alert dialog box makes sure you don't inadvertently delete artwork when you delete a layer.*

You can also create new layers automatically when you paste items from one document to another. This behavior is controlled by the Paste Remembers Layers command.

To create new layers while pasting:

1. Choose Paste Remembers Layers from the Layers palette menu. If there is a check mark next to the command, then it is already turned on.

TIP When turned on, this command is applied to all open documents.

2. Drag and drop or copy and paste the items from one document into a second document. New layers are created in the second document ❹.

TIP If Paste Remembers Layers is turned off, the items are pasted onto the single active layer in the second document.

As you work, you may want to delete the layers in a document.

To delete a layer:

1. Select the layer you want to delete.

TIP Shift-click to select multiple layers.

2. Click the Delete layer icon. If there are items on the layer a alert box appears ❺.

TIP Opt/Alt-click the Delete layer button to bypass the alert box.

If you have layers with no objects on them, you can quickly delete those layers.

To delete all unused layers:

◆ Choose Delete All Unused layers.

Creating and Deleting Layers

Setting the Layer Options

The Layer Options dialog box contains some housekeeping options that make it easier to organize and work with layers ❻. *(See the previous section for how to open the Layer Options dialog box.)*

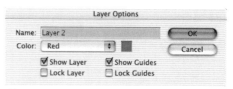

❻ *The* **Layer Options dialog box** *is the command center for all the attributes of a layer.*

To name a layer:

◆ Use the Name field to name the layer.

TIP If you have many layers, you may want to use descriptive names instead of the default names Layer 1, Layer 2, etc.

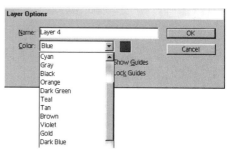

Each layer has a color associated with it. This is the color used to highlight object frames and paths.

❼ *The* **Color list** *contains all the choices for highlighting objects.*

To set the highlight color for a layer:

◆ Choose a color from the Color list ❼.

TIP Each new layer appears with the next color listed in the Color list.

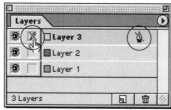

Layers help you organize your documents in several ways. For instance, if you lock a layer you lock all the objects on the layer. This protects them from being selected, moved, modified, or deleted.

❽ *Click the* **Toggle Lock space** *to lock the layer. The circled icons indicate the layer is locked.*

To lock a layer:

1. Choose Lock Layer from the Layer Options dialog box.

   or

   Click the Toggle Lock space in the Layers palette ❻. A pencil with a slash indicates that the layer is locked. A black space indicates the layer is unlocked.

TIP Use the Lock Others command from the Layers palette menu or Opt/Alt-click the Toggle Lock space in one layer to lock all the other layers in the document ❾.

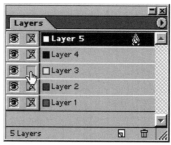

❾ *Opt/Alt-click the* **Toggle Lock space** *to lock all the other layers in the document.*

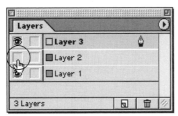

⓾ *Click the* **Toggle visibility space** *to hide and show the layer.*

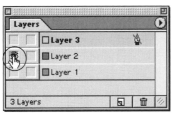

⓫ *Opt/Alt-click the Toggle visibility space to hide all the other layers in the document.*

You can also use layers to hide and show the information on the layer. This can make it easy to focus on certain information. Hidden layers do not print.

To hide a layer:

◆ Deselect Show Layer from the Layer Options dialog box.

   or

   Click the Toggle visibility icon in Layers palette so that the space is blank ⓾. When the space is blank, the layer is invisible.

TIP You cannot work on invisible layers.

TIP Use the Hide Others command from the Layers palette menu or Opt/Alt-click the Toggle visibility space in one layer to hide all the other layers in the document ⓫.

To show a layer:

◆ Select Show Layer from the Layer Options dialog box.

   or

   Click the Toggle visibility icon in Layers palette. When the eyeball is visible, the layer is visible.

The Layer Options dialog box also lets you control the guides on a layer. This lets you show and hide or lock the guides on a specific layer.

To control the guides on a layer:

1. Choose Show Guides in the Layer Options dialog box to display the guides for that layer.

2. Choose Lock Guides to protect the guides on the layer from being changed.

Setting the Layer Options

Working with Layers

Once you have created additional layers in your document, you can move objects onto the new layers.

To apply objects to layers:

◆ Click the layer so that it is highlighted, and then create the object.

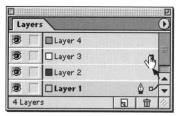

⑫ Drag the proxy square *to move an object from one layer to another.*

Rather than cutting the object, selecting the new layer, and pasting, you can use the Layers palette to move the object between layers.

To move objects from one layer to another:

1. Select the object. A square object proxy appears next to the name of the layer in the Layers palette.

2. Drag the object proxy from one layer to another ⑫. This moves the object to a new layer.

TIP Hold the Opt/Alt key as you drag the proxy to create a copy of the object on the new layer ⑬.

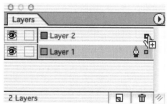

⑬ *Hold the Opt/Alt key as you drag the proxy square to copy an object from one layer to another.*

To reorder layers:

◆ Drag one layer above or below another to change the order that objects appear in the document ⑭.

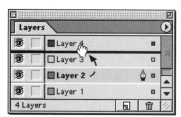

⑭ *Drag a layer up or down in the Layers palette to change the order of the layers.*

You may want to combine the contents of one layer with another. This is called *merging* layers.

To merge layers:

1. Select the layers you want to merge.

2. Choose Merge Layers from the Layers palette submenu. All the objects on the layers are combined onto one layer.

LIBRARIES 12

As you work on your layout, you may find yourself using the same objects throughout a document. For instance, if you are working on a magazine, you might want to have a series of different-sized frames to hold frequently used ads.

Rather than copying and pasting the frames from one part of the document to another, you can use a library to hold those frames — neatly labeled, sorted, and ready to use at a moment's notice.

Then, anytime you need an element, you just drag it out of the library onto your page.

Storing Items in a Library

Another important utility for working with long documents is the Library feature. A library allows you to store elements, such as text frames, images, or empty frames. When elements are in a library, they can be dragged easily into open documents.

To create a library:

1. Choose **File** > **New** > **Library.** This opens the New Library dialog box.

2. Use this dialog box to name the library file and select its location.

TIP The name of the library file appears in the tab of the Library palette.

3. Click Save. The library appears as a floating palette ❶.

To add items to a library:

1. With a library open, select the item you want to insert in the library.

2. Click the Add Item button at the bottom of the Library palette.

   or

   Drag the item into the library ❷. The item appears in the Library palette.

   or

   Choose Add Item from the Library palette submenu.

TIP Multiple items are always entered as a single library item. If you want individual items, you need to select and add them one by one.

Item Information Show Subset

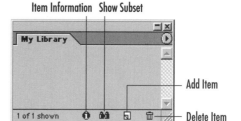

Add Item

Delete Item

❶ *A new* **Library palette** *does not contain any items.*

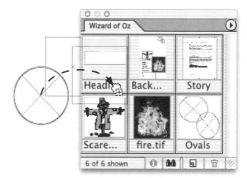

❷ *You can add items to a library by dragging them from the page into the Library palette.*

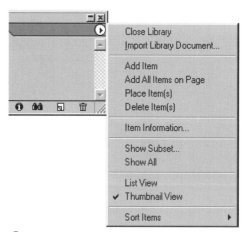

Close Library
Import Library Document...

Add Item
Add All Items on Page
Place Item(s)
Delete Item(s)

Item Information...

Show Subset...
Show All

List View
✓ Thumbnail View

Sort Items ▶

❸ *The* **Library palette menu** *contains the commands for working with a Library.*

❹ *Items can be dragged from a library onto a document.*

Strategies for Using Libraries

Libraries can be used in many different ways. I use a library to store items that I use often in a document.

For instance, I have one library labeled for this VQS book. One of the elements is a graphic frame with a text frame underneath. I drag that out for the illustrations and captions.

Other elements are the empty circles, lines, and curved arrows I use to point to elements in the figures.

Another element is a gray text frame with a stroke around it. I drag it out when I write sidebars such as this.

You can also add all the items on a page.

To add a page to a library:

1. With a library open, move to the page you want to add to the library.
2. Choose Add All Items on Page from the Library palette submenu.

TIP The Add All Items on Page command automatically labels the entry as a page in the library Item Information dialog box *(see page 234).*

Libraries can be opened and the elements in the libraries dragged onto any InDesign documents.

To add library items to a document:

1. Select the item in the library.

TIP Shift-click to select multiple contiguous entries in the Library palette.

TIP Cmd/Ctrl-click to select multiple non-contiguous entries in the Library palette.

2. Drag the items from the library onto the page **❹**.

   or

   Choose Place Item(s) from the Library palette submenu.

To delete items from a library:

1. Select the item in the library.
2. Click the Delete Item icon.

   or

   Choose Delete Item(s) from the Library palette menu.

3. A dialog box appears asking for confirmation that you want to delete the items. Click Yes.

TIP Hold the Opt/Alt key to bypass the dialog box when you delete a library item.

Setting the Library Display

If you have many items in a library, you may want to change how the items are displayed.

To change the library display:

- Choose List View to see the item name and an icon that indicates the type of item ❺.

  or

  Choose Thumbnail View to see the name and a small preview of the item ❻.

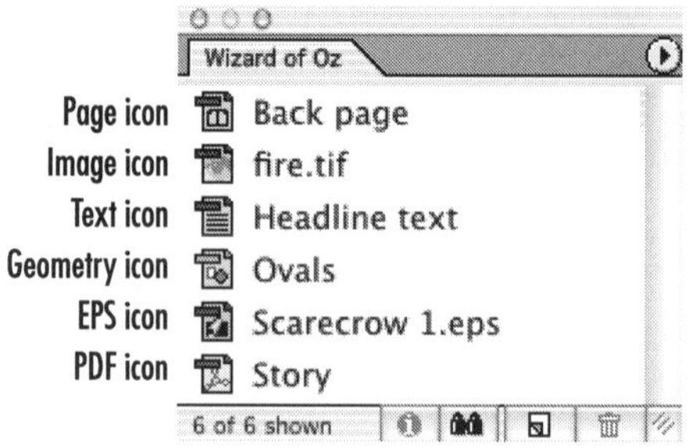
Wizard of Oz
Page icon
Image icon
Text icon
Geometry icon
EPS icon
PDF icon
Back page
fire.tif
Headline text
Ovals
Scarecrow 1.eps
Story
6 of 6 shown

❺ *The* **List View** *shows the name of the item and an icon that shows the type of item.*

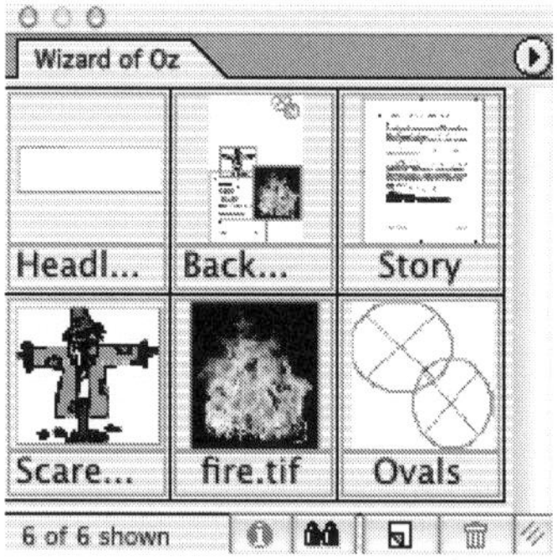
Wizard of Oz
Headl...
Back...
Story
Scare...
fire.tif
Ovals
6 of 6 shown

❻ *The* **Thumbnail View** *shows the name of the item and a preview of the item.*

You can also add information that makes it easy to search for library entries.

To add to the library item information:

1. Select the item.
2. Click the Library Item Information icon.

   or

   Choose Item Information from the Library palette menu. This opens the Item Information dialog box ❼.
3. Enter the name in the Item Name field.
4. Use the Object Type list to choose the following categories ❽:
   - **Image** contains images, such as Photoshop or TIFF files.
   - **EPS** contains EPS files.
   - **PDF** contains PDF files.
   - **Geometry** includes frames and rules that do not contain images or text.
   - **Page** is an entire page.
   - **Text** contains text frames.

   TIP InDesign assigns a category when items are entered into a library. You can change that listing to any category you want.
5. Enter a description for the item.

   TIP The description can be keywords or other information that helps identify the item.

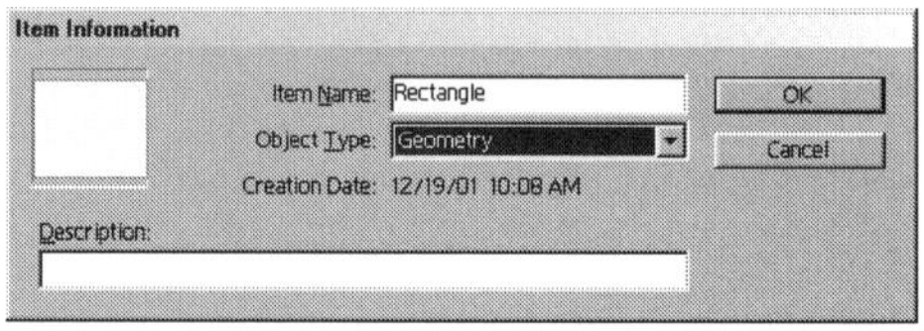
Item Information
Item Name: Rectangle
Object Type: Geometry
Creation Date: 12/19/01 10:08 AM
Description:
OK
Cancel

❼ *The* **Item Information dialog box** *lets you change the information assigned to each item.*

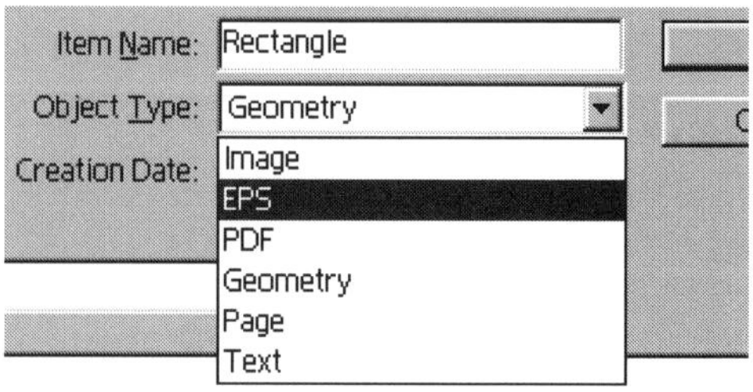
Item Name: Rectangle
Object Type: Geometry
Creation Date:
Image
EPS
PDF
Geometry
Page
Text

❽ *Use the* **Object Type list** *to apply a label for the library element.*

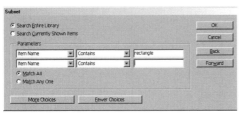

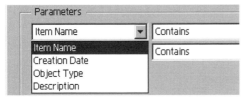

⑩ *The* **Subset dialog box** *lets you find specific library items.*

⑪ *The* **search criteria** *in the Subset dialog box let you specify where to search in the Library.*

⑫ *The* **Parameters menu** *lets you choose what part of the Item Information is searched for.*

⑬ *The* **match criteria** *in the Subset dialog box control how the search items are matched.*

Searching and Sorting Libraries

If you have many items in a library, you may find it difficult to find specific library entries. InDesign has a powerful search feature that makes it easy to locate specific items in a library.

To search within a library:

1. Click the Show Library Subset icon.

   or

   Choose Show Subset from the Library palette submenu. The opens the Subset dialog box **⑩**.

2. Choose Search Entire Library to search all the entries in the library **⑪**.

   or

   Choose Search Currently Shown Items to search through only those items currently displayed in the library.

3. Use the Parameters menu and fields to set the criteria **⑫**.

4. Click More Choices to add up to five choices to the parameters list.

5. Choose Match All to choose only those items that match all the search parameters **⑬**.

   or

   Choose Match Any One to find items that meet at least one of the search parameters.

6. Click OK to display the items that meet the search criteria.

TIP Use the Back or Forward buttons to move to previous search settings in the Subset dialog box.

To display all the library entries:

◆ Choose Show All from the Library palette submenu.

Searching and Sorting Libraries

To sort library entries:

◆ Choose the Sort Items options from the
Library palette menu:

- **By Name** arranges the items in
alphabetical order.
- **By Oldest** arranges the items in the
order they were added with the oldest
items first.
- **By Newest** arranges the items in the
order they were added, with the newest
items first.
- **By Type** arranges the items in
groups according to their categories
(see page 234).

TABS AND TABLES 13

Before tabs and tables, there was chaos. Well, perhaps not chaos, but it was difficult to line columns of text in an orderly fashion.

The word "tab" comes from the tabulator key on a typewriter. (Does anyone still use a typewriter?) The tabulator key moved the carriage return a certain number of spaces.

The tabulator key was named because it allowed typists to create tabular data. Tabular data is information arranged in systematic rows and columns—otherwise known as a table.

Accountants create a lot of tables. They like to line up information so it's easy to read both across and up and down.

However, mathematical information isn't the only thing arranged in tables. Resumes, menus, train schedules, calendars, and even classified ads are all arranged in some form of table.

Anytime you need to keep text or graphics aligned in either columns or rows, consider using the tabs and tables features in InDesign.

Inserting Tab Characters

There are two parts to working with tabs. The first part is to insert the *tab characters* that force the text to jump to a certain position.

To insert tab characters into text:

1. Position the insertion point where you want the tab character to be located.

2. Press the tab key on the keyboard. This creates a tab character in the text ❶.

TIP Choose **Type** > **Show Hidden Characters** to see the display of the tab character within the text (*see page 57*).

TIP InDesign recognizes tab characters in imported text.

InDesign also has a special type of tab character called a right tab. This tab character automatically sets the text to the right-most position in the frame ❷.

To insert a right tab character:

1. Place the insertion point where you want the right tab character.

2. Press Shift+Tab.

or

Use the Contextual menu to insert a right tab character from the Insert Special Character menu.

Frank»Writer

❶ *A* **tab character** *is displayed as part of the hidden characters in text.*

Chapter·one   ⸗   5¶
Chapter·two   ⸗   45¶
Chapter·three ⸗   62#

❷ *The* **right tab character** *automatically moves the text to the right side of the text frame.*

Inserting Tabs in Text

It's actually very simple to insert a tab character into text. Just tap the Tab key. However, there are some guides for working with tabs.

Insert only one tab character for each column. Even if the text doesn't line up correctly, don't add another tab key. Use the Tab palette and tab stops to line up the columns.

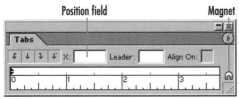

③ *The* **Tabs palette** *contains the controls for inserting tab stops and aligning the tabs.*

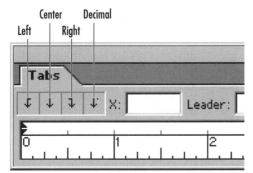

④ *Choose one of the four* **tab alignment icons** *to control how the text is aligned.*

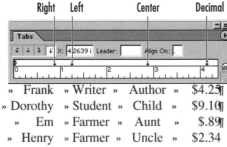

⑤ *Examples of how the four tab alignments control the text.*

Setting Tab Stops

The next—and most important—part to working with tabs is to set the *tab stops* or the formatting controls that set where the text should stop after it is forced to jump to a new position. This is controlled using the Tabs palette.

To open the Tabs palette:

1. Choose **Type** > **Tabs.** The Tabs palette appears above the text frame **③**.

TIP The Tabs palette can be kept onscreen like any other palette.

TIP If the Tabs palette is not positioned above the text, click the Magnet icon in the palette to automatically move the palette to the correct position.

To set tab stops:

1. Select the text.

2. Choose the type of tab alignment from the four tab icons in the ruler **④**. The four alignments work as follows **⑤**:

   - **Left** aligns the left side of the text at the tab stop.
   - **Center** centers the text on either side of the tab stop.
   - **Right** aligns the right side of the text at the tab stop.
   - **Decimal** aligns the text at the decimal point or period of the text.

3. Click the ruler area where you want the tab stop to be positioned.

   or

   Type a number in the Position field. A small tab arrow appears that indicates the position of the tab stop.

TIP The default tab stops are invisible left-aligned tabs every half inch. Adding tab stops to the ruler overrides all tab stops to the left of the new tab.

To change tab settings:

1. Select the text.

2. Open the Tabs palette.

3. To change the alignment of a tab stop, select the tab arrow and then click a new alignment icon.

   or

   Hold the Opt/Alt key and click the tab arrow in the ruler.

4. To change the position of a tab stop, drag the tab arrow to a new position.

TIP As you move a tab stop along the ruler, a line extends through the text, even if the Tabs palette is not aligned to the text frame ⑥. This helps you judge the position of the tab stop.

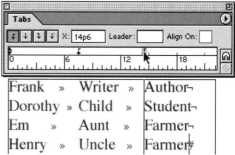

⑥ *As you move a tab stop,* **a line extends through the text** *to help you position the tab stop correctly.*

Many times you will want to have tab stops repeated at the same interval. InDesign makes it easy to set repeating tabs.

To set a repeating tab:

1. Position the first tab stop on the ruler.

2. With the tab stop still selected, choose Repeat Tab from the Tabs palette menu ⑦. This adds new tab stops at the same interval along the ruler ⑧.

TIP The tab stops created by the Repeat Tab command are not linked and move independently.

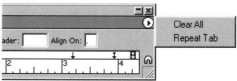

⑦ *The* **Tabs palette menu** *gives you two important commands for working with tabs.*

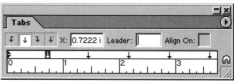

⑧ *The* **Repeat tab command** *allows you to easily add tab stops at the same interval along the ruler.*

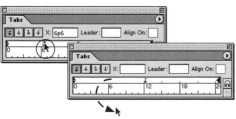

⑨ *To remove a tab stop, drag it off the Tabs palette ruler.*

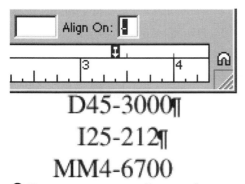

⑩ *You can enter a custom alignment character for the* **Align On field**. *Here the text aligns to the hyphen.*

Once you have added tab stops to the Tabs palette ruler, you can remove them easily.

To remove tab stops:

1. Select the tab stop on the Tabs palette ruler.

2. Drag the tab stop off the ruler. This deletes the tab stop.

TIP If there are no tab stops to the left of the one you removed, this restores the invisible, default tab stops at the nearest half inch position **⑨**.

If you have many tab stops on the Tabs palette ruler, it may be easier to delete all the tab stops with a single command.

To clear all the tabs off the ruler:

◆ Choose Clear All from the Tabs palette ruler **⑨**. This restores the invisible, default tab stops at every half inch mark.

The Decimal tab aligns numerical data to a decimal point. However, you may need to align text to a different character. For instance, some European currency uses a comma instead of a decimal. InDesign lets you set a custom alignment character.

To set a custom alignment character:

1. Choose the Decimal tab icon.

2. Add a tab stop to the ruler.

3. Replace the period in the Align On field with a different character. The text aligns around that character **⑩**.

Creating Tab Leaders

A *tab leader* allows you to automatically fill the space between the tabbed material with a repeating character. Tab leaders are often used in the tables of contents of books *(such as the table of contents in this book)*.

TIP Tab leaders are added when the reader needs to move along a wide column from one entry to another. The tab leader helps the reader's eye stay on the correct line of text.

To add tab leaders:

1. Select the tab stop arrow on the Tabs palette ruler.

2. Type up to eight characters in the Leader field of the Tabs palette.

TIP Add spaces to the Leader field for a more pleasing look for the leader characters ⓫.

TIP Press the tab key on the keyboard to preview the characters in the Leader field.

TIP You can select the characters in a tab leader like ordinary text and change the point size, kerning, or other attributes.

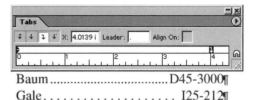

Baum ....D45-3000¶
Gale. . . . . I25-212¶
Cohen MM4-6700

⓫ *An example of adding spaces to separate the tab leader.*

Choosing Between Tabs and Tables

For as long as I can remember, designers have wanted an easy way to create tables in page-layout documents. Now that InDesign lets you create tables, is there any reason to still use tabs?

Absolutely! I use tabs in this book to separate numbers from the text in the exercises. I also use tabs with leaders for the listings in the table of contents.

I use tables whenever I need side-by-side paragraphs such as in a resume. I also use tables whenever I need to separate the information with horizontal and vertical lines.

Creating Tab Leaders

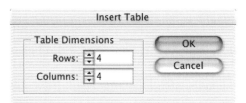

⑫ *Use the* **Insert Table dialog box** *to create an empty table in a text frame.*

April » May » June¶
12 » 67 » 54¶
6 » 7 » 2#

April#	May#	June#
12#	67#	54#
6#	7#	2#

⑬ *The* **Convert Text to Table command** *transforms tabs and paragraphs into rows and columns.*

Creating and Using Tables

Tabs limit you to lining up only a single line of text. Tables let you line up text so it can extend down into several lines. Tables also let you create strokes around the cell that contains the text or add fills of color behind the text.

To create a new table in a text frame:

1. Place an insertion inside a text frame.

2. Choose **Table > Insert Table**. The Insert Table dialog box appears ⑫.

3. Use the Rows control to set the number of rows in the table.

4. Use the Columns control to set the number of columns.

5. Click OK. InDesign creates a table that fills the text frame as follows:

   • The width of the table is set to fill the width of the text frame.

   • The table columns are distributed evenly across the table.

   • The height of the table is set at the size of the default text size plus 8 points to accomodate the cell inset *(see page 254)*.

   • If the default height of the table is greater than the size of the text frame, an overflow symbol appears indicating that the table can flow to another frame *(see page 41)*.

To convert text into a table:

1. Select the text.

2. Choose **Table > Convert Text to Table**. The text is inserted into a table that is created as follows ⑬:

   • Each paragraph return creates a new table row.

   • Each tab character creates a new table column.

Most people use Microsoft Word and Excel to create text and spreadsheets. InDesign lets you import the tables created by both Word and Excel.

To import a table from Microsoft Word:

1. Select a text frame by placing an insertion point inside a text frame.

   or

   Deselect any text frame. (This will create a loaded text cursor.)

2. Choose **File > Place** and navigate to the Word file.

3. The imported Word table is inserted into the selected text frame.

   or

   Click or drag the loaded text cursor.

To import a table from Microsoft Excel:

1. Click to place an insertion point inside a text frame.

   or

   Deselect any text frame. (This will create a loaded text cursor.)

2. Choose **File > Place** and navigate to the Excel file.

3. Use the Import Options dialog box to control which cells in the Excel worksheet that will be imported ⓮.

   TIP The import options automatically choose all the cells in the worksheet that contain data.

4. The imported Excel table is inserted into the selected text frame.

   or

   Click or drag the loaded text cursor.

   TIP InDesign retains the formatting applied in Excel.

   TIP If no formatting has been applied in Excel, InDesign adds a stroke around each cell.

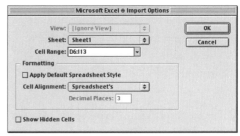

⓮ *The* **Microsoft Excel® Import Options dialog box** *let you choose which worksheet and cells are imported from an Excel document.*

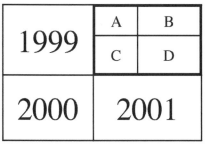

⑮ *An example of how a table can be inserted inside a cell of another table.*

Summer Schedule#	Closed#	
June#	July#	July 4#
Aug.#	Sept#	Sept. 1#

Summer Schedule » Closed¶
June » July » July 4¶
Aug. » Sept » Sept. 1#

⑯ *The* **Convert Table to Text command** *transforms table rows and columns into tabs and paragraph returns.*

InDesign's tables are extremely flexible in that you can insert a table inside the cell of another table. This lets you use a table as the grid structure for a page and then insert smaller tables within the cells. For instance, a calendar might be laid out as an entire page with smaller tables within the cells.

To place a table in a table cell:

1. Click with the Text tool to place an insertion point inside a table cell.

2. Use the Insert Table command or a Place command to create a table within that cell **⑮**.

To convert a table to text:

1. Place an insertion point in any cell inside the table.

2. Choose **Table > Convert Table to Text**. This converts the table as follows **⑯**:

   • Table columns are converted to tab characters.

   • Table rows are converted to paragraph returns.

Changing the Content in Tables

If you create an empty table, you can easily
fill it with content.

To insert text into table cells:

1. Place an insertion point inside a table cell.

2. Type the text for the cell.

   or

   Choose **File** > **Place** to insert imported
   text in the cell.

TIP Press the Tab key to jump forward from
one cell to another.

TIP Press Shift-Tab to move backwards from
one cell to another.

TIP Press Opt/Alt-Tab to insert a tab
character inside a cell.

Because many tables are long, it is helpful to
be able to jump to a specific row.

To jump to a specific row:

1. Choose **Table** > **Go to Row**. The Go to
   Row dialog box appears **⑰**.

2. Enter the number for the row you want
   to move to.

If a table extends longer than a text frame,
you get a text frame overflow. You can easily
flow the rest of the table from frame to frame
across pages.

To flow tables between frames:

1. Use the Selection tool to load the
   overflow cursor **⑱**.

2. Click the overflow cursor inside the new
   frame to flow the table the rest of the
   table into the frame **⑲**.

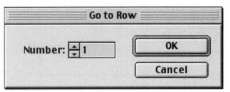

⑰ *The **Go to Row dialog box** lets you quickly
jump from one row to another.*

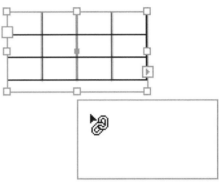

⑱ *Click the overflow symbol in a text frame to
load any overflow from a table.*

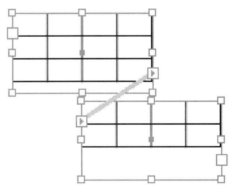

⑲ *The text threads show how tables can flow
from one frame to another.*

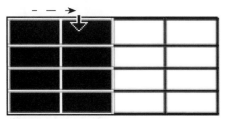

⑳ *The* **down arrow cursor** *indicates you can click to select an entire column in a table.*

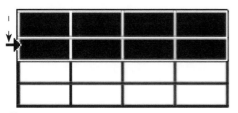

㉑ *The* **left arrow cursor** *indicates you can click to select an entire row in a table.*

To select text in a table cell:

1. Place an insertion point inside a table cell.

2. Choose **Edit** > **Select All** to select all the text within that cell.

To select text in multiple table cells:

◆ Use the Text tool to drag across the cells you want to select.

To select a table column:

1. Place the Text tool cursor at the top of the table. A down arrow cursor appears.

2. Click the down arrow. The entire column is selected **⑳**.

3. Drag across with the down arrow cursor to select any additional columns.

or

Move the down arrow to another column and Shift-click to select multiple columns.

To select a table row:

1. Place the Text tool cursor at the left side of the table. A left arrow cursor appears.

2. Click the left arrow. The entire row is selected **㉑**.

3. Drag down with the left arrow cursor to select any additional rows.

or

Move the down arrow to another row and Shift-click to select multiple rows.

Changing the Content in Tables

To use the table selection commands:

1. Place the insertion point in a cell in the table.

2. Choose one of the following commands:
   - **Table > Select > Cell** selects the cell.
   - **Table > Select > Row** selects the row that contains the cell.
   - **Table > Select > Column** selects the column that contains the cell.
   - **Table > Select > Table** selects the entire table.

TIP The table selection commands are very helpful for applying borders and fills to table cells *(see page 257)*.

To insert a graphic into a table cell:

1. Place an insertion point inside a table cell.

2. Choose **File > Place** to insert a placed image into the cell 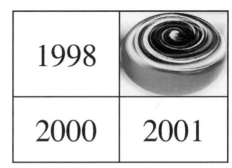.

   or

   Paste a graphic copied to the clipboard into the cell.

TIP Graphics in cells are pasted as inline graphics *(see page 161)*.

If the graphic is larger than the size of the cell, some of the graphic may stick out beyond the cell. You use the Clipping setting to control if placed graphics are seen outside a cell.

To control the display of a graphic inside a cell:

1. Place your insertion point inside the cell that contains the placed graphic.

2. Choose **Table > Cell Options > Text**.

3. Choose Clip Contents to Cell to limit the display of the graphic inside the cell.

An example of how a placed image can be inserted into a table cell.

Changing the Content in Tables

Number of Rows   Number of Columns

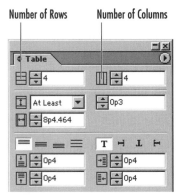

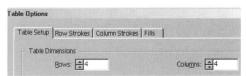

❷❸ *The* **Table palette** *contains many of the controls for working with tables.*

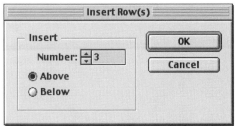

❷❹ *The* **Table Dimensions controls** *in the Table Options dialog box lets you set the number of rows and columns in a table.*

❷❺ *The* **Insert Row(s) dialog box** *allows you to add rows to a specific location in a table.*

Setting the Table Options

Once you have created a table, there are many modifications you can make to the table. Some of these modifications are made using the Table palette.

To open the Table palette:

◆ Choose **Window** > **Table**. This opens the Table palette **❷❸**.

To change the number of rows and columns:

1. Select the table by placing an insertion point in any cell.

2. Use the Number of Rows controls in the Table palette to increase or decrease the number of rows in the table.

3. Use the Number of Columns controls in the Table palette to increase or decrease the number of columns in the table.

TIP You can also change the number of rows and columns using the Table Dimensions fields in the Table Setup section of the Table Options dialog box. **❷❹**.

The Table palette adds rows and columns to the end of the table. You can also insert rows and columns into a specific location.

To insert rows into a table:

1. Place an insertion point where you want to insert the rows.

2. Choose **Table** > **Insert** > **Row**. The Insert Row(s) dialog box appears **❷❺**.

   or

   Choose **Insert** > **Row** from the Table palette menu.

3. Use the Number field to set the number of rows.

4. Choose either Above or Below to position where the new rows should be inserted.

Setting the Table Options

To insert columns into a table:

1. Place an insertion point where you want to insert the columns.

2. Choose **Table** > **Insert** > **Column**. The Insert Columns(s) dialog box appears **26**.

   or

   Choose **Insert** > **Column** from the Table palette menu.

3. Use the Number field to set the number of rows.

4. Choose either Left or Right to position where the new rows should be inserted.

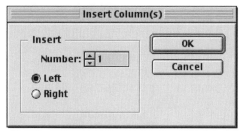

26 *The* **Insert Columns(s)** *dialog box lets you add columns to a specific location in a table.*

To delete table columns:

1. Select the columns you want to delete.

   or

   Place an insertion point in the column you want to delete.

2. Choose **Table** > **Delete** > **Column**.

   or

   Choose **Delete** > **Column** from the Table palette menu.

To delete table rows:

1. Select the rows you want to delete.

   or

   Place an insertion point in the row you want to delete.

2. Choose **Table** > **Delete** > **Row**. The row that contained the cell is deleted.

   or

   Choose **Delete** > **Row** from the Table palette menu.

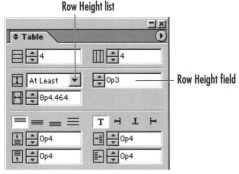

② *The* Up/ **Down arrow** *indicates you can adjust the row height.*

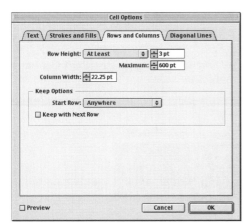

Row Height list

Row Height field

③ *The numerical controls for setting the* **height** *of a table row.*

Cell Options

Text \ Strokes and Fills \ **Rows and Columns** \ Diagonal Lines \

Row Height: At Least ‖ 3 pt

Maximum: 600 pt

Column Width: 22.25 pt

Keep Options

Start Row: Anywhere

☐ Keep with Next Row

☐ Preview   Cancel   OK

④ *The* **Rows and Columns category** *of the Cell Options dialog box.*

April	May	June
12	67	↔54
6	7	2

⑤ *The* **Left/ Right arrow** *indicates you can adjust the column width.*

To delete the entire table:

1. Place an insertion point in any cell of the table you want to delete.

2. Choose **Table > Delete > Table**. The table is deleted.

   or

   Choose **Delete > Table** from the Table palette menu.

When you create a table, all the columns and rows are evenly spaced. However, you can modify the size of the rows and columns.

To change the row height visually:

1. With the Text tool selected, place the cursor along the border of the row you want to adjust. The cursor changes to an up/down arrow **②**.

2. Drag to adjust the height of the row.

To set the row height numerically:

1. Select the rows you want to adjust.

2. In the Table palette, set the Row Height list as follows **③**:

   • **At Least** sets a row height that can increase to hold text or an image.

   • **Exactly** sets a row height that does not change.

3. Enter an amount in the Row Height field.

TIP A red dot in the cell indicates an overflow.

TIP You can also set the row height using the Row Height controls in the Cell Options dialog box **④**. Choose **Table > Cell Options > Rows and Columns**.

To change the column width visually:

1. With the Text tool selected, place the cursor along the border of the column you want to adjust. The cursor changes to a left/right arrow **⑤**.

2. Drag to adjust the width of the column.

Setting the Table Options

To set the column width numerically:

1. Select the columns you want to adjust.
2. Enter an amount in the Column Width field ❸❶.

TIP You can also set the column width using the Rows and Columns Column Width field in the Cell Options dialog box ❷❾.

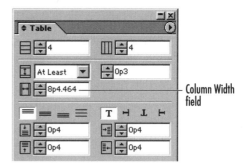

— Column Width field

❸❶ *The numerical controls for setting the* **width of a table column.**

You can adjust columns or rows so they are evenly distributed.

To automatically distribute columns:

1. Set the right-most column to the position it should be after the adjustment.
2. Select the columns you want to adjust.
3. Choose **Table > Distribute Columns Evenly**. The column widths are automatically adjusted ❸❷.

   or

   Choose Distribute Columns Evenly from the Table palette.

April	May	June
12	67	54
6	7	2

April	May	June
12	67	54
6	7	2

❸❷ *The results of using the* **Distribute Columns Evenly** *command.*

To automatically distribute rows:

1. Set the bottom-most column to the position it should be after the adjustment.
2. Select the rows you want to adjust.
3. Choose **Table > Distribute Rows Evenly**. The row heights are automatically adjusted ❸❸.

   or

   Choose Distribute Rows Evenly from the Table palette.

April	May	June
12	67	54
6	7	2

April	May	June
12	67	54
6	7	2

❸❸ *The results of using the* **Distribute Rows Evenly** *command.*

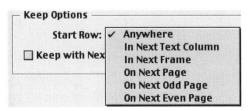

③④ *The Keep Options menu lets you choose when and where rows break across frames.*

Here are the dates for the Spring classes.¶

April#	May#
12#	67#

No space around table

Here are the dates for the Summer classes.¶

June#	July#
12#	22#

Space around table

③⑤ *Add some space around a table to keep it from colliding with text.*

③⑥ *The Table Spacing controls lets you set the amount of space before and after a table.*

If you want, you can control when and how the rows of a table break across text frames. This is called the *keep options* for rows.

To set the keep options for rows:

1. Select the rows you want to control.
2. Choose **Table** > **Cell Options** > **Rows and Columns**.
3. Choose from the Start Row list as follows ③④:
   - **Anywhere** lets the row start anywhere in a text frame.
   - **In The Next Text Column** forces the row to the next column in the frame or the next text frame.
   - **In Next Frame** forces the row to the next text frame.
   - **On Next Page** forces the row to the next page.
   - **On Next Odd Page** forces the row to the next odd-numbered page.
   - **On Next Even Page** forces the row to the next even-numbered page.
4. Check Keep with Next Row to make sure one row is not separated from another.

You can adjust the space around the table ③⑤.

To set the spacing around a table:

1. Select the table.
2. Choose **Table** > **Table Options** > **Table Setup**. The Table Options dialog box appears set to Table Setup.

   or

   Choose **Table Options** > **Table Setup** from the Table palette.
3. Use the Table Spacing control for Space Before to set the amount of space between text and the top of the table ③⑥.
4. Use the Table Spacing control for Space After to set the amount of space between the bottom of the table and the text that follows it.

Setting the Table Options

Setting the Table Cell Options

In addition to the controls for the entire table, you can also make settings for individual cells. For instance, you can control the *cell insets*, or how much space is maintained between the edges of the cells and the content inside the cells.

To set the cell insets:

1. Select the cells you want to adjust.

2. Use the four Cell Inset fields to adjust the amount of space at the top, bottom, left, and right sides of the cells ③.

TIP You can also change the cell insets using the Cell Insets fields in the Cell Options dialog box.

You can customize the pattern of rows and columns by merging or splitting cells.

To merge cells:

1. Select the cells you want to merge.

2. Choose **Table** > **Merge Cells**.

   or

   Choose Merge Cells from the Table palette.

TIP If the merged cells contain text, the resulting text will be divided into paragraphs.

To split cells:

1. Select the cell you want to split.

2. Choose **Table** > **Split Cells Vertically** or **Split Cells Horizontally** ③.

   or

   Choose **Split Cells Vertically** or **Split Cells Horizontally** from the Table palette.

TIP If you select multiple cells, only the Split Cells Vertically command is available ③.

Top inset
Bottom inset

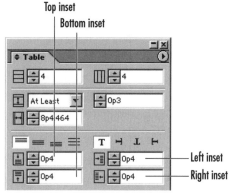

Left inset
Right inset

③ *The* **Cell Inset controls** *for setting the space within a cell.*

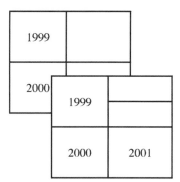

③ *The results of using the* **Split Cells Horizontally command.**

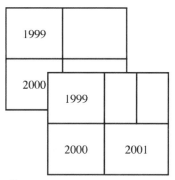

③ *The results of using the* **Split Cells Vertically command.**

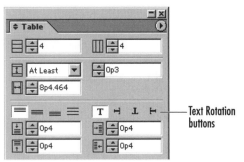

Text Rotation buttons

40 *The* **Text Rotation buttons** *for rotating text within a cell.*

Top

Center

Bottom

Justify

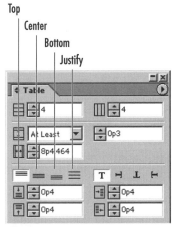

41 *The* **Vertical Alignment controls** *position text within a cell.*

Text doesn't have to sit horizontally in a cell. You can rotate text to help fit lines in thin columns.

To set the text orientation:

1. Select the cells you want to adjust.

2. Click one of the four buttons to rotate the text in 90° increments 40.

TIP You can also change the text orientation using the Text Rotation pop-up list in the Cell Options dialog box.

You can also set the vertical alignment for where the text is positioned in the cell.

To set the text vertical alignment:

1. Select the cells you want to adjust.

2. Click one of the four alignment buttons in the Text palette as follows 41:

   • **Align Top** positions the text at the top of the cell.
   • **Align Center** positions the text in the middle of the cell.
   • **Align Bottom** positions the text at the bottom of the cell.
   • **Justify** distributes the lines of text evenly so that it extends from the top to the bottom of the cell.

TIP The Justify setting overrides any leading applied to the text.

Setting the Table Cell Options

If you choose Justify for the vertical alignment, you can then control the space between
the lines or paragraphs.

To vertical justification spacing:

1. Select the cells you want to adjust.

2. Choose **Table** > **Cell Options** > **Text**. This
   opens the text controls for the cells.

3. Choose Justify from the Vertical
   Justification list.

4. Set an amount for the Paragraph Spacing
   Limit **42**.

TIP Increase the value for the paragraph
spacing to avoid increasing the space
between the lines within the paragraph.
This is similar to setting the Vertical
Justificatiion for text frames *(see page 62)*.

Just as you can control where the first baseline of text appears in a text frame, you
can also control the position of the baseline
within a cell.

To control the first baseline in a cell:

1. Select the cells you want to control.

2. Choose **Table** > **Cell Options** > **Text**. This
   opens the text controls for the cells.

3. In the First Baseline area, use the Offset
   list to choose a setting **43**.

4. In the Min field, set the minimum
   amount of space for the first baseline.

TIP For more details on working with the first
baseline, see page 61.

42 *The* **Paragraph Spacing Limit** *lets you
control how space is added when text is justified
vertically.*

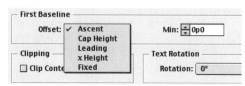

43 *The* **First Baseline controls** *let you set the
position of the first baseline of text within a cell.*

Setting the Table Cell Options

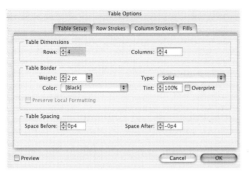

44 *The* **Table Setup dialog box** *lets you apply a border around the entire table.*

45 *You can format the stroke around a table with the* **Table Border controls.**

Setting the Table Strokes and Fills

One of the benefits of using tables instead of tabs is how easy it is to add lines and colors to the table. (The line around a table is called the *border*. Lines around cells are called *strokes*. Colors inside the cells are called *fills*.)

To add a border around the table:

1. Select at least one cell in the table.

2. Choose **Table > Table Options > Table Setup.** The Table Options dialog box appears set to Table Setup **44**.

   or

   Choose **Table Options > Table Setup** from the Table palette.

3. Use the Table Border field for Weight to set the thickness of the stroke **45**.

4. Use the Color list to set the color of the stroke.

5. Use the Tint field to apply a screen to the color.

6. If desired, check overprint for the color *(see page 110)*.

7. Use the Type list to set a stripe pattern for the border.

TIP If you have applied a stroke to a cell that touches the table border, use the the Preserve Local Formatting checkbox to control if the table border changes the local settings to cells.

Setting the Table Strokes and Fills

Many people who work with tables find it helpful to set strokes or fills for entire rows or columns in repeating patterns. This can help readers easily navigate down the column or across the row in lengthy tables.

TIP Even if you insert or delete rows or columns, the Alternating Pattern feature automatically applies the correct pattern to your table.

To set repeating strokes for rows:

1. Select at least one cell in the table.

2. Choose **Table > Table Options > Alternating Row Strokes**. The Table Options dialog box appears set to Row Strokes ⁴⁶.

   or

   Choose **Table Options > Alternating Row Strokes** from the Table palette.

3. Use the Alternating Pattern list to choose how many row strokes will alternate ⁴⁷.

4. Set the controls on the left side of the Alternating area to format the stroke appearance for the first set of rows.

5. Set the controls on the right side of the Alternating area to format the appearance of the stroke for second set of rows.

6. Use the Skip First and Skip Last fields to omit certain columns at the start and end of the table from the alternating count.

TIP If you have applied custom strokes to individual cells and want to override the local formatting, uncheck the Preserve Local Formatting checkbox.

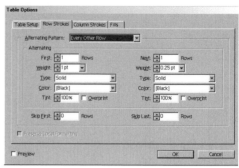

⁴⁶ *The* **Row Strokes** *controls under Table Options let you apply automatic alternating strokes to table rows.*

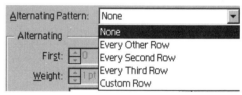

⁴⁷ *The* **Alternating Pattern** *menu for setting table rows.*

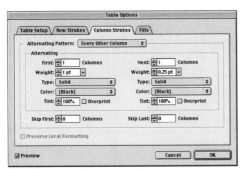

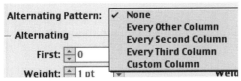

48 *The* **Column Strokes controls** *under Table Options let you apply automatic alternating strokes to table columns.*

49 *The* **Alternating Pattern menu** *for table columns.*

To set repeating strokes for columns:

1. Select at least one cell in the table.

2. Choose **Table > Table Options > Alternating Column Strokes**. The Table Options dialog box appears set to Column Strokes **48**.

   or

   Choose **Table Options > Alternating Column Strokes** from the Table palette.

3. Use the Alternating Pattern list to choose how many column strokes will alternate **49**.

4. Set the controls on the left side of the Alternating area to format the appearance of the stroke for the first set of columns.

5. Set the controls on the right side of the Alternating area to format the appearance for the second set of columns.

6. Use the Skip First and Skip Last fields to omit certain columns at the start and end of the table from the alternating count.

TIP If you have applied strokes to individual cells, the Preserve Local Formatting command controls if the alternating strokes for columns override that local formatting.

Setting the Table Strokes and Fills

To set repeating fills:

1. Select at least one cell in the table.

2. Choose **Table** > **Table Options** > **Alternating Fills.** The Table Options dialog box appears set to Fills .

   or

   Choose **Table Options** > **Alternating Fills** from the Table palette.

3. Use the Alternating Pattern list to choose how many row or column fills will alternate 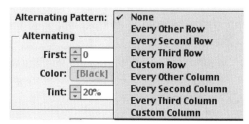.

   TIP You cannot alternate the fills for both rows and columns in the same table.

4. Set the controls on the left side of the Alternating area to format the appearance of the fill for the first set of columns or rows.

5. Set the controls on the right side of the Alternating area to format the appearance for the second set of columns or rows.

6. Use the Skip First and Skip Last fields to omit certain rows or columns at the start and end of the table from the alternating count.

   TIP If you have applied fills to individual cells, the Preserve Local Formatting command controls if the alternating fills override that local formatting.

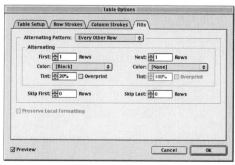

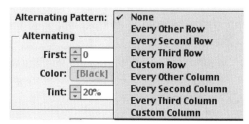

 The **Fills controls** *under Table Options let you apply automatic alternating fills to table rows or columns.*

 The **Alternating Pattern menu** *for setting table fills.*

Setting the Table Strokes and Fills

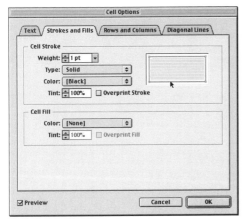

52 *The* **Strokes and Fills controls** *under Cell Options let you format individual cells in a table.*

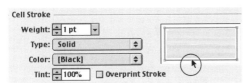

53 *Click the* **proxy lines for the cell stroke** *to control which edges of the cell are stroked.*

54 *The* **Cell Fill controls** *let you apply colors to individual cells in a table.*

Tables are automatically created with strokes around the cells. You can remove those cell strokes or customize them.

To customize the strokes around individual cells:

1. Select the cells you want to modify.

2. Choose **Table** > **Cell Options** > **Strokes and Fills**. The Cell Options dialog box appears set to Strokes and Fills **52**.

   or

   Choose **Cell Options** > **Strokes and Fills** from the Table palette.

3. Click the proxy lines in the cell preview to select which edges of the selected cells should be formatted **53**.

4. Set the controls under Cell Stroke to format the appearance of the selected edges.

To customize the fill inside individual cells:

1. Select the cells you want to modify.

2. Choose **Table** > **Cell Options** > **Strokes and Fills**. The Cell Options dialog box appears set to Strokes and Fills.

   or

   Choose **Cell Options** > **Strokes and Fills** from the Table palette.

3. Set the controls under Cell Fill to format the color inside the selected cells **54**.

Setting the Table Strokes and Fills

Adding Diagonal Lines in Cells

Many people who design tables use diagonal lines to indicate empty data or corrected information. InDesign lets you apply diagonal lines inside cells.

To add diagonal lines in cells:

1. Select the cells you want to modify.

2. Choose **Table** > **Cell Options** > **Diagonal Lines**. The Cell Options dialog box appears set to Diagonal Lines **55**.

   or

   Choose **Cell Options** > **Diagonal Lines** from the Table palette.

3. Choose between Draw in Front or Draw in Back to control if any text appears behind or in front of the diagonal line.

4. Click one of the buttons to control the direction of the lines.

5. Set the Line Stroke options to format the appearance of the line.

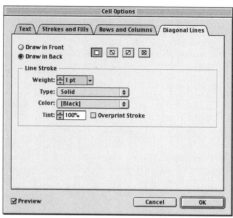

55 *The* **Diagonal Lines controls** *under Cell Options let you add diagonal lines to cells.*

If You Work With Many Tables

As you have seen there are quite a few controls for working with tables. Unfortunately, InDesign itself does not provide a way to save complex table formatting as a table style.

Fortunately, Woodwing Software (http://www.woodwing.com) has created Smart Tables, a plug-in that automates the creation of tables in InDesign.

Smart Tables lets you apply a table style to completely format a table, including all of the table, row, column, cell, paragraph and character attributes.

Smart Tables can also be used to do basic math within InDesign tables including calculating the sum, product or average of all cells in a column.

If you anticipate frequently working with tables, I suggest purchasing a copy of Smart Tables to help automate your work.

AUTOMATING TEXT 14

I have a general rule about working with a computer. Anytime you find yourself doing the same thing more than ten times in a row, stop. Most likely there is a command or tool that can automate the process.

That's what this chapter is all about—learning how to automate InDesign so that the application does the dull, tedious chores for you. (Sadly, I can't apply this rule to other parts of my life, such as washing dishes or folding socks.)

Some of these automation features, such as Find/Change and Spell Check, are very straightforward. You simply choose the command and let InDesign do its stuff.

Others, such as style sheets, need a little bit of preparation to make them work their magic.

Of course you're not required to learn any of these automation features. You are perfectly welcome to modify text by hand one word at a time—especially if you don't care about doing anything else in your life.

Changing Case

InDesign gives you a command to quickly change text case.

To change text case:

1. Select the text you want to change.
2. Choose Type > Change Case and then choose lowercase, Title Case, Sentence case, or UPPERCASE from the submenu ❶.

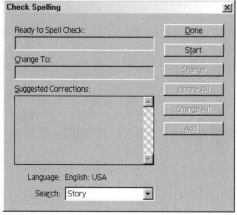

changing case — Lowercase

Changing Case — Title Case

Changing case — Sentence Case

CHANGING CASE — Uppercase

❶ *The* **Change Case options** *change text as shown.*

Checking Spelling

One of the most popular features of page layout programs is the Spelling Checker that checks a document for misspelled words.

To use the spell check command:

1. To check the spelling in a specific text frame or linked frames, click to place an insertion point within the text.
2. Choose Edit > Check Spelling. The Check Spelling dialog box appears ❷.
3. In the Search list, choose where the spelling check should be performed ❸:
   - **All Documents** checks all open documents.
   - **Document** checks the entire document.
   - **Story** checks all the linked frames of the selected text.
   - **To End of Story** checks from the insertion point.
   - **Selection** checks only the selected text.
4. Click Start to begin the spell check. InDesign searches through the text, then stops and displays each error it finds.

TIP InDesign displays words not in its dictionary, duplicate words, and capitalization errors.

❷ *The* **Check Spelling dialog box** *is the command center for a spell check.*

❸ *The* **Search list** *allows you to specify where the spell check is performed.*

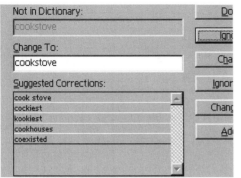

④ *InDesign gives you a list of* **suggested corrections** *for the unknown words found during a spell check.*

The Limitations of the Spell Check

Every once in a while, I read an article about how the use of spelling checkers in computers is contributing to the death of proper writing and language.

It's true; too many people run a spell check and don't bother to actually read their document. Consider the following text:

Their is knot any thing wrung with using a spell cheque on a sent tents in a doc you mint. Ewe just haft to clique the write butt ends.

Obviously the paragraph is utter nonsense. Yet InDesign's Spell Check (as well as the Spell Check in most other programs) wouldn't flag a single word as being incorrect.

A Spell Check only flags words it doesn't recognize; but since everything in the paragraph is an actual word, InDesign doesn't see any problems.

So, please, don't skip a session with a proofreader just because you've run a spell check.

The spell check may display a word that is correctly spelled. This could be a specialized term (like *InDesign*) or a proper name (like *Sandee*). If you have words like that, you will want to instruct the spell check to ignore a specialized word.

To ignore specialized words:

◆ Click Ignore to continue the check without changing that instance of the text.

or

Click Ignore All to continue the spell check without changing any instance of that text.

TIP Once you press the Start button, it then turns into the Ignore button.

Of course, the spell check wouldn't be very helpful if it couldn't make changes to suspected words.

To correct the error displayed:

1. Type a correction in the Change To box.

or

Select a word from the Suggested Corrections list **④**.

2. Click Change to change only that instance of the word in the text.

or

Click Change All to change all instances of the word in the text.

The Ignore commands only work during a particular session of InDesign. If you use specialized words frequently, you will want to add them to the dictionary that InDesign uses during a spell check.

To add words to the spell check dictionary:

◆ Click Add when the word is displayed during the spelling check.

To edit the dictionary:

1. Choose **Edit** > **Edit Dictionary** to open the Dictionary dialog box ❺.

2. Choose the language from the Language list.

TIP If you have only one language in the Language list, you need to do a custom installation of InDesign to install the rest of the language dictionaries.

3. Choose Added Words or Removed Words from the Dictionary List.

4. Type the word you want to add in the Word field.

   or

   Click the word you want to remove.

5. Click the Add or Remove button.

TIP The words in the Dictionary also help you control their hyphenation. *(For more information on working with hyphenation, see Chapter 15, "Typography Controls.")*

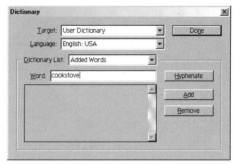

❺ *The* **Dictionary dialog box** *allows you to add or remove words from the dictionary used during a spell check.*

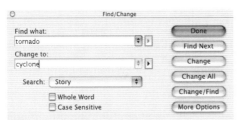

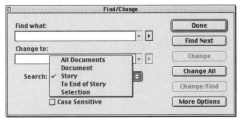

⑥ The **Find/Change dialog box** *allows you to set the controls for searching for and replacing text.*

⑦ The **Search** *list in the Find/Change dialog box allows you to set where the search takes place.*

Finding and Changing Text

InDesign has a powerful Find/Change command that lets you find all instances of text or formatting and make changes to the found items. The simplest Find/Change command looks for certain characters of text, called *text strings,* and changes them. For instance, you can change *Sept.* into *September.*

To set the Find/Change text strings:

1. To find and change within a specific text frame or linked frames, click to place an insertion point within the text.

2. Choose **Edit** > **Find/Change**. The Find/Change dialog box appears **⑥**.

3. In the Search pop-up list, choose where the search should be performed **⑦**:
   - **All Documents** checks all open documents.
   - **Document** checks the entire document.
   - **Story** checks all the linked frames of the selected text.
   - **To End of Story** checks from the insertion point.
   - **Selection** checks only the selected text.

4. In the Find What field, type or paste the text you want to search for.

5. In the Change To field, type or paste the text to be inserted.

6. Select Case Sensitive to limit the search to text with the same capitalization. For instance, a case-sensitive search for "InDesign" does not find "Indesign".

7. Select Whole Word to disregard the text if it is contained within another word. For instance, a whole-word search for Design omits the instance in InDesign.

8. Click Start. InDesign looks through the text and selects each matching text string it finds.

Finding and Changing Text

As you run a Find/Change search, you can choose whether or not to apply the changes.

To apply the Find/Change changes:

◆ Click Change to change the text without moving to the next instance.

or

Click Change/Find to change the text and move to the next instance.

or

Click Change All to change all the instances in the text.

❽ *The* **metacharacters menu** *for the Find what field.*

You can tell InDesign to ignore or skip the change of a Find/Change instance.

To ignore a Find/Change instance:

◆ Click Find Next to avoid changing that instance of the found text and skip to the next occurrence.

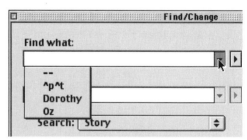

❾ *InDesign keeps a record of the past 15 text strings in the Find what or Change to fields.*

InDesign also lets you search for special characters such as spaces, hyphens, paragraph returns, tab characters, or inline graphic markers. These are called *metacharacters* for the Find/Change commands.

To Find/Change metacharacters:

1. Choose the character you want to look for in the Find what menu **❽**.

2. Choose the character you want to substitute in the Change to menu.

3. Apply the Find/Change commands as described on the opposite page.

TIP InDesign also keeps a list of the past 15 text strings for both the Find what and the Change to fields. You can use that list to quickly reapply searches **❾**.

⑩ *The* **expanded options** *in the Find/Change dialog box.*

Working with Wildcard Characters

You cannot insert wildcard characters in the Change to field. However, that should not discourage you from working with wildcard characters.

The numbers for the steps of this book are an example of how I can format using wildcard characters. In the Find what field I enter ^9.^t, which is the code for any digit followed by a period and a tab.

I set the formatting for the number style in the Change to field. InDesign searches for any number followed by a period and a tab and applies the proper formatting.

In addition to text strings, you can also Find/Change formatting. This helps when making changes to text imported from word-processing programs.

The Find what menu has three special meta-characters called *wildcard* characters. The wildcard characters allow you to search for items that you do not know the specific characters for.

To search for wildcard characters:

1. Choose one of the wildcard characters from the Find what menu:
   - **Any Character** finds any character including spaces, tabs, returns, or text.
   - **Any Digit** searches for any number (0–9).
   - **Any Letter** searches for any alphabetical letter (a–z).
2. Set the Change to options.
3. Run the search.

TIP You can only use wildcard characters in the Find what field, not in the Change to field.

The Find/Change dialog box has additional options that let you search for more than just text strings. You can use the Find/Change dialog box to search for formatting options.

To expand the Find/Change options:

◆ Click More Options in the Find/Change dialog box. This opens the format options for searches ⑩. *(See the next exercises for setting the format options.)*

Finding and Changing Text

With the Find/Change dialog box expanded, you can set the formatting options for either the Find or Change fields.

To search for formatting options:

1. Click the Format button in the Find Format Settings area of the Find/Change dialog box. This opens the Find Format Settings dialog box ⓫.

2. Choose those formatting categories on the left side of the Find Format Settings dialog box ⓬.

   - **Style Options** changes character and paragraph styles. *(See the next page for information on working with styles.)*
   - **Basic Character Formats** changes the character formatting options *(see page 45)*.
   - **Advanced Character Formats** searches for the language and distortion formatting, such as skewing *(see page 50)*.
   - **Indents and Spacing** searches for alignment, indents, and paragraph spacing *(see page 53)*.
   - **Keep Options** changes the Keep With Next paragraph formatting *(see page 286)*.
   - **Drop Caps and Composer** searches for Drop Caps and Composer settings *(see page 56)*.
   - **Character Color** searches for colors from the Swatch palette *(see page 95)*.
   - **OpenType** searches for attributes that are available in OpenType typefaces *(see page 297)*.

3. Enter the criteria you want to search for in the fields for the chosen category.

   TIP For instance, if you want to search for all 12-point text, you would choose the Basic Character category and then enter 12 point in the point size.

4. Click OK. The search criteria are displayed in the Find Style Settings area ⓭.

   TIP Leave the Find what field blank to search for formatting without looking for specific text.

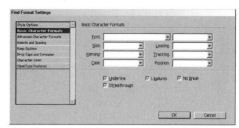

⓫ *The* **Find Format Settings** *dialog box lets you search for specific formatting options.*

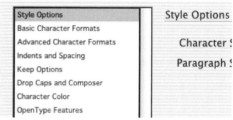

⓬ *The categories for the Find Format Settings and Change Format Settings dialog boxes.*

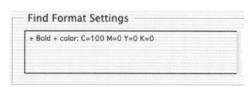

⓭ **Formatting criteria** *appear in the Find Format Settings area of the Find/Change dialog box.*

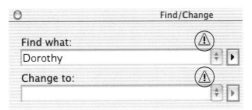

⓮ *The alert symbol next to the Find what and Change to fields indicates that formatting options have been chosen as part of Find/Change.*

⓯ *Click the Clear button to delete all the format options from the Find/Change criteria.*

With the Find/Change dialog box expanded, you can set the formatting options for either the Find or Change fields.

To set the replacement formatting options:

1. Click the Format button in the Change Format Settings area of the Find/Change dialog box. This opens the Change Format Settings dialog box.

TIP This dialog box is identical to the Find Format Settings dialog box ⓫.

2. Choose those formatting categories on the left side of the Change Format Settings dialog box.

3. Click Format to open the Change Format Settings dialog box. Choose the options from the pop-up menu or click Prev or Next.

4. Enter the criteria you want to replace in the fields for the chosen category.

TIP An alert symbol next to the Find what or Change to fields indicates that formatting options are part of the Find/Change criteria ⓮.

TIP If you click the Fewer Options button, you reduce the size of the Find/Change box, although you can still search for the Formatting options that are hidden.

To delete the formatting options:

♦ Click the Clear button to delete all the formatting in the Find Format Settings or Change Format Settings areas ⓯.

Defining Styles

Styles are the most powerful feature for applying formatting. InDesign has two types of styles. *Paragraph styles* apply formatting for both character and paragraph attributes. *Character styles* apply formatting for only character attributes. *(For more information on working with character and paragraph attributes, see Chapter 3, "Basic Text.")*

You can use the Paragraph Styles palette to define new paragraph styles for a document.

To define a paragraph style manually:

1. Choose **Type** > **Paragraph Styles.** This opens the Paragraph Styles palette **⑯**.

2. Choose New Style from the Paragraph Styles palette menu **⑰**. This opens the New Paragraph Style dialog box **⑱**.

3. Use the Style Name field to name the style.

4. Set the Based On, Next Style, and Shortcuts as described on pages 273, 275, and 276.

5. Click each category on the left side of the dialog box **⑲**.

6. Set the criteria for each category.

7. Click OK to define the style. The name of the style appears in the Paragraph Styles palette.

New style

⑯ *The* **Paragraph Styles** palette *lets you define and apply paragraph styles.*

Delete style

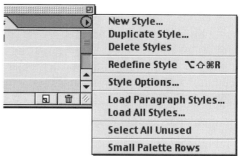

⑰ *The* **Paragraph Styles** palette menu *contains the commands for paragraph styles.*

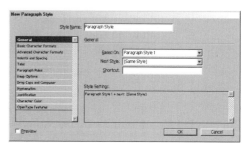

⑱ *The* **New Paragraph Style** dialog box *contains the settings for defining a paragraph style.*

Defining Styles

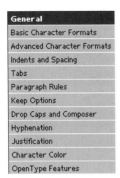

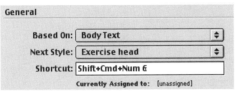

⑲ *Click each* **category in the Paragraph Styles** *dialog box to set the format of the style.*

⑳ *The* **General options** *in the New Paragraph Style dialog box.*

The easier way to define a style is to format the text and define the style by example.

To define a paragraph style by example:

1. Select a sample paragraph.

2. Use the Character and Paragraph palettes and any other commands to format the text.

3. Leave the insertion point in the formatted paragraph.

4. Choose **Type** > **Paragraph Styles.**

5. With the insertion point blinking in the formatted text, click the New Style icon. This adds a new style to the Paragraph Styles palette.

TIP Double-click to rename the style created by the New Style icon.

The Next Style command allows you to automatically switch to a new style as you type text. For instance, when I press the paragraph return after this paragraph, I automatically switch to the style for the exercise header.

To set the next paragraph style:

1. Select the General category in the New Paragraph Style dialog box **⑳**.

2. Choose a style from the Next Style list in the New Paragraph Style dialog box.

TIP The Next Style is applied to the next paragraph when you press the Return key.

Defining Styles

Character styles allow you to set specific attributes that override the paragraph style character attributes. For instance, the bold text within the captions of this book overrides the normal text of the captions.

To define a character style:

1. Choose Type >Character Styles. This opens the Character Styles palette ❷❶.

2. Choose New Style from the Character Styles palette menu ❷❷. This opens the New Character Style dialog box ❷❸.

3. Name the style.

4. Set the Based On and Shortcut controls as described on page 275 and 276.

5. Set each of the character attributes listed in the pop-up list ❷❹.

6. Click OK to define the style. The name of the style appears in the Character Styles palette.

You can also format the text and then define a character style by example.

To define a character style by example:

1. Select a sample paragraph.

2. Use the Character palette and other commands to format the text.

TIP It does not matter what paragraph attributes are applied to this text.

3. Leave the insertion point in the newly formatted text.

4. Choose Type >Character Styles.

5. Click the New Style icon. This adds a new style to the Character Styles palette.

New style

Delete style

❷❶ *The* **Character Styles palette** *lets you define and apply character styles.*

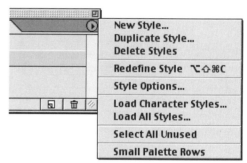

❷❷ *The* **Character Styles palette menu** *contains the commands for character styles.*

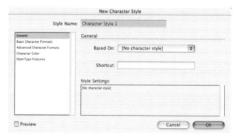

❷❸ *The* **New Character Style dialog box** *contains the settings for defining character styles.*

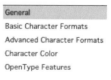

❷❹ *Click each* **category** *in the Character style dialog box to set the format of the style.*

Style Settings:

Body Text + next: Exercise head + size: 18 pt

25 *When you base a new style on an existing style, you can read how they differ in the Style Settings field of the New Style dialog box.*

Basing Styles

The style for the numbers of the exercises in this book is based on the style of the subheads. If I change the style for the subheads, the numbers change automatically.

Similarly, the style for the exercises is based on the style for the body copy. So if my publisher asks me to make the copy a little smaller, I only have to change the point size for one style.

Limit how many levels you go when you base one style on another. Theoretically you can base one style on another, which is based on another, which is based on another, and so on. However, this can be confusing if you go down too many levels. I always use one style as the main one and base others on it. I think of the main style as the hub of a wheel, and the others are the spokes around it.

Basing one style on another makes it easy to coordinate multiple styles.

To base one style on another:

1. Start with at least one paragraph or character style.

2. Open the dialog box to define a new style.

3. From the Based On pop-up menu, choose the style you want to use as the foundation of the new style.

4. Make changes to define the second style attributes.

TIP The changes to the second style are displayed in the Style Settings area **25**.

TIP Any changes you make later to the original style also affect the second style.

Rather than create a new style from scratch, it may be easier to duplicate an existing style and then redefine it.

To duplicate a style:

1. Select the style.

2. Drag the style onto the New Style icon in the Paragraph Styles palette.

   or

   Choose Duplicate Style from the Paragraph Styles palette menu.

Defining Styles

You can also set keyboard shortcuts for paragraph and character styles. This makes it easy to apply styles as you type.

To set style keyboard shortcuts:

1. Open the New Paragraph Style or New Character Style dialog box.

   or

   Double-click the name of the style to open the Modify Paragraph Style or Modify Character Style dialog box.

2. Place an insertion point in the Shortcut field.

3. Press a number from the number pad plus a keyboard modifier.

- **TIP** Macintosh keyboard shortcuts can use Cmd or Shift modifiers.

- **TIP** Windows keyboard shortcuts can use Ctrl or Shift modifiers.

- **TIP** In Windows, the Num Lock must be turned on to set keyboard shortcuts.

- **TIP** The keyboard shortcut appears next to the style name in the Paragraph Styles or Character Styles palettes **26**.

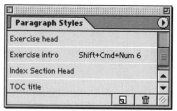

26 *The* **keyboard shortcut for a style** *is listed next to the name of the style.*

Style Guidelines

Styles are listed alphabetically in the two styles palettes. So if you want styles to be listed together, give them similar name.

For instance, I have three different paragraph styles for the numbered lists in this book. Each style starts with the name *list item* and is followed by a descriptive word such as *list item body, list item bullet,* and so on. This groups the styles together in the Paragraph Styles palette.

If you use keyboard shortcuts, keep them in groups. For instance, the styles for the list items all use the keypad number 2 with variations of the keyboard modifiers. So *list item plain* is Shift-2, while *list item body* is Shift-Cmd/Ctrl-2.

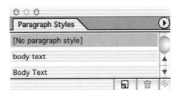

27 *Style names are case sensitive. So two styles can have the same name but different character cases.*

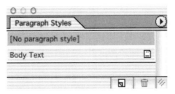

28 *The disk icon indicates that the style definition came from an imported text file.*

If you have defined styles in one document, you can transfer or load those styles into another document.

To transfer styles from an InDesign document:

1. Choose one of the following from the Styles palette menus:
   - **Load Character Styles** transfers the character styles.
   - **Load Paragraph Styles** transfers the paragraph styles.
   - **Load All Styles** transfers both character and paragraph styles.
2. Navigate to find the document that contains the styles you want to import.
3. Click Open. The styles are automatically added to the current document.

TIP Style names are case sensitive. A style name of *Body Text* will be added to a document that already has a style named *body text* **27**.

When you place text into InDesign, the styles from the imported text are added to the document.

To import styles with placed text:

◆ Choose **File** > **Place** and navigate to find the text file.

TIP A disk icon indicates that the style definition came from the imported text **28**.

TIP The disk icon disappears if you modify the imported style.

Working with Styles

Defining styles is just half of the process. You take advantage of your planning when you apply styles to text.

You can apply styles as you type new text, or you can add styles to existing text.

To apply paragraph styles:

1. Select the paragraphs.

TIP You do not need to select entire paragraphs. As long as a portion is selected, the paragraph style will be applied to the entire paragraph.

2. Click the name of the paragraph style.

   or

   Type the keyboard shortcut.

When you apply a paragraph style to text, the character attributes are controlled by the paragraph style. You can override the style by applying a character style **29**.

To apply character styles:

1. Select the text.

TIP You must select all the text you want to format with a character style.

2. Click the name of the character style.

   or

   Type the keyboard shortcut.

Character styles

2. Navigate to find the document that ——Paragraph style
   contains the styles you want to import.

3. Click **Open**. The styles are *automatically* added to the current document.

29 *An example of paragraph and character styles applied to text.*

Character Style Strategies

InDesign character styles only need to be defined with a single change from the paragraph attributes.

For instance, if you want to change text to italic, define a character attribute with just italic as the definition.

You can then apply the italic character attribute to many different paragraph styles, even if they are different typefaces or point sizes.

This is very different from the character style sheets in QuarkXPress. In that program you need a different character style sheet to apply italic to different typefaces.

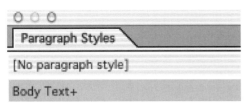

㉚ *The plus sign next to the style name indicates that local formatting has been applied to the text.*

Original text with
local formatting

> Dorothy lived with **Uncle Henry**, and **Aunt Em**. Their house was small.

Opt/Alt-click removes
local formatting

> Dorothy lived with Uncle Henry, and Aunt Em. Their house was small.

㉛ *Opt/Alt-click a paragraph style name to remove local character formatting applied to text.*

Original text with
character style applied

> Their house was small. There were four *walls*, a *floor*, and a *roof*.

Opt/Alt-Shift-click
converts to local
formatting

> Their house was small. There were four *walls*, a *floor*, and a *roof*.

Opt/Alt-click
removes local
formatting

> Their house was small. There were four walls, a floor, and a roof.

㉜ *Opt/Alt-Shift-click a paragraph style name to convert character styles to local formatting.*

Once you have paragraph styles applied to text, you can override the style by applying local formatting to the text characters.

To override paragraph styles:

1. Select the text you want to modify.
2. Apply character attributes from the Character palette. A plus sign (+) next to the paragraph style name indicates that local character formatting has been applied to the text **㉚**.

   or

   Apply a character style sheet from the Character Styles palette.

When you apply a paragraph style sheet, InDesign maintains any local character formatting that was applied to the text. However, you can override local character formatting when you apply a paragraph style.

To override local character formatting:

◆ Hold the Opt/Alt keys as you click the name of the paragraph style **㉛**.

There is a two-step process to override any character style sheets that have been applied to text.

To override character style sheets:

1. Hold the Opt/Alt + Shift keys as you click the name of the paragraph style. This converts the character style sheet to local character formatting, indicated by a plus sign (+).
2. Hold the Opt/Alt keys and click the name of the paragraph style. This deletes the local character formatting and leaves the default paragraph style **㉜**.

Working with Styles

One of the advantages of using paragraph or character styles is that when you redefine the style, it changes all the existing text that has that style applied to it.

To redefine a paragraph or character style:

1. Double-click the style name in the palette. This opens the Modify Style Options dialog box, where you can change the attributes of the style 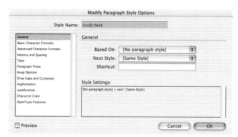.

2. Click OK. The style is redefined, and the text updates to reflect the new definition of the style.

33 *The* **Modify Paragraph Style Options dialog box** *lets you change the style attributes.*

To redefine a style by example:

1. Make any changes to a paragraph that has the style applied to it.

2. Select the modified text.

3. Choose Redefine Style from the Styles palette. The style is redefined based on the modified example.

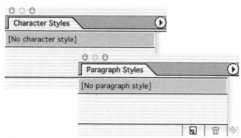

34 *The* **[No paragraph style]** *and* **[No character style]** *listings indicate that no style is applied to the text.*

You may have styles that you do not need in your InDesign document. You can shorten the styles list by deleting unused styles.

To delete styles:

1. Select the styles.

2. Drag the styles onto the Delete Style icon.

   or

   Choose Delete Styles from the Style palette menu.

TIP If you delete a style that was applied to text, the appearance of the text does not change. The No Paragraph Style or No Character Style is applied to the text, but the text is no longer associated with any style **34**.

TIP Use Select All Unused Styles to delete all the unused styles from a document.

Working with Styles

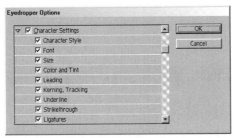

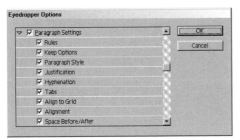

③⑤ *The* **Eyedropper tool** *in the Toolbox lets you sample and apply text formatting.*

③⑥ *The* **Eyedropper Options dialog box** *set to choose the* **Paragraph Settings**.

③⑦ *The* **Eyedropper Options dialog box** *set to choose the* **Character Settings**.

Using the Eyedropper on Text

Paragraph and character styles are the most efficient ways to apply and change text formatting for long documents. However, the Eyedropper tool lets you quickly sample formatting from one set of text and apply it to another. *(See Chapter 5 and Chapter 6 for more information on how to use the eyedropper to sample colors, fills, and stroke attributes.)*

To set the eyedropper options for text:

1. Double-click the Eyedropper tool in the Toolbox **③⑤**. This opens the Eyedropper Options dialog box.
2. Click the triangle control to open the Paragraph Settings from the list **③⑥**.
3. Check which paragraph attributes you want the Eyedropper tool to sample.
4. Click the triangle control to open the Character Settings from the list **③⑦**.
5. Check which character attributes you want the Eyedropper tool to sample.

Using the Eyedropper on Text

Once you have set the eyedropper options, you can sample and apply paragraph or character attributes.

To sample and apply paragraph attributes:

1. Choose the Eyedropper tool.

2. Click the white eyedropper inside the paragraph that you want to sample ❸❽. The eyedropper changes from white to black.

3. Click the black eyedropper inside the paragraph that you want to change ❸❾. This changes the paragraph attributes.

TIP The black eyedropper does not apply character attributes when clicked unless a paragraph style was already applied to the sampled text.

4. Click the eyedropper inside any additional paragraphs that you want to change.

To sample and apply character attributes:

1. Choose the Eyedropper tool.

2. Click the white eyedropper inside the text that you want to sample ❹❶. The eyedropper changes from white to black.

3. Drag the black eyedropper across the text you want to change. This highlights the text ❹❶.

4. Release the mouse to apply the changes.

To sample new text attributes:

1. Hold the Opt/Alt key. The eyedropper changes to white.

2. Click the eyedropper inside the new text that you want to sample.

The·Wizard·of· Oz.¶
By·L.·Frank·Baum¶

❸❽ *Click the white eyedropper to sample the right alignment of the paragraph attributes.*

The·Wizard·of· Oz.¶
By·L.·Frank·Baum¶

❸❾ *Click the black eyedropper to apply the right alignment of the paragraph attributes.*

The·**Munchkins**· and·the·Witch.¶

❹❶ *Click the white eyedropper to sample local character attributes.*

The·**Munchkins**· and·the·Witch.¶

❹❶ *Drag the black eyedropper to apply character attributes to text.*

```
<ASCII-MAC>
<dps:Normal=<Nextstyle:Normal><ct:>>
<ctable:=<Black:COLOR:CMYK:Process:0.0000
00,0.000000,0.000000,1.000000>>
<pstyle:Normal>The <ct:Bold>Scarecrow<ct:>
did not mind how long it took him to fill the
basket, for it enabled him to <ct:Italic>keep
away from the fire.<ct:> So he kept a good
distance away from the flames.
```

42 *The tagged text codes as they appear outside InDesign.*

The **Scarecrow** did not mind how long it took him to fill the basket, for it enabled him to *keep away from the fire.* So he kept a good distance away from the flames.

43 *The same text as it appears on the InDesign page.*

44 *The* **Export Options** *dialog box for setting the Tagged Text options.*

Creating Tagged Text

If you import text from Microsoft Word, InDesign reads the paragraph and character styles applied in Word. However, what happens if you want to import text from an application such as a database that doesn't have style sheets? Tags let you add the codes for styles **42** so that the correct formatting imports with the text **43**.

You can learn the correct tags for different formatting by exporting tags from InDesign.

To export tags from InDesign:

1. Select the text you want to export.
2. Choose **File > Export**.
3. Choose InDesign Tagged Text from the Save as File Type (Win) or Formats (Mac) menu.
4. Click Save. The Export Options dialog box appears **44**.
5. Choose the type of tag:
    *   **Verbose** shows the longer version of the tags.
    *   **Abbreviated** shows the short version of the tags.
6. Choose the type of encoding:
    *   **ASCII**, for most English language files.
    *   **ANSI**, for most international characters.
    *   **Unicode**, a standard for most languages.
    *   **Big 5**, for Chinese characters.
    *   **Shift-JIS**, for Japanese characters.

Creating Tagged Text

You can import tagged text as ordinary text. However, there are some special import options for tagged text.

To import tagged text:

1. Choose File > Place.

2. Navigate to find the text-only file with the tagged text codes.

3. If you want to control how the text is placed, click Show Import Options.

4. Click Open.

45 *The* InDesign Tags Import Options dialog box *is used to control how tagged text is imported.*

The tagged-text import options control how any conflicts and missing tags are treated **45**.

To set tagged-text import options:

1. Select a choice for resolving conflicts between the styles in the InDesign Tags Import Options dialog box:

   • **Publication Definition** uses the style as it is already defined in the document.
   • **Tagged File Definition** uses the style as defined in the tagged text. This adds a new style to the document with the word "copy" added to the style name.

2. Check Show List of Problem Tags before Place to display a list of incorrect or unrecognized tags.

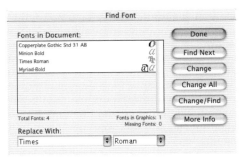

④⑤ *The* **Find Font** *dialog box lets you make global changes to the fonts in a document.*

④⑦ *The* **Find Font** *icons tell you the status and type of fonts used in the document.*

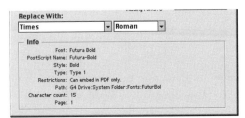

④⑧ *The* **Info** *area of the Find Font dialog box gives you more information about the font.*

Using Find Font

In addition to the Find/Change commands for text, InDesign lets you make global changes for font families. This is helpful when you open documents that contain missing fonts.

TIP The Find Font list lets you quickly check what fonts are used in a document.

To make changes using Find Font:

1. Choose **Type** > **Find Font**. The Find Font dialog box appears **④⑤**.

2. Select the font in the list that you want to change.

TIP The icons next to each font display the type of font and its status **④⑦**.

3. Use the Replace With list to choose a replacement for the selected font.

4. Click Find First to find the first instance of the font. InDesign highlights the first place the font is used.

TIP When you find the first instance, the Find First button changes to Find Next.

5. Click one of the following options:
   - **Find Next** skips that instance.
   - **Change** replaces that instance.
   - **Change/Find** replaces that instance and finds the next instance.
   - **Change All** changes all the instances of the font.

6. Use the More Info button to find more information, such as if the fonts can be embedded in PDF documents **④⑧**.

7. Click Done to return to the document.

To replace missing fonts:

1. Open the document. If fonts are missing, an alert box appears.

2. Click Find Font to open the Find Font dialog box.

3. Choose the missing font and follow the steps in the previous exercise.

Keeping Lines Together

Another automation technique is to specify
how many lines of text must remain together
in a column or page. InDesign does this using
the Keep Options controls.

To set the keep options for a paragraph:

1. Choose Keep Options from the
   Paragraph palette menu. This opens the
   Keep Options dialog box 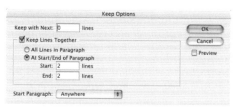.

2. Enter a number in the Keep With Next
   Lines field to force the last line in a
   paragraph to stay in the same column or
   page with the specified number of lines.

   TIP This option ensures that subheads or
   titles remain in the same column as the
   body copy that follows.

3. Click Keep Lines Together and set one of
   these options **50**:

   - **All Lines in Paragraph** prevents the
     paragraph from ever breaking.
   - **At Start/End of Paragraph** lets you set
     the number of lines that must remain
     together for the start and the end of the
     paragraph.

4. Use the Start Paragraph pop-up list to
   choose where the lines must jump to **51**.

   - **Anywhere** allows the text to jump
     anywhere.
   - **In Next Column** forces the text to the
     next column or page.
   - **In Next Frame** forces the text to the
     next frame or page.
   - **On Next Page** forces the text to the next
     page.
   - **On Next Odd Page** forces the text to the
     next odd-numbered page.
   - **On Next Even Page** forces the text to
     the next even-numbered page.

49 *The* **Keep Options dialog box** *controls how
paragraphs break across columns or pages.*

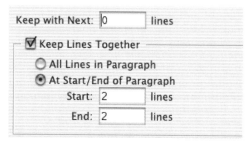

50 *The* **Keep Lines Together controls** *of the
Keep Options dialog box.*

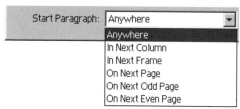

51 *The* **Start Paragraph list** *lets you choose
where the next lines of the paragraph appear.*

Keeping Lines Together

TYPOGRAPHY CONTROLS 15

The one thing that truly separates the amateurs from the experts in page layout is the control they take over their text. Amateurs are pleased if they can apply simple formatting such as fonts, sizes, alignment, tracking, and so on.

Experts, though, want more from a page-layout program. They want sophisticated control over kerning. This includes the ability to move one character in so that it tucks under the stroke of another.

They want to control how lines are justified within a text frame. This means that if one line looks too crowded and the next has big gaps between the words, the experts tell the program to reapportion the spaces.

The experts also want to work with the newest typefaces that give more choices for how letters look and act together.

These are advanced text effects. Once you apply these features, you move from being an ordinary designer to a typographer.

Hanging Punctuation

One of the most sophisticated text effects in InDesign is the ability to apply hanging punctuation to justified text. Hanging punctuation is applied by setting the *optical margin adjustment*. This moves punctuation characters slightly outside the text margin. It creates the illusion of a more uniform edge for the text ❶. In addition, optical margin adjustment also moves portions of serifs outside the margin ❷.

Optical margin adjustment is set using the Story palette.

To set optical margin adjustment:

1. Select the text.

2. Choose **Type > Story**. This opens the Story palette ❸.

3. Check Optical Margin Adjustment. The text reflows so that the punctuation and serifs lie outside the margin edges.

4. Enter a size for the amount of overhang.

TIP As a general rule, set the overhang the same size as the text.

Off	On
"From the Land of Oz," said Dorothy gravely. "And here is Toto, too. And oh, Aunt Em! I'm so glad to be at home again!	"From the Land of Oz," said Dorothy gravely. "And here is Toto, too. And oh, Aunt Em! I'm so glad to be at home again!"

❶ **Optical margin adjustment** *moves punctuation outside the margin edges.*

he Lion shook the dust out of his mane, and the Scarecrow patted himself into his best shape, and the Woodman polished his tin

❷ *The* **Optical Margin Alignment** *also moves the serifs of letters slightly outside the margin.*

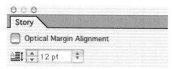

❸ *The* **Story palette** *lets you set the Optical Margin Alignment to hang punctuation in the margin.*

> The road was still paved with yellow brick, but these were much covered by dried branches and dead leaves from the trees, and the walking was not at all good.

Off

> The road was still paved with yellow brick, but these were much covered by dried branches and dead leaves from the trees, and the walking was not at all good.

On

❹ *Turn on* **Adobe Paragraph Composer** *to improve the spacing between words.*

When to Use Paragraph Composition?

Why would anyone want to turn off the miracle of paragraph composition? Well first you have to understand that paragraph composition does require some power from your computer—especially if you've got lots of long paragraphs.

So one way to cut down on processing power is to turn off Adobe Paragraph Composer.

Basically, you don't need paragraph composition for any text that contains lots of single-line paragraphs. Statistical data, single-line tables, headlines, indexes, table of contents, and callouts are good examples of information that doesn't need paragraph composition.

Using Paragraph Composer

InDesign has two ways of compositing (laying out) text. Single-line composition looks at the current line and evaluates the best place to break the line or apply hyphenation. Paragraph composition looks at the all the text in a paragraph—forward and backward—when it evaluates the best place to break lines. When paragraph composition is turned on, the result is more even spacing for the text and fewer hyphens ❹.

To apply paragraph composition:

1. Select the text.
2. Choose **Type** > **Paragraph** to open the Paragraph palette.
3. Choose Adobe Paragraph Composer from the Paragraph palette menu. The text reflows.

TIP Adobe Paragraph Composer is a paragraph attribute and is applied to all the text in a paragraph.

TIP Adobe Paragraph Composer is turned on by default when you first open InDesign.

TIP Choose Adobe Single-line Composer to apply standard line-by-line composition.

Using Paragraph Composer

Applying Justification Controls

Justification determines how lines fit between margins. (See the sidebar below for information on how justification affects text.) InDesign provides three different ways to control justification. *Word spacing* changes the space between words.

To set word spacing:

1. Select the text.
2. Choose **Type** > **Paragraph** to open the Paragraph palette.
3. Choose Justification from the Paragraph palette menu. This opens the Justification dialog box **⑤**.
4. Set the Word Spacing options as follows **⑥**:
    *   **Desired** controls the preferred amount of space between words. 100% indicates that you want the same amount that the designer of the typeface created.
    *   **Minimum** controls the smallest amount of space you want between words. For instance, a value of 80% means that you are willing to allow the space to be 80% of the normal space.
    *   **Maximum** controls the largest amount of space you want between words. A value of 120% means that you are willing to allow the space to be 120% of the normal space.
5. Click OK to apply the changes **⑦**.

TIP The Minimum, Desired, and Maximum settings apply only to text that is set to one of the Justified settings. Other alignments, such as left-aligned text, use only the Desired setting.

⑤ *The* **Justification** dialog box *controls the word and letter spacing.*

	Minimum	Desired	Maximum
Word Spacing:	80%	100%	133%
Letter Spacing:	0%	0%	0%
Glyph Scaling:	100%	100%	100%

⑥ *The* **spacing controls** *in the Justification dialog box.*

Welcome, my child, to the Land of Oz

Min: 80, Desired: 100, Max: 120

Welcome, my child, to the Land of Oz

Min: 80, Desired: 100, Max: 100

⑦ *The effects of changing the* **word** *spacing.*

Understanding Justification

The lines in this paragraph are justified — that is, both ends of the line are aligned with the paragraph margins. Of course not all lines fit evenly between the margins. So some sentences have a bit more space between the words and others have less. The justification settings control how much space is added.

Welcome, my child, to the Land of Oz

Min: 0,
Desired: 0,
Max: 0

Welcome, my child, to the Land of Oz

Min: -4,
Desired: 0,
Max: 4

⑧ *The effect of changing the* **letter spacing.**

What Are the Best Justification Settings?

Perhaps the most debated issue in desktop publishing is what are the best settings for the Justification controls. The answer depends on a variety of factors. The typeface, width of the columns, even the type of text all need to be considered in setting the Justification controls.

For body text, such as the text here, I use word spacing of 70%, 100%, and 110%. (Here in New York City, most designers like to set copy tightly.) However, for headlines, I fit letters tighter, with word spacing of 60%, 90%, and 100%.

I keep all the letter spacing values at 0%. I set the glyph spacing values at 100%. I don't like to scrunch up the space between letters and I definitely don't like to change the shape of the text which happens with glyph scaling *(see the next page)*.

But that's just me. And that's why they call them preferences!

The space between letters is *letter spacing*. This is sometimes called character spacing. InDesign lets you change the letter spacing for text.

To set letter spacing:

1. Select the text.

2. Choose **Type** > **Paragraph** to open the Paragraph palette.

3. Choose Justification from the Paragraph palette menu.

4. Set the Letter Spacing options as follows:
   - **Desired** controls the preferred amount of space between letters. 0% indicates that you do not want to add or subtract any space.
   - **Minimum** controls the smallest amount of space between words. A value of –5% allows the space to be reduced by 5% of the normal space.
   - **Maximum** controls the largest amount of space between words. A value of 5% allows the space to be increased by 5% of the normal space.

5. Click OK to apply the changes **⑧**.

TIP If a paragraph cannot be set using the justification controls you choose, InDesign violates the settings by adding or subtracting spaces. Set the Composition preferences to have those violations highlighted *(see page 359)*.

Applying Justification Controls

Another way to control justification is to use *glyph scaling*. Glyph scaling applies horizontal scaling to the text so that it takes up more or less space within the line.

To set glyph scaling:

1. Select the text.

2. Choose **Type** > **Paragraph** to open the Paragraph palette.

3. Choose Justification from the Paragraph palette menu.

4. Set the Glyph Scaling options as follows:

   - **Desired** controls the preferred amount of scaling. 100% indicates that you do not want to apply any scaling to the character shape.

   - **Minimum** controls the smallest amount of scaling that you are willing to apply to the text. A value of 98% means that you are willing to allow the characters to be reduced by 98% of their normal width.

   - **Maximum** controls he amount that you are willing to expand the space between words. A value of 105% means that you are willing to allow the characters to be increased by 5% of their normal width.

5. Click OK to apply the changes **9**.

TIP Glyph scaling distorts the shape of letters. Most people say you can't see the slight distortion. However, typographic purists (such as this author) try to avoid distorting the letterforms whenever possible **10**.

The road was still paved with yellow brick, but these were much covered by dried branches and dead leaves from the trees, and the walking was not at all good.

Min: 100
Desired: 100
Max: 100

The road was still paved with yellow brick, but these were much covered by dried branches and dead leaves from the trees, and the walking was not at all good.

Min: 80
Desired: 100
Max: 120

9 *The effects of changing the* glyph scaling.

10 *The black area shows the original shape of the character. The gray area shows the effects of 80% glyph scaling.*

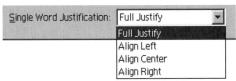

⓫ *The* **Auto Leading field** *controls how InDesign calculates the leading when set to Auto.*

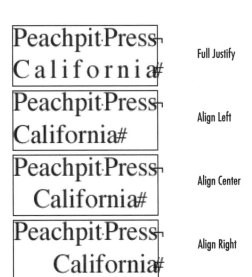

⓬ *The* **Single Word Justification menu** *controls what happens when a single word occupies a line of justified text.*

The Auto Leading field controls how much space is put between the lines whenever auto leading is chosen *(see page 48)*.

To set the Auto Leading percentage:

1. Choose Justification from the Paragraph palette menu.

2. Enter an amount in the Auto Leading field ⓫.

TIP The Auto Leading percentage is based on the point size of the text. So an Auto Leading of 120% applied to 12-point text creates a leading of 14.4 points (12 × 1.20 = 14.4).

TIP Most professional designers use an absolute amount for leading, rather than the automatic leading.

Have you ever seen a paragraph of justified text where a single word stretched out along the entire line? InDesign lets you control what happens to a single word in a justified paragraph.

To set the single word justification:

1. Choose Justification from the Paragraph palette menu.

2. Choose a setting from the Single Word Justification menu ⓬. Any text that is set to Justify in the Paragraph palette will be set according to the menu command ⓭.

Peachpit·Press¬ C a l i f o r n i a#	Full Justify
Peachpit·Press¬ California#	Align Left
Peachpit·Press¬ California#	Align Center
Peachpit·Press¬ California#	Align Right

⓭ *The effects of the* **Single Word Justification** settings.

Controlling Hyphenation

InDesign lets you turn on hyphenation in the Paragraph palette. Once hyphenation is turned on, you can then control how the hyphenation is applied. *(See the sidebar on the opposite page for comments on setting the hyphenation controls.)*

To turn on hyphenation:

1. Select the text.
2. Check Hyphenate in the Paragraph palette ⓮.

TIP The Hyphenate check box is also controlled from within the Hyphenation dialog box *(see the next exercise).*

To control the hyphenation:

1. Choose Hyphenation from the Paragraph palette menu. The Hyphenation dialog box appears ⓯. The Hyphenate check box displays the controls ⓰.
2. **Words Longer Than** controls the minimum number of letters a word must be before it can be hyphenated.
3. **After First** sets the minimum number of letters that must appear before the hyphen.
4. **Before Last** sets the minimum number of letters that must appear after the hyphen.
5. **Hyphen Limit** sets how many consecutive lines that end with hyphens can appear.
6. **Hyphenate Capitalized Words** allows those words to be hyphenated.
7. **Hyphenation Zone** controls the amount of whitespace at the end of a non-justified line. This option only affects Single-Line Composer text.
8. Adjust the slider to control the total number of hyphens in the paragraph.
9. Click OK to apply the settings.

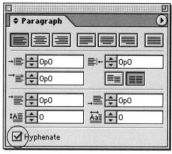

⓮ *Click the* **Hyphenate check box** *to turn on automatic hyphenation for a paragraph.*

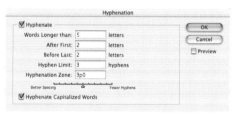

⓯ *The* **Hyphenation dialog box** *lets you control how hyphenation is applied.*

Words Longer than:	5	letters
After First:	2	letters
Before Last:	2	letters
Hyphen Limit:	3	hyphens
Hyphenation Zone:	3p0	

Better Spacing   Fewer Hyphens

⓰ *The Hyphenation controls let you enter values for how words are hyphenated.*

Hyphenation Units are Nigels

The units in the hyphenation slider are called Nigels in honor of Nigel Tufnel (Christopher Guest), the Spinal Tap guitarist, whose amplifier went to 11.

Behold! I am the great and mighty, all-power-ful Oz.

Behold! I am the great and mighty, all-powerful Oz.

🔞 *In the bottom example the word powerful was selected and the* **No Break command** *was applied to prevent the text from hyphenating.*

A·document· can·not·be·

🔞 *A* **discretionary hyphen** *appears within the word but prints only when it appears at the end of a line.*

Setting Hyphenation Controls

My own preference is to set Words Longer Than to six or more. This allows a word such as *person* to be hyphenated.

I also prefer a minimum of three letters before the hyphen and three after. This avoids breaking words as *un-excited* or *relunctant-ly*.

Hyphenate Capitalized Words?

Some people automatically turn this off. I don't. The command doesn't distinguish between proper nouns and words that begin a sentence. So I would rather set proper nouns not to break by using the No Break command or by inserting a discretionary hyphen before the word.

Sometimes you may want to prevent words or phrases from being hyphenated or breaking across lines. For instance, you might not want the words *Mr. Cohen* to be separated at the end of a line. You might not want a compound word such as *self-effacing* to be broken with another hyphen 🔞.

To apply the no break command:

1. Select the text.
2. Choose **Type** > **Character** to open the Character palette.
3. Choose No Break from the Character palette menu.

You can also control hyphenation by inserting a *discretionary hyphen,* which forces the word to hyphenate at that point if it falls at the end of a line.

To use a discretionary hyphen:

1. Place the insertion point where you want the hyphen to occur.
2. Press Command/Ctrl-Shift-(hyphen).

   or

   Control/Right-click and choose **Insert Special Character** > **Discretionary Hyphen** from the contextual menu.

TIP The discretionary hyphen prints only when it appears at the end of the line 🔞.

TIP Insert a discretionary hyphen before a word to prevent that instance of the word from being hyphenated.

Controlling Hyphenation

You can also edit the dictionary to control where a word is hyphenated.

To edit the hyphenation in the dictionary:

1. Choose **Edit** > **Edit Dictionary**.

2. Type the word you want to modify in the Word field as follows :
   - **One tilde** (~) indicates the best possible hyphenation position.
   - **Two tildes** (~~) indicates the next best possible position.
   - **Three tildes** (~~~) indicates the least acceptable position.
   - A tilde before the word prevents the word from being hyphenated.

4. Click Add to add the new hyphenation to the dictionary.

⑲ *The tilde characters control the preference for where hyphenation should occur.*

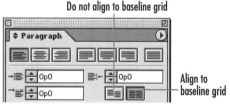

⑳ *The* **Align to Baseline Grid buttons** *in the Paragraph palette.*

Using the Baseline Grid

As mentioned in Chapter 2, InDesign has a electronic baseline grid that you can force text to align to. The grid ensures that the text baselines line up correctly in two separate frames.

TIP Aligning text to baselines is a design decision. As you can see from the pages of this book, not all designers insist on aligning text to a baseline grid.

To align text to a baseline grid:

1. Select the text.

2. Click the Align to Baseline Grid icon in the Paragraph palette **⑳**. The text aligns to the grid **㉑ – ㉒**.

TIP When you align text to the baseline grid, the baseline grid overrides the leading. As a general rule, most designers set the baseline grid to the same amount as the leading for the text.

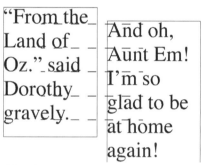

㉑ *When the Align to Baseline Grid is turned off, the text in different frames can be misaligned.*

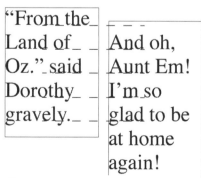

㉒ *When the Align to Baseline Grid is turned on, the text in two different frames lines up.*

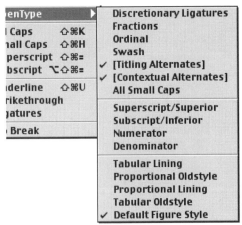

②③ *The OpenType submenu in the Character palette lets you set the special glyphs in OpenType fonts.*

Kin
King
Kingd
Kingdom

②④ *As you add more letters to an OpenType font, the previous letters change.*

②⑤ *Press a glyph with a triangle to see the alternate glyphs.*

Using OpenType

One of the more exciting advances in fonts is OpenType. Instead of the paltry 256 glyphs (characters) in Type 1 or TrueType fonts, OpenType fonts can have thousands of glyphs. InDesign has special commands that help you get the most out of OpenType fonts. For instance, you can set the commands to automatically swap ordinary characters with special OpenType glyphs.

To set automatic OpenType alternate characters:

1. Select the text.

2. Choose **Type** > **Character** to open the Character palette.

3. Choose the settings from the OpenType submenu in the Character palette menu **②③**. InDesign automatically swaps characters with the alternate glyphs in each category.

TIP Some OpenType fonts swap one glyph for another, depending on the position of the letter in the text **②④**.

You can also manually choose alternate glyphs for each character in the font.

To choose the alternate glyphs:

1. Select the character in the text.

2. Choose **Type** > **Insert Glyphs** to open the Glyphs palette.

3. Press the triangle next to the selected character in the palette **②⑤**. The alternate glyphs for the selection appear.

4. Choose one of the alternate characters. This replaces the selected text with the alternate character in the Glyphs palette.

You can also control the Glyphs palette so that you see just certain categories of glyphs.

To display certain categories in the Glyphs palette:

1. Press the Show list in the Glyphs palette.
2. Choose the category of OpenType characters that you want to display 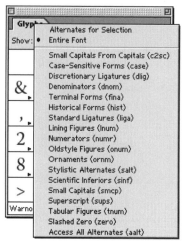.

Alternates for Selection
• Entire Font

Small Capitals From Capitals (c2sc)
Case-Sensitive Forms (case)
Discretionary Ligatures (dlig)
Denominators (dnom)
Terminal Forms (fina)
Historical Forms (hist)
Standard Ligatures (liga)
Lining Figures (lnum)
Numerators (numr)
Oldstyle Figures (onum)
Ornaments (ornm)
Stylistic Alternates (salt)
Scientific Inferiors (sinf)
Small Capitals (smcp)
Superscript (sups)
Tabular Figures (tnum)
Slashed Zero (zero)
Access All Alternates (aalt)

26 *The Show list in the Glyphs palette contains the 18 categories of specialized glyphs.*

COLOR MANAGEMENT 16

I remember when my family got our first color television set. Back then, there weren't many programs broadcast in color, so a color television was a strange and mysterious thing.

No one in the family understood how it worked. We didn't know how to make the pictures look realistic. We jumped up to adjust the image whenever we changed channels. My sister and I spent most of our time fiddling with the TV controls rather than just watching the shows. Or if we couldn't get acceptable color, we changed the channel and watched something in black and white.

Well, that's a lot like controlling color in desktop publishing. Not many people understand how color is managed. They don't know how to make colors look better or how to control images from different applications. Basically they spend most of their time fiddling with the knobs. Or, if they can't deal with color management, they do nothing.

The truth is that color is an extremely deep and complex subject—far too deep for the scope of this book. In this chapter I give you some basic steps for managing color in InDesign.

If you are interested in learning more about color management, I suggest getting *Real World Color Management* by Bruce Fraser, to be published by Peachpit Press in July 2002.

Choosing Color Settings

The first step for color management is to set up the color system. Fortunately, Adobe provides predefined color settings that are suitable for many users.

To turn on color management:

1. Choose **Edit** > **Color Settings**. This opens the Color Settings dialog box ❶.

2. Check Enable Color Management. This opens the color settings controls.

3. Choose one of the predefined settings from the Settings menu ❷:

   - **Custom** uses the settings you choose in the Color Settings dialog box *(see the exercises that follow)*.
   - **Color Management Off** uses minimal color management. Use this for video or on-screen presentations.
   - **ColorSync Workflow (Mac)** manages color using the ColorSync 3.0 CMSl.
   - **Emulate Photoshop 4** simulates the color workflow used by Adobe Photoshop 4.0 and earlier.
   - **Europe Prepress Defaults** manages for typical European press conditions.
   - **Japan Prepress Defaults** manages for typical Japanese press conditions.
   - **Photoshop 5 Default Spaces** manages using the default working spaces for Photoshop 5.0 and later.
   - **U.S. Prepress Defaults** manages for typical U.S. press conditions.
   - **Web Graphics Defaults** manages for display on the World Wide Web.

4. Check Advanced Mode only if you want to set the added color controls *(see page 303)*.

5. Click OK to apply the color settings. In many cases, this is all you need to do to set color management in InDesign.

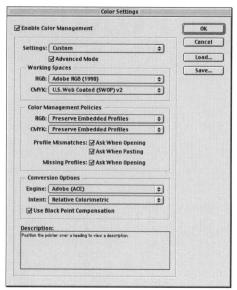

❶ *The* **Color Settings** *dialog box contains the controls for managing how colors are displayed and printed.*

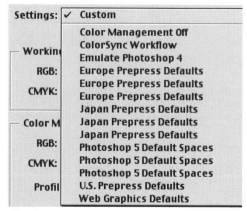

❷ *The* **Settings** *menu lets you choose one of the predefined color management settings.*

☐ Advanced Mode

Workin☐

RGB: ✓ **Adobe RGB (1998)**
       Apple RGB
CMYK: **ColorMatch RGB**
       sRGB IEC61966-2.1

Color M   **Monitor RGB - Generic RGB Profile**

RGB: **ColorSync RGB - Generic RGB Profile**

❸ *The* Working Space RGB menu *lets you choose the display options for RGB colors.*

ings: Other

     Euroscale Coated v2
     Euroscale Uncoated v2
orkin☐ **Japan Standard v2**
     U.S. Sheetfed Coated v2
RGB: **U.S. Sheetfed Uncoated v2**
MYK: ✓ **U.S. Web Coated (SWOP) v2**
     U.S. Web Uncoated v2

lor M   **ColorSync CMYK - Generic CMYK Profile**

❹ *The* Working Space CMYK menu *lets you choose the output destination for printing CMYK colors.*

Talk to Your Print Shop

Most designers I know are embarrassed to admit they don't understand color management. It's nothing to be ashamed of. What you need to do is talk to your print shop. Ask them what settings they recommend for color management. And remember, color management also needs to be set in image-creation applications such as Adobe Illustrator and Adobe Photoshop that you use to create images placed in InDesign.

The working space applies the default color profiles for RGB and CMYK colors *(see Chapter 5, "Working in Color").*

To set the RGB working space:

◆ Use the RGB menu to choose one of the following RGB display settings **❸**:

- **Adobe RGB (1998)** has a large color gamut. Use it if you do print work with a broad range of colors.
- **Apple RGB** reflects the characteristics of the Apple Standard 13-inch monitor. Use for files displayed on Mac OS monitors or for working with older desktop publishing files.
- **ColorMatch RGB** matches the color space of Radius Pressview monitors.
- **sRGB IEC61966-2.1** reflects the characteristics of the average PC monitor. It is recommended for Web work, but is too limited for prepress.
- **Monitor RGB** sets the working space to the color profile of your monitor. Use this if your other applications do not support color management.
- **ColorSync RGB (Mac)** matches the RGB space specified in the control panel for Apple ColorSync 3.0 or later.

TIP When the Advanced Mode is chosen, the RGB Working Space menu displays additional options.

To set the CMYK working space:

◆ Use the CMYK menu to choose the CMYK output settings **❹**:

- **Euroscale (Coated) v2.**
- **Euroscale (Uncoated) v2.**
- **Japan Standard v2.**
- **U.S. Sheetfed Coated v2.**
- **U.S. Sheetfed Uncoated v2.**
- **U.S. Web Coated (SWOP) v2.**
- **U.S. Web Uncoated v2.**
- **ColorSync CMYK (Mac)** matches the CMYK space specified in the control panel for Apple ColorSync 3.0 or later.

TIP Each setting describes the type of ink and paper used in the printing.

Choosing Color Settings

You can also set what happens when placed images contain different color profiles than the current working spaces.

To set the Color Management Policies:

1. Choose a setting in the RGB and CMYK Color Management Policies menus as follows ⑤:
   - **Off** turns off color management for imported images or documents.
   - **Preserve Embedded Profiles** maintains the profile in the imported image or document.
   - **Convert to Working Space** converts placed images and document to the working spaces of the InDesign document.

2. Check Ask When Opening under Profile Mismatches to give a choice when opening documents with different profiles ⑥.

3. Check Ask When Pasting under Profile Mismatches to give a choice when pasting information from documents with different profiles.

4. Check Ask When Opening under Missing Profiles to give a choice when pasting information from documents that have no color profiles.

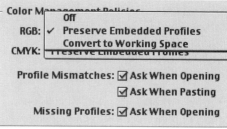

⑤ *The* RGB and CMYK Color Management Policies menus *let you choose what to do with different color profiles.*

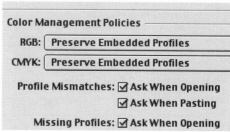

⑥ *The* Color Management Policies *control what happens when two different profiles appear in the same document.*

Conversion Options

Engine: Adobe (ACE)

Intent: Relative Colorimetric

☑ Use Black Point Compensation

⑦ *The* **Conversion Options** *are displayed in the Color Settings when the Advanced Mode is checked.*

Conversion Options

Engine: ✓ Adobe (ACE)
Apple ColorSync

Intent:

⑧ *The* **Engine menu** *lets you choose the system that is used to control color management.*

Conversion Options

Engine: Perceptual
Saturation

Intent: ✓ Relative Colorimetric
Absolute Colorimetric

☑ Use Black Point Compensation

⑨ *The* **Intent menu** *lets you choose how the final color display should look.*

Black and White Points?

A *white point* is the most extreme highlight in an image. This is the part of the image that should be totally white without any ink.

A *black point* is the most extreme black part of an image.

When you check Advanced Mode, you get additional options for managing color. The Conversion Options control how objects and color data are converted **⑦**.

To set the conversion options:

1. Choose one of the settings in the Engine menu **⑧**:
   - **Adobe (ACE)** uses the Adobe color management system and color engine. This is the default setting for most preset color configurations.
   - **Apple ColorSync (Mac)** uses the color management system provided for Mac OS computers.
   - **Microsoft ICM (Win)** uses the color management system provided for Windows computers.

   TIP Choose Adobe CMS engine if you are working with other Adobe products.

2. Choose one of the settings in the Intent menu **⑨**:
   - **Perceptual** preserves the relationships between colors in a way that is perceived as natural by the human eye.
   - **Saturation** is suitable for business graphics, where the exact relationship between colors is not as important as having vivid colors.
   - **Absolute Colorimetric** maintains color accuracy at the expense of preserving relationships between colors.
   - **Relative Colorimetric** is more accurate than absolute colorimetric if the image's profile contains correct white point information. This is the default rendering intent used by all predefined color management configurations.

3. Check Use Black Point Compensation to adjust for differences in black points.

   TIP Adobe strongly recommends you keep the Use Black Point Compensation option selected.

Choosing Color Settings

Working with Profiles

You can also set profiles and color management for individual imported images.

To control a placed image's color management:

1. If the graphic has already been placed into the layout, select it, and then choose **Object > Image Color Settings** to open the Image Color Settings dialog box 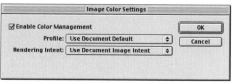.

   or

   If you're about to import the graphic, choose Color Settings on the left side of the Image Import Options dialog box. This opens the Color Settings for the Image Import Options 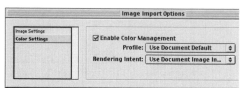.

2. Select Enable Color Management to apply color management to the image, or deselect it to exclude the image from color management.

3. Use the Profile menu to choose the source profile to apply to the graphic.

4. Use the Rendering Intent menu to choose a rendering intent.

⑩ *The* Image Color Settings dialog box *allows you to assign a specific profile and rendering intent to an imported image.*

⑪ *The* Color Settings in the Image Import Options dialog box *allows you to assign a specific profile and rendering intent to an image that is about to be imported.*

Working with Profiles

OUTPUT 17

Several years ago the title of this chapter would have been *Printing*. That was what you did with page-layout documents: You printed them using a desktop printer. Today, however, there are many more choices for publishing your InDesign documents.

These days, the notion of printing is too limited. InDesign files are created as part of the professional prepress process. (For more information on professional printing, see *The Non-Designer's Scan and Print Book* by Sandee Cohen and Robin Williams published by Peachpit Press.) You need to know more than just how to print to a desktop printer. You need to know how to make sure your document has been setup correctly. You need to know what files are necessary to send to a print shop.

So this chapter is called Output. Output refers to preparing documents and printing them—to either an ordinary desktop printer or with a high-end imagesetter.

Printing a Document

When a document is printed, there are many different instructions that are sent to the printer. You need to set all those instructions correctly.

TIP You may be used to setting certain options in the Page Setup (Mac) dialog box or the Printer Properties (Win) dialog box. Adobe recommends not using those controls with InDesign; instead only use the Print dialog box.

To print a document:

1. Choose **File > Print.** This opens the Print dialog box 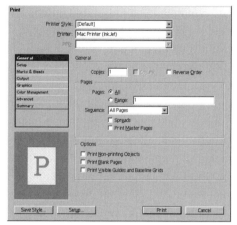❶.

2. If necessary, click each of the categories on the left side of the dialog box to set the following options ❷:
   - **General** sets the basic printing options *(see the next page).*
   - **Setup** controls the paper properties *(see page 308).*
   - **Marks & Bleeds** sets the print control marks and print area *(see page 311).*
   - **Output** controls colors and separations *(see page 312).*
   - **Graphics** sets how images are printed *(see page 314).*
   - **Color Management** controls how colors are handled. (Talk to your service bureau before setting color management controls.)
   - **Advanced** controls image replacement options and how transparency effects are printed *(see page 315).*
   - **Summary** lets you see a summary of all the print settings *(see page 319).*

TIP You do not need to set all the controls every time you print unless you need to change a specific setting.

3. Click the Print button to print the document according to the settings.

❶ *The* **Print dialog box** *contains all the settings for printing documents.*

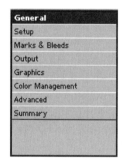

❷ *Click each of the categories to display the settings in the Print dialog box.*

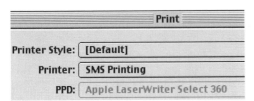

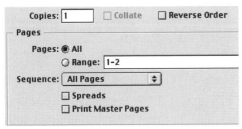

③ *The* **Printer list** *lets you choose the printer to print a document.*

④ *The* **Copies and Pages area** *of the General controls for printing.*

⑤ *The* **Options area** *of the General controls for printing.*

Setting the General Print Options

If you are printing to an desktop printer, the options in the General category may be all you need to set to print a document.

To choose the printer:

◆ Choose the printer from the Printer list at the top of the dialog box **③**.

To control the copies:

1. Set the number of copies in the Copies field **④**.

2. Choose Collate to print multiple copies as complete sets.

3. Choose Reverse Order to print the copies back to front.

TIP Use Reverse Order for printers that print documents face up.

To control the pages:

1. Choose All to print all the pages **④**.

 or

 Select Range to enter a range of pages.

TIP Use a hyphen to specify a range of pages, such as *4-6*. Use a comma to specify individual pages, such as *8, 9*.

2. Choose Collate to print copies as sets.

3. Use the Sequence menu to choose All Pages, Even Pages, or Odd Pages.

4. Check Spread to print the pages in spreads together.

5. Choose Print Master Pages to print any master pages in the document.

To set the general options:

1. Check Print Non-printing Objects to print objects set to not print **⑤**.

2. Check Print Blank Pages to print pages that have no visible items.

3. Check Print Visible Guides and Baseline Grids to print the guides and grids.

Setting the General Print Options

Choosing the Setup Controls

The Setup options contain the controls to set the paper size and orientation.

To set the paper size and orientation:

1. Use the Paper Size menu to choose the size of the paper to print the document on .

TIP This menu changes depending on the type of printer chosen.

2. Click one of the Orientation buttons. This changes the rotation of the document on the printed page.

To choose the setup options:

1. Set the Scale amount for either Height or Width to change the size of the printed document on the paper .

2. Click the Scale to Fit button to have the document automatically resized to fit the chosen paper size.

3. Use the Page Position menu to choose where to position the document on the printed page 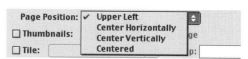.

4. Check Thumbnails to print small versions of the pages on a single page.

5. If you have chosen Thumbnails, use the Thumbnails menu to choose how many pages are printed on each page .

TIP See the next exercises for information on how to use the Tile controls.

6 *The* **Paper Size and Orientation controls** *in the Setup category of the Print dialog box.*

7 *The* **Options controls** *in the Setup category of the Print dialog box.*

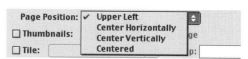

8 *The* **Page Position menu** *in the Setup category of the Print dialog box.*

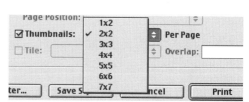

9 *The* **Thumbnails menu** *in the Setup category of the Print dialog box.*

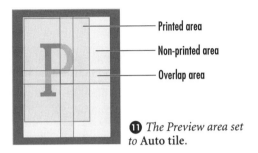

⑩ *The* **Tile menu** *in the Setup category of the Print dialog box.*

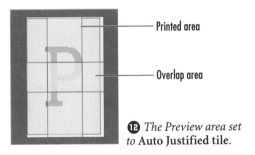

- Printed area
- Non-printed area
- Overlap area

⑪ *The Preview area set to* **Auto tile.**

- Printed area
- Overlap area

⑫ *The Preview area set to* **Auto Justified tile.**

Tiling Pages

If your document is larger than the paper in the printer, you can print portions of the document on different pages. You can then assemble the pages together. This is called *tiling*. Auto tiling automatically divides the page into smaller segments.

To set automatic tiling:

1. Check Tile in the Setup category of the Print dialog box.

2. Choose Auto from the Tiling menu **⑩**.

3. Set the amount in the Overlap field. This controls how much of one page is repeated on the tile for a second section of the page.

TIP The Preview area in the lower left portion of the Print dialog box shows how the page will be tiled **⑪**.

Auto justified tiling divides the pages so that the right edge of the document lies on the right side of a printed page and the bottom edge of the document lies on the bottom edge of a printed page **⑫**.

TIP The Auto setting ensures that there are no white spaces on the right side and bottom of the tiled pages.

To set auto justified tiling:

1. Check Tile in the Setup category of the Print dialog box.

2. Choose Auto Justified from the Tiling menu.

Tiling Pages

You can also tile pages manually. This lets you make sure that the edge of the paper does not cut across an important portion of the document.

To set manual tiling:

1. Use the zero-point crosshairs on the ruler to set the upper-left corner of the area you want to print ⓭. *(See Chapter 2, "Document Setup" for more information on setting the zero point of the ruler.)*

2. Choose File > Print.

3. Click the Setup category of the Print dialog box.

4. Choose Manual from the Tiling menu.

TIP The Preview area of the Print dialog box shows the area that will be printed ⓮.

5. Click Print to print that one page.

6. Reposition the zero-point crosshairs to set a new area to be printed.

7. Follow steps 2 through 5 to define and print the second tile.

8. Repeat the process until the entire page has been printed.

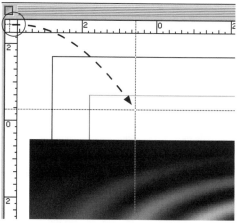

⓭ **Move the zero-point crosshairs** *to set the area to print as a tile on one page.*

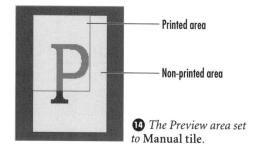

Printed area

Non-printed area

⓮ *The Preview area set to* **Manual tile.**

Why Do I Need To Bleed?

Why do you need to position objects so they bleed off the page layout *(see the opposite page)*? The reason is that the machines that trim books and pages don't always cut perfectly. Take a look at the thumbtabs on the sides of this book. If you flip from page to page you will see that the gray area isn't always the same size. That's because when the paper for the book is trimmed, some of the pages are cut slightly different from the others. (Yes, I know this will happen, even before the book is printed.)

So instead of trusting that the trim position is always perfect, I set a bleed by extending the gray area outside the edge of the page. That way I don't have to worry if the trim is slightly off. I know that the gray area will still be visible outside the trim.

Unless your print shop is trying to trim pages in the middle of an earthquake, you shouldn't need more than a quarter-inch bleed. However, if you are in doubt, ask your print shop for the size they would like for a bleed.

Tiling Pages

*The **Marks** settings in the Marks & Bleeds category of the Print dialog box.* **⑮**

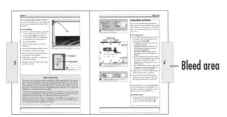

*The **page marks and information** as they appear on the printed page.* **⑯**

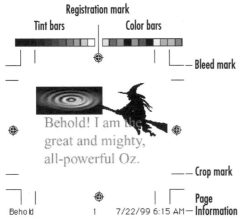

An example of creating an object that bleeds off a page. **⑰**

*The **Bleed controls** in the Marks & Bleeds category of the Print dialog box.* **⑱**

Setting Marks and Bleeds

You can also add information that shows where the page is trimmed, the document name, and so on. This information is sometimes called *printer's marks* or *page marks.*

To set the page marks:

1. Check All Printer's Marks to turn on all the marks or use the checkboxes to set each one individually **⑮ – ⑯**.
   - **Crop Marks** indicates where the page should be trimmed.
   - **Page Information** prints the name of the file, page number, and time the document was printed.
   - **Registration Marks** adds crosshair targets that are used to line up pieces of film.
   - **Color Bars** provides boxes that display the colors used in the document as well as the tint bars that can be used to calibrate the printing press for correct tints of colors.
   - **Bleed Marks** shows how far outside the crop marks you must put graphics so that they are trimmed correctly.
   - **Type** lets you pick a custom set of marks such as those used in Japanese printing.

2. Enter an amount in the Weight field for the thickness for the crop marks:

3. Enter an amount in the Offset field to determine how far away from the trim the page marks should be positioned:

You set a bleed to create an area that allows objects that extend off the page to print **⑰**. *(See the sidebar on the opposite page for why you need a bleed area.)*

To set the bleed area:

◆ Set an amount for each edge of the page in the Bleed area of the Marks & Bleed category of the Print dialog box **⑱**.

Setting the Output Controls

You may need to set the color controls to choose how color documents are printed.

To control how colors are printed:

1. Choose one of the following from the Color menu ⓲:
   - **Composite Gray** prints all the colors as a gray image. Use this when printing on one-color laser printers.
   - **Composite RGB** prints all the colors as an RGB image. Use this when printing on RGB ink jet printers.
   - **Composite CMYK** prints all the colors as a CMYK image. Use this when printing on CMYK printers.
   - **Separations** prints all the colors onto separate plates (pages).

   TIP Separations printed on a laser printer are commonly called *paper separations* and are used to make sure the proper number of plates will be printed by service bureau.

2. If you choose one of the composite settings, you can check Text as Black.

   TIP The Text as Black command is helpful if you have color text that you want to be more readable when printed on a one-color printer.

You can also change the screen frequency and angle of halftones in the image.

To change the screen settings:

◆ Use the Screening menu to set the frequency and angle for the halftone screens ⓲.

   or

   Select a color in the Inks area and then use Frequency and Angle fields ⓳.

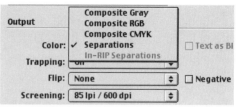

⓲ *The* **Color menu** *in the Output category of the Print dialog box.*

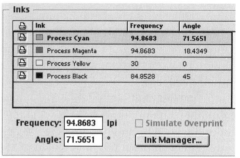

⓳ *The* **Frequency and Angle fields** *in the Output category of the Print dialog box.*

Setting Traps

Trapping *(see the next page)* is like buying a boat. If you have to ask the price of a boat, you can't afford it. If you have to ask what trapping is, you shouldn't do it.

If a service bureau asks you turn on trapping, they should give you information about how to set the traps.

Don't be afraid to ask for the information. You're not expected to know what values to enter, but you'll look pretty smart if you do ask.

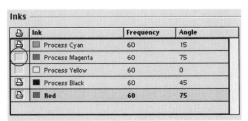

㉑ *Click the* **printer icon next to an ink color** *to prevent that ink from printing.*

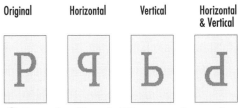

㉒ *Use the* **Flip menu** *to change how a document reads.*

Original	Horizontal	Vertical	Horizontal & Vertical

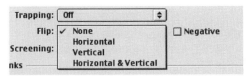

㉓ *Examples of how the* **Flip menu** *changes the readability of a document.*

㉔ *The* **Trapping menu** *lets you choose how the trapping is applied.*

You can also control the individual inks that are printed when you choose Separations.

TIP This makes it easy to see exactly which colors are printing in a document.

To set the inks to be printed:

◆ Click the small printer icon next to the name of each color **㉑**. If the icon is visible, the color will print. If the icon is not visible, the color will not print.

Ordinarily you want to read your document right side up and as a positive image. However, if you create film separations you may need to flip the image and create a negative version.

To flip the direction of a document:

◆ Choose one of the choices from the Flip menu in the Output category of the Print dialog box **㉒** – **㉓**.

To create a negative version of a document:

◆ Check the Negative box in the Output category of the Print dialog box.

Trapping refers to the various techniques that are used to compensate for the misregistration of printing plates. However, if you don't understand trapping, you must consult with the service bureau that will print your file before you set the trapping.

To turn on basic trapping:

◆ Choose Application Built-in from the Trapping menu **㉔**.

Setting the Graphics Options

The Graphics options control how much information is sent to the printer. You can control the data that is sent for placed images.

To control the data sent for images:

◆ Choose one of the following from the Image Send Data menu 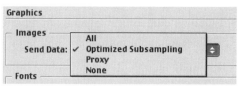:
- **All** sends all the information for the graphics. This is the slowest setting.
- **Optimized Subsampling** sends only the amount of information necessary for the chosen output device. Use this option if you proofing high resolution images on a desktop printer.
- **Proxy** sends only a 72 ppi version of the image.
- **None** replaces the image with crosshairs within the frame. Use this option when you want to proof only the text in the file.

You can also control how much of the font information is sent to the printer.

To control the font information sent for printing:

1. Choose one of the following from the Download menu 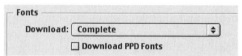:
- **None** sends no font information, only a reference to the font. Do not use this option unless you understand how to replace the reference in the PostScript stream.
- **Complete** sends the entire set of glyphs for the font. This is the longest option.
- **Subset** sends only those glyphs used in the document.
2. Choose Download PPD Fonts to send all fonts, even if they have been installed on the printer 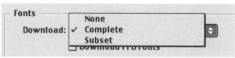. This option is helpful if use use a variation of the fonts installed on the printer.

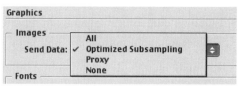
❷❺ *Use the* **Send Data menu** *in the Graphics category to control how images are printed.*

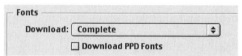
❷❻ *Use the* **Download menu** *in the Graphics category to control how much of a font is sent to the printer.*

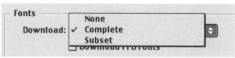
❷❼ *Choose* **Download PPD Fonts** *to send printer fonts as part of the print information.*

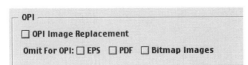

28 *Set the* **OPI Image Replacement options** *to control how images are handled during prepress.*

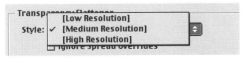

29 *Set the Gradients* **Force Continuous Tone Behavior** *to improve how gradients print.*

30 *Use the* **Style menu** *in the Transparency Flattener area to set the resolution for transparency effects that create rasterized images.*

Setting the Advanced Options

If you print to a desktop printer, you can most likely skip this section. If you print to a high-end imagesetter, you probably already understand everything here. OPI stands for Open Prepress Interface. The OPI controls are used when files are sent to Scitex and Kodak prepress systems.

To set the OPI controls:

1. In the OPI area, click the OPI Image Replacement checkbox **28**.

2. Choose which types of images should be replaced during an OPI workflow. (An OPI workflow uses low-resolution images for the layout and swaps them with high-resolution images just before printing.)

Certain imagesetters may not print gradients as smoothly as you like. If this happens, you may need to change the settings for printing gradients.

To set how gradients print:

♦ In the Gradients area, check Force Continuous Tone Behavior **29**.

When you use the transparency, drop shadow, and feather effects, you create rasterized images. The Transparency Flattener area controls the resolution of the rasterized images. *(See the next page for how to create your own transparency flattener styles.)*

To set the transparency flattener:

1. Use the Style menu to choose a resolution for the rasterized images **30**.

2. If you have used the Pages palette to flatten individual spreads, you can check Ignore Spread Overrides to override that setting.

Using Transparency Flattener Styles

The transparency flattener styles control how the transparency effects, drop shadows, and feathers are handled during output. The three default styles cannot be edited, but you can create your own flattener style.

To create a transparency flattener style:

1. Choose **Edit > Transparency Flattener Styles**. This opens the Transparency Flattener Styles dialog box **31**.

2. Click the New button. The Transparency Flattener Style dialog box appears **32**.

3. Use the Name field to name the style.

4. In the Options area, move the Raster/Vector Balance slider to create either vector or rasterized artwork **33**.

5. Set an output resolution for rasterized artwork in the Flattener Resolution field.

TIP 300 dpi is sufficient for most output.

6. Set an output resolution for gradient objects in the Gradient Resolution field.

TIP 150 dpi is sufficient for most output.

7. Check Force Text to Outlines to expand all text to outlines.

TIP If this is not checked only transparent portions of the text may be converted to outlines which may make that text thicker than other text. This option makes all the text width consistent.

8. If you have strokes that pass through different transparencies, you may want to choose Convert Strokes to Outlines to convert all strokes in the document to outlines.

9. Check Clip Complex Regions to ensure that any differences in raster and vector objects always fall along existing paths.

TIP This can result in complex clipping paths, which may not print on some devices.

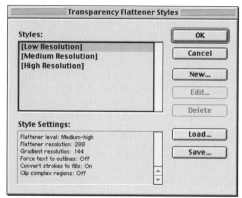

31 *The* **Transparency Flattener Styles dialog box** *lets you define new styles for printing transparency effects.*

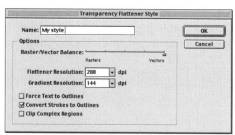

32 *The* **Transparency Flattener Style dialog box** *contains the settings for a custom transparency flattener style.*

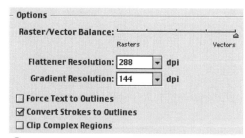

33 *The* **Options area** *in the Flattener Style dialog box.*

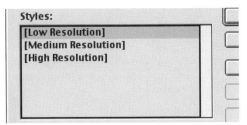

Styles:

[Low Resolution]
[Medium Resolution]
[High Resolution]

34 *The* **three default transparency flattener styles** *cannot be edited or deleted.*

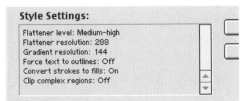

Style Settings:

Flattener level: Medium-high
Flattener resolution: 288
Gradient resolution: 144
Force text to outlines: Off
Convert strokes to fills: On
Clip complex regions: Off

35 *The* **Style Settings area** *displays a read out of the settings for a particular transparency flattener style.*

To edit a transparency flattener style:

1. Choose the style you want to edit.

TIP The three default styles, surrounded by brackets, cannot be edited **34**.

2. Click the Edit button.

3. Edit the style in the Transparency Flattener Style dialog box.

TIP The Style Settings area displays a read out of the settings for each style **35**.

To delete transparency flattener styles:

1. Choose the styles you want to edit.

TIP The three default styles, surrounded by brackets, cannot be deleted **34**.

TIP Use the Shift key to select multiple adjacent styles. Use the Cmd/Ctrl key to select multiple non-adjacent styles.

2. Click the Delete button.

You can also save transparency flattener styles to share among others. Once saved, the styles can then be loaded onto other machines.

To save a transparency flattener style:

1. Choose the styles you want to save.

TIP Use the Shift key to select multiple adjacent styles. Use the Cmd/Ctrl key to select multiple non-adjacent styles.

TIP The three default styles, surrounded by brackets, cannot be edited.

2. Click the Save button.

3. Name the file.

To load a transparency flattener style:

1. Click the Load button.

2. Navigate to find the file that contains the styles.

3. Click Open. The styles appear in the Transparency Flattener Styles dialog box.

Using Transparency Flattener Styles

Working with Print Styles

With all the areas in the Print dialog box, you wouldn't want to have to set all the controls each time you have a new document. InDesign lets you save the print settings to easily apply later.

36 *Use the* **Save Style dialog box** *to name your own printer style.*

To save a print style:

1. Set all the categories in the Print dialog box to the settings you want to save.

2. Click the Save Style button at the bottom of the Print dialog box. The Save Style dialog box appears **36**.

3. Enter a name for Style.

4. Click OK. This saves the style.

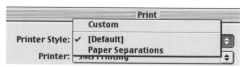

37 *Saved styles are listed in the* **Printer Style** menu.

To apply a print style:

1. Choose a saved style from the Printer Style menu **37**.

You don't need to go through the Print dialog box to create and save a print style.

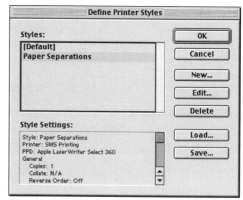

38 *Saved styles are listed in the* **Printer Style** menu.

To define a printer style:

1. Choose File > Printer Styles > Define. The Define Printer Styles dialog box appears **38**.

2. Click the New button to define a new style. This opens a version of the Print dialog box that lets you set the various print categories.

   or

   Click the Edit button to make changes to the selected print style.

To delete a printer style:

1. Select the styles you want to delete in the Define Printer Styles dialog box.

2. Click the Delete button.

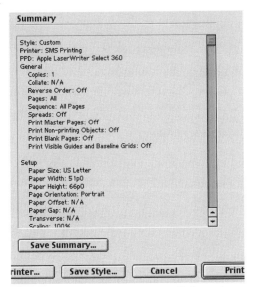

Summary

Style: Custom
Printer: SMS Printing
PPD: Apple LaserWriter Select 360
General
    Copies: 1
    Collate: N/A
    Reverse Order: Off
    Pages: All
    Sequence: All Pages
    Spreads: Off
    Print Master Pages: Off
    Print Non-printing Objects: Off
    Print Blank Pages: Off
    Print Visible Guides and Baseline Grids: Off

Setup
    Paper Size: US Letter
    Paper Width: 51p0
    Paper Height: 66p0
    Page Orientation: Portrait
    Paper Offset: N/A
    Paper Gap: N/A
    Transverse: N/A
    Scaling: 100%

[Save Summary...]

[rinter...] [Save Style...] [Cancel] [Print]

39 *Use the **Summary** area to see all the settings applied to printing a document.*

One of the benefits of working with printer styles is that you can export them so others can print documents with the same settings.

To export printer styles:

1. In the Define Printer Styles dialog box, select the styles you want to export.

TIP Use the Shift key to select adjacent multiple styles. Use the Cmd/Ctrl key to select non-adjacent multiple styles.

2. Click Export. A dialog box appears where you can name the document that contains the exported styles.

Your service bureau can provide you with printer styles that you can import to use for printing or packaging documents.

To import printer styles:

1. In the Define Printer Styles dialog box, click Import.

2. Use the dialog box to select the document that contains the styles exported from another machine.

3. Click OK. The styles appear in the Define Printer Styles dialog box.

Creating a Print Summary

With all the settings in the Print dialog box, you may want to keep track of how a document has been printed. The Summary area gives you a report of all the print settings.

To use the Summary area:

◆ Scroll through the summary area to read all the settings applied to a print job **39**.

or

Click the Save Summary button to save a text file listing all the print settings.

Creating a Print Summary

Creating PostScript Files

Instead of sending the InDesign document to a service bureau, you can create a PostScript file that contains all the information necessary to print the file. (This is sometimes called *printing to disk*.) A standard PostScript file contains all the information necessary to print the file as well as the specific information about the printer.

⓴ *Choose* **PostScript® File** *from the Printer menu to create a file that contains all the information necessary to print the document.*

To create a standard PostScript file:

1. Choose File > Print.
2. Choose PostScript® File from the Printer menu **⓴**.
3. Choose the type of printer that will print the file.
4. Set all the options in the print categories in the Print dialog box.

   TIP Check with the service bureau that will print your file for the correct options.

5. Choose a name and location for the file.

   TIP (Mac) Add the suffix *.ps* to the file name to indicate that it is a PostScript file.

6. Click Save.

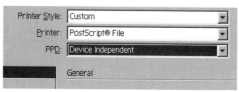

㉑ *Choose* **Device Independent** *from the PPD menu to create a PostScript file that can be printed to any printer.*

A device independent PostScript file does not contain any information about the type of printer or output device.

TIP This lets you create a PostScript file even if you don't know the type of printer that your document will be printed on.

To create a device independent PostScript file:

1. Choose File > Print.
2. Choose Device Independent from the PPD menu **㉑**.
3. Follow steps 3–6 in the previous exercise.

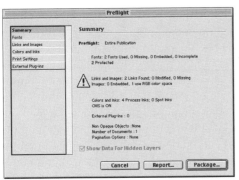

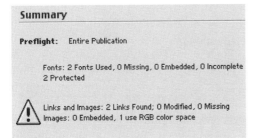

The Preflight dialog box lets you choose each of the categories for the various aspects of printing a document.

Summary

Preflight: Entire Publication

    Fonts: 2 Fonts Used, 0 Missing, 0 Embedded, 0 Incomplete
    2 Protected

    Links and Images: 2 Links Found; 0 Modified, 0 Missing
    Images: 0 Embedded, 1 use RGB color space

The Summary area of the Preflight dialog box gives you an overview of the categories checked during a preflight.

The preflight categories let you see the details of the preflight report.

Creating a Preflight Report

When you create an InDesign document, you have two jobs: designer and production manager. As the production manager, you need to know if there could be any problems printing your job. Fortunately, InDesign has a built-in preflight utility that checks all the elements in your document to make sure they print correctly. (The name comes from the list that airline pilots complete before they take off.)

To run the preflight utility:

1. Choose **File > Preflight**. InDesign takes a moment to check all the elements of the document and then opens the Preflight dialog box.

2. Review the information in the Preflight Summary ⓰.

   TIP Any potential printing problems are flagged with an alert symbol in the Preflight Summary ⓱.

3. Click each of the categories in the Preflight dialog box ⓲. *(See the following exercises for details on these categories.)*

4. Click the Report button to create a report of the preflight status.

   or

   Click the Package button to copy all the files necessary to print the document.

   TIP The Package button is the same as the Package command located on the File menu. *(See page 324 for more information packaging a document.)*

   TIP You can open the preflight report in a text editor.

Your Service Bureau may ask you to use only Type 1 fonts. The Fonts area lets you make sure that your have used the correct fonts and that they are correctly installed.

To review the Fonts information:

1. Choose Fonts from the categories on the left of the Preflight dialog box. This opens the Fonts area, which shows the type of font and whether it is installed in the system ⑮.

2. If you want to replace a non-standard or missing font, click the Find Font button. This opens the Find Font dialog box that lets you replace fonts *(see page 285)*.

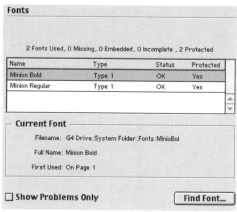

⑮ *The* **Fonts area of the Preflight dialog box** *shows you the status of the fonts used in a document.*

You also want to make sure that no placed graphics are of the wrong type or are missing or modified.

To review the Links information:

1. Choose Links and Images from the categories on the left of the Preflight dialog box. This opens the Links area, which shows the placed images ⑯.

2. Choose the modified or missing image.

3. If the image is modified, click the Update button.

    or

    If the image is missing, click the Relink button. This opens the Find dialog box.

4. Navigate to choose the missing image.

5. Click the Repair All button to have InDesign update all modified images or open the dialog box for all missing images.

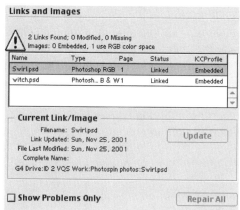

⑯ *The* **Links and Images area** *of the Preflight dialog box shows you the status of the placed images in the document.*

Colors and Inks

4 Process Inks; 0 Spot Inks
CMS is ON

Name And Type	Angle	Lines/Inch
Process Cyan	71.565	94.868
Process Magenta	18.434	94.868
Process Yellow	0.000	30.000
Process Black	45.000	84.852

47 *The* **Colors and Inks area** *of the Preflight dialog box shows the process and spot color plates in the document.*

Print Settings

Print Settings
PPD: Apple LaserWriter Select 360, (SMS Printing)
Printing To: Printer
Number of Copies: 1
Reader Spreads: No
Even/Odd Pages: Both
Pages: All
Proof: No
Tiling: None
Scale: 100%, 100%
Page Position: Upper Left
Printer's Marks: None
Bleed: 0 in, 0 in, 0 in, 0 in
Color: Composite CMYK
Trapping Mode: None
Send Image Data: Optimized Subsampling

48 *The* **Print Settings area** *of the Preflight dialog box shows you the current print settings applied to the document.*

External Plug-ins

External Plug-ins

49 *The* **External Plug-ins area** *of the Preflight dialog box shows any third party plug-ins that have been installed. (Sadly, I don't own any.)*

You should also check the colors and inks to make sure that the right number of colors print.

To review the Colors and Inks information:

◆ Choose Colors and Inks from the categories on the left of the Preflight dialog box. This shows the colors used within the document **47**.

You can also look at the Print Settings for a complete list of all the print settings currently applied to the docuemnt.

To review the Print Settings information:

◆ Choose Print Settings from the categories on the left of the Preflight dialog box. This shows the print settings applied to the document **48**.

You can also look to see if there are any external plug-ins that were used in creating the document. You may need to alert your print shop that these plug-ins are necessary for outputting the document.

TIP You don't need to worry about the plug-ins unless you have installed any special third-party plug-ins.

To review the external plug-ins information:

◆ Choose External Plug-ins from the categories on the left of the Preflight dialog box. This shows any third party plug-ins that have been installed **49**.

Creating a Preflight Report

Packaging a Document

A package is a folder that contains everything necessary to print a document. Instead of manually collecting all the files, the Package command assembles the files for you.

To package files for printing:

1. Choose File > Package. InDesign looks through the document and then opens the Printing Instructions dialog box ⑤⓪.

2. Fill out the contact and file information.

TIP The information in the Printing Instructions dialog box is kept if you repackage the document later.

3. Click Continue. This opens the Create Package Folder dialog box ⑤①.

4. Enter a name for the folder that will hold the files.

5. Check the following options for the package:
   - **Copy Fonts (roman only)** copies the fonts used in the document. *(See the sidebar on the next page for a discussion of copying fonts.)*
   - **Copy Linked Graphics** copies placed images that are not embedded in the file.
   - **Update Graphic Links in Package** automatically updates any modified graphics.
   - **Use Document Hyphenation Exceptions Only** limits the hyphenation exceptions to only those added to the document.
   - **Include Fonts and Links from Hidden Layers** adds the fonts and graphics from layers that are not visible.
   - **View Report** launches a text editor to open the report created with the document.

6. Click Package to assemble all the necessary files in the folder.

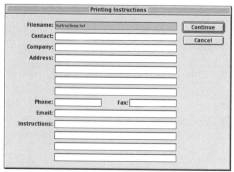

⑤⓪ *The* **Printing Instructions** *dialog box lets you create a text file with contact information and instructions about the document package.*

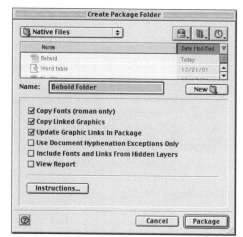

⑤① *The* **Create Package Folder** *dialog box lets you choose which items should be included in the package folder.*

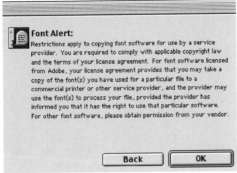

Font Alert:
Restrictions apply to copying font software for use by a service provider. You are required to comply with applicable copyright law and the terms of your license agreement. For font software licensed from Adobe, your license agreement provides that you may take a copy of the font(s) you have used for a particular file to a commercial printer or other service provider, and the provider may use the font(s) to process your file, provided the provider has informed you that it has the right to use that particular software. For other font software, please obtain permission from your vendor.

Back   OK

52 *The* **Font Alert** *is a gentle reminder that both you and the service bureau need to own a copy of a font before you can copy and send it with a file.*

Copying Fonts: Legal or Not?

If you choose to send fonts, a warning notice appears about the legalities of copying fonts **52**. You may have heard stories of people carted off to prison for illegally copying software. While there have been people arrested for software piracy, the rules about fonts are more intricate.

Ssome font companies, such as Adobe, allow you to send a copy of the font along with your document provided that the service bureau that is going to print your file also has its own copy of the font. Other companies let you send the font along with your file, but the font can only be used to print *your* documents. You must check the license that came with the font.

So why would a service bureau want a copy of your font if it already has a copy? They want to make sure they uses exactly the same font as the one you used to create the document.

This is why most survice bureaus spend thousands of dollars to buy complete font libraries. If the bureau doesn't have a copy of the font, you should not send the font along with the file. Either the service bureau buys the font or you should create a prepress package.

Of course, if you use a program such as FontLab to make your own fonts, you have total permission to copy the fonts and give them to anyone you want. For instance, the tip bullet in this book is a font I created—I have no problem getting permission to copy that font.

However, the figure numbers are a specialized font I bought. I will have to buy another license to send that font to my service bureau.

Packaging a Document

EXPORTING 18

Printing your document on paper is only one way in which your InDesign files can be published. Today there are many more options for publishing documents.

For instance, you might want clients to read your document electronically—even if they don't have the InDesign application. Or you might want to take a design that you created with InDesign and use it as the graphic in another page-layout program. Or you may want to turn your InDesign document into Web pages.

When you convert InDesign documents into other formats, you use the export features of the program. Using export lets you change InDesign documents into other types of publications such as portable document format (PDF) files or Web hypertext markup language (HTML) pages.

Setting the Export File Options

InDesign gives you many export options. In each case you choose a file format, name the file, and save it to a location.

To choose a file format:

1. Choose **File** > **Export**. The Export dialog box appears **❶**.

TIP You will not see the options for exporting text unless your insertion point is inside a text frame.

2. Give the file a name and set the location.

3. Choose one of the following from the Save as File Type (Win) or Formats (Mac) menu:

 - **Adobe InDesign Tagged Text** creates a text file formatted with codes. *(See page 283 for working with tagged text.)*
 - **Adobe PDF** creates an Acrobat file. *(See the next page to set the PDF options.)*
 - **EPS** creates an encapsulated PostScript file that can be placed as a graphic. *(See page 338 to set the EPS options.)*
 - **HTML** creates text and graphics that can be viewed on the World Wide Web. *(See page 341 to set the HTML options.)*
 - **Rich Text Format** exports selected text with formatting that can be read by most word processing applications.
 - **SVG** and **SVG Compressed** create scalable vector graphics that can be viewed on the World Wide Web. *(See page 347 for how to set the SVG options.)*
 - **Text** exports selected text without any formatting *(See page 349.)*
 - **XML** creates text formatted with the extensible markup language that offers customizable definitions and tags. *(Working with XML is beyond the scope of this book. I recommend "Real World InDesign 2" by David Blatner and Olav Martin Kvern for more information on working with XML.)*

4. Click Save. This opens the options dialog box for each format.

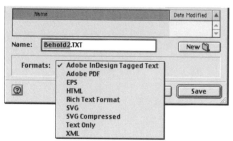

❶ *The* **options** *for exporting* InDesign *documents.*

Other Uses for Exported Files

The Export command could be one of the most useful features in InDesign.

For instance, let's say you have a document that you want to feature as an illustration in a Microsoft Word file. You can use the EPS Export command to convert the file into an EPS file. Then use Word's Insert > Picture from File command to bring the EPS into the Word document.

You can even be a little more creative with how you use the Export command. For instance, let's say you want all the TIFF images in an InDesign document to be converted to GIF files. Insteady of opening Photoshop to convert the TIFF images, run the HTML export and you will get a graphics folder of GIF images.

I think of the Export commands as translation devices for InDesign.

Setting the Export File Options

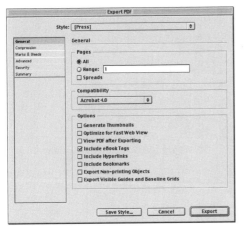

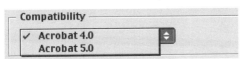

*The **Export PDF dialog box** is the command center for creating PDF files.*

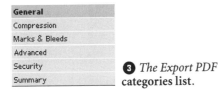

The Export PDF **categories list.**

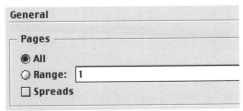

*The **Pages** options in the General category of the Export PDF dialog box.*

*The **Compatibility menu** in the General category of the Export PDF dialog box.*

Creating PDF Files

You can convert your InDesign documents into PDF files so that others can read the files—even if they do not have the InDesign application.

To set the general PDF Options:

1. Choose Adobe PDF from the Save as File Type (Win) or Formats (Mac) menu. The Export PDF dialog box appears **②**.

2. Click General from the categories on the left of the Export PDF dialog box **③**.

TIP InDesign ships with four PDF styles that you can use for most exports *(see page 336 for information on using PDF styles).*

To set the pages for a PDF:

1. In the Pages area, select All to export all the pages in the document **④**.

   or

   Select Range to enter specific pages.

TIP Use the hyphen to select a range of pages such as *4-9*, or use commas to enter individual pages such as *3, 8*.

2. Check Spreads to keep pages that are within spreads together in the Acrobat file.

You need to choose which version of Acrobat can open your PDF document.

To set the PDF version:

◆ Use the Compatibility menu to choose one of the following **⑤**:

  • Adobe Acrobat 4.0 files can be opened by more people.

  • Adobe Acrobat 5.0 preserves transparency, text, and spot colors, if the PDF is placed into another page layout program.

To set the general options:

◆ Choose one of the following from the Options area in the General category ⑥:

- **Generate Thumbnails** creates a thumbnail image for each page being exported.
- **Optimize for Fast Web View** restructures the file to prepare for downloading from Web servers.
- **View PDF after Exporting** opens the finished Adobe PDF file in Acrobat.
- **Include eBook Tags** tags elements in the story using the Acrobat 5.0 tags that InDesign supports.
- **Include Hyperlinks** creates Acrobat hyperlinks for InDesign hyperlinks, table of contents entries, and index entries.
- **Include Bookmarks** creates bookmarks for table of contents entries, preserving the TOC levels.
- **Export Non-printing Objects** exports objects which have the Nonprinting option applied.
- **Export Visible Guides and Baseline Grids** exports the guides and grids currently visible in the document.

To open the compression controls:

1. Click Compression from the categories on the left of the Export PDF dialog box. The Compression controls appear ⑦.

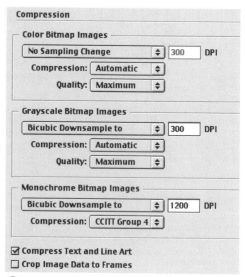

⑥ *The* Options *controls in the General category of the Export PDF dialog box.*

⑦ *The* compression controls *in the Export PDF dialog box.*

Talk to your Service Bureau

If you create PDF files for onscreen viewing or to be downloaded from the Web, you can use the compression settings to reduce the file size.

However, if you create PDF files to be output by a service bureau for print work, you should not apply too much downsampling or compression.

Ask your service bureau for the correct settings. Better yet, ask them to create a PDF style that you can load onto your machine (*see page 336*).

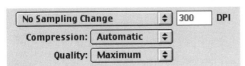

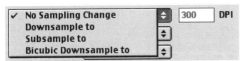

The compression controls for color and grayscale bitmap images.

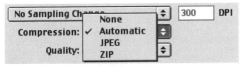

The Sampling menu for color and grayscale bitmap images.

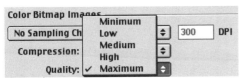

The Compression menu for color and grayscale bitmap images.

The Quality menu for color and grayscale bitmap images.

One of the benefits of creating PDF files is that they can be compressed to take up less space.

To set the color and grayscale downsampling:

1. Choose one of the following from the Sampling menu:
   - **No Sampling Change** does not throw away any pixel information. Use this setting if you want to maintain all the information in the image.
   - **Downsampling** averages the pixels in a sample area.
   - **Subsampling** significantly reduces processing time compared with downsampling, but results in images that are less smooth.
   - **Bicubic downsampling** is the slowest but most precise method, resulting in the smoothest tonal gradations.
2. When you have set a downsampling method, enter an amount in the resolution field.

TIP For print work this is usually 1.5 times the line screen of the printing press.

TIP For onscreen viewing this is usually 72 DPI.

To set the color and grayscale compression:

1. Choose one of the following from the Compression menu:
   - **None** applies no compression to the image.
   - **Automatic** lets InDesign judge whether or not JPEG or ZIP compression should be applied.
   - **JPEG** applies a compression that is best for images with tonal changes.
   - **ZIP** applies a compression that is best for images with large areas of flat color.
2. Choose a setting from the Quality menu: Maximum sets the least amount of compression. Minimum sets the most.

TIP Use Maximum for high-end output.

The compression options for monochrome bitmap images (such as 1-bit scanned art) are slightly different from those for color and grayscale images .

To set the monochrome bitmap options:

1. Choose one of the following from the Sampling menu 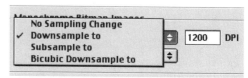:

   - **No Sampling Change** does not throw away any pixel information. Use this setting if you want to maintain all the information in the image.
   - **Downsampling** averages the pixels in a sample area.
   - **Subsampling** is faster than downsampling, but creates images that are less smooth.
   - **Bicubic downsample** is the slowest but most precise method, resulting in the smoothest tonal gradations.

2. When you have set a downsampling method, enter an amount in the resolution field.

   TIP For print work this is usually the resolution of the output device with a limit of 1500 DPI.

3. Choose one of the following from the Compression menu 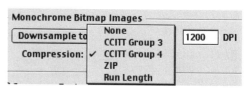:

   - **None** applies no compression to the image.
   - **CCITT Group 3** is similar to the compression used for faxes.
   - **CCITT Group 4** is a general-purpose method that produces good results for most monochromatic images.
   - **ZIP** works well for black-and-white images that contain repeating patterns.
   - **Run Length** produces the best results for images that contain large areas of solid black or white

To set the rest of the compression options:

1. Check Compress Text and Line Art to further reduce the size of the file .

2. Check Crop Image Data to Frames to delete the image outside the frame .

*The compression controls for **monochrome bitmap** images.*

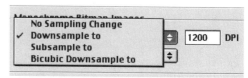

*The **Sampling** menu for monochrome bitmap images.*

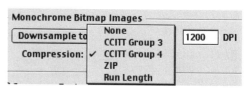

*The **Compression** menu for monochrome bitmap images.*

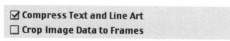

*The compression controls for **text and line art** and the parts of **images** outside of frames.*

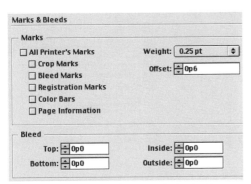

⑯ *The* **Marks & Bleeds controls** *in the Export PDF dialog box.*

The Marks & Bleeds category allows you to add printer's marks to documents and to set the bleed area.

To open the marks and bleeds controls:

◆ Click Marks & Bleeds from the categories on the left of the Export PDF dialog box. The Mark & Bleeds controls appear **⑯**.

TIP These are the same as the marks and bleeds controls available in the Print dialog box. *(See page 311 for details on how to set the Marks & Bleeds controls.)*

The Advanced category contains the controls for handling colors, fonts, and setting the transparency flattener options.

To open the advanced controls:

◆ Click Advanced from the categories on the left of the Export PDF dialog box. The Advanced controls appear **⑰**.

TIP The OPI controls are the same as the ones in the Print dialog box. *(See page 315 for details on how to set the OPI controls.)*

TIP The Transparency Flattener controls are the same as the ones in the Print dialog box. *(See page 316 for details on how to set the Transparency Flattener controls.)*

⑰ *The* **Advanced controls** *in the Export PDF dialog box.*

Creating PDF Files

To set the color controls:

1. Choose one of the following from the Color menu 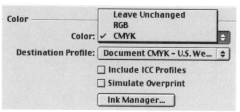:
   - **Leave Unchanged** does not convert the colors in the document.
   - **RGB** converts all colors to RGB which is best for onscreen viewing.
   - **CMYK** converts all colors to CMYK which is appropriate for process color separations.

2. Choose a profile for the type of output device from the Destination Profile.

3. Check Include ICC Profiles to keep embedded profiles with the document.

4. Check Simulate Overprint to show onscreen a representation of how overprinting will look when printed.

 The **Color controls** *in the Advanced area of the Export PDF dialog box.*

 *The* **Subset Fonts Below field** *in the Advanced area of the Export PDF dialog box.*

The Advanced PDF Options let you embed fonts within your document and control how the color and resolution of the file are handled.

To control how much of a font is embedded:

♦ Enter an amount in the Subset Fonts field for the threshold amount . That threshold determines how many characters of the font will be embedded.

TIP If the threshold is 35%, InDesign embeds only the characters used in the document to a maximum of 35% of the characters. If you use more than 35% of the characters, then InDesign embeds all the characters in the font.

TIP The default setting of 100% means that only a subset of the font will be embedded unless you have used all the characters in the font.

(sidebar) **Creating PDF Files**

Security

Passwords

☑ Password Required to Open Document

User Password: [   ]

☑ Password Required to Change Permissions and Passwords

Master Password: [   ]

Permissions

Encryption Level: 40-bit RC4

☐ No Printing
☐ No Changing the Document
☐ No Content Copying or Extraction, Disable Accessibility
☐ No Adding or Changing Comments and Form Fields

㉟ *The* **Security area** *of the Export PDF dialog box.*

Summary

General
  Pages: All
  Spreads: Off
  Compatibility: Acrobat 4.0
  Generate Thumbnails: Off
  Optimize PDF: Off
  View PDF after Exporting: Off
  Include eBook Tags: On
  Include Hyperlinks: Off
  Include Bookmarks: Off
  Export Nonprinting Objects: Off
  Export Visible Guides and Baseline Grids: Off

Compression
  Color Bitmap Images
    No Sampling Change
    Compression: Automatic
    Quality: Maximum

  Grayscale Bitmap Images
    Bicubic Downsample at: 300 DPI
    Compression: Automatic
    Quality: Maximum

  Monochrome Bitmap Images
    Bicubic Downsample at: 1200 DPI
    Compression: CCITT Group 4

[Save Summary...]

㉡ *The* **Summary area** *of the Export PDF dialog box.*

You can also set security options for PDF files to restrict who can open the file or to limit what they can do to it.

To set the Security options:

1. Choose Security from the categories area of the Export PDF dialog box **㉟**.

2. Check Password Required to Open Document if you want to require the user to enter a password before the document can be opened.

3. Type a password for step 2 in the User Password field.

4. Check Password Required to Change Permissions and Passwords to limit who can change the passwords and security options once the PDF is open.

5. Type a password for step 4 in the Master Password field.

6. Check the actions you do not want:
   - **No Printing** disables the Print command.
   - **No Changing the Document** keeps anyone from changing text.
   - **No Content Copying or Extraction, Disable Accessibility** prevents anyone from copying or exporting the text or images for use elsewhere.
   - **No Adding or Changing Comments and Form Fields** keeps anyone from adding or modifying annotations.

You can also get a summary of the settings.

To read the summary of the PDF settings:

1. Choose Summary from the categories area of the Export PDF dialog box **㉡**.

2. Scroll through the list to read the summary.

3. Click the Save Summary button to create a text file that contains a list of all the settings.

Creating PDF Files

Working with PDF Styles

Just as you can create printer styles for printing documents *(see pages 318–319)*, you can also create PDF styles that contain settings for different PDF documents.

To save the current PDF settings as a PDF style:

1. Set the options in the Export PDF dialog box.
2. Click the Save Style button ㉒. This opens the Save Style dialog box ㉓.
3. Enter a name for the style and click OK. The new style appears at the top of the Export PDF dialog box.

Once you have saved a style, you can easily apply it.

To apply a PDF style:

♦ Choose a saved style from the Style menu at the top of the Export PDF dialog box ㉔.

You can also define PDF styles without going through the Export PDF dialog box.

To create a PDF style:

1. Choose File > PDF Styles to open the PDF Styles dialog box ㉕.
2. Click New. This opens the New PDF Style dialog box.
3. Name the style.
4. Choose each of the categories and set them as described earlier in this section.

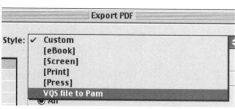

㉒ *Click the* Save Style button *to create a style based on the current settings in the Export PDF dialog box.*

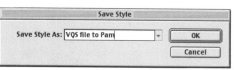

㉓ *Enter a name for a PDF style in the* Save Style dialog box.

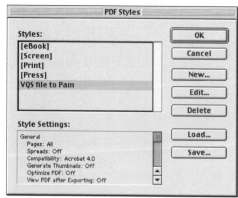

㉔ *Choose a style to apply to a PDF from the* Style menu *in the Export PDF dialog box.*

㉕ *The* PDF Styles dialog box *lets you manage custom PDF styles.*

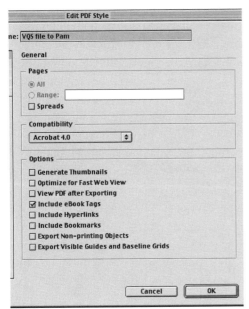

⑳ *The* **Edit PDF dialog box** *lets you create a PDF style without exporting the file.*

To edit a PDF style:

1. Select the style you want to edit in the PDF Styles dialog box.

2. Click the Edit button. This opens the Edit PDF Style dialog box ⑳.

TIP There is no difference between the New PDF dialog box and the Edit PDF dialog box except the name in the title bar.

3. Choose each of the categories and make changes as described earlier in this section.

To delete a PDF style:

1. Select the style you want to delete in the PDF Styles dialog box ㉕.

TIP Use the Shift key to select multiple adjacent styles.

TIP Use the Cmd/Ctrl key to select multiple non-adjacent styles.

2. Click the Delete button.

3. Click OK to confirm your choice.

To export PDF styles:

1. In the PDF Styles dialog box, select the styles you want to export ㉕.

TIP Use the Shift key to select multiple adjacent styles.

TIP Use the Cmd/Ctrl key to select multiple non-adjacent styles.

2. Click the Save button. This creates a new document that contains the exported styles.

To import PDF styles:

1. Click the Load button in the PDF Styles dialog box ㉕.

2. Use the dialog box to select the document that contains the styles exported from another machine.

3. Click OK. The styles appear in the PDF Styles dialog box.

Working with PDF Styles

Creating EPS Files

You might create a special shape or design in InDesign that you would like to use in another layout program. Export the file as an EPS, or *Encapsulated PostScript*, file so that you can use it in other applications.

TIP Most of today's layout programs import PDF files. Use the EPS format for older programs than can't import PDF files.

To create an EPS file:

1. Choose EPS from the Save as File Type (Win) or Formats (Mac) menu.

2. Click Save. This opens the Export EPS dialog box **㉗**.

3. Click the General tab to display the pages, bleed, and general controls.

    or

    Click the Advanced tab to display the production controls **㉘**. *(See pages 315–317 for information on setting the production controls.)*

To set the EPS pages options:

1. In the General area, choose All Pages to export all the pages in the document as EPS files **㉙**.

TIP Each page is exported as its own EPS file.

    or

    Choose Ranges and enter the numbers of the pages you want to export.

TIP Use hyphens to export a range of pages such as *4-9*.

TIP Use commas to export individual pages such as *3, 8*.

2. Check Spreads to export spreads as a single EPS file.

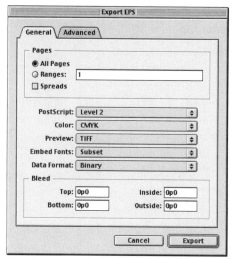

㉗ *The* **Export EPS dialog box** *lets you create an EPS file that can be placed in other programs.*

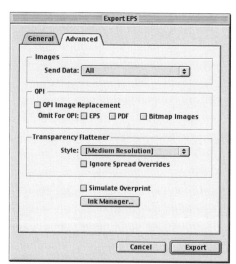

㉘ *The* **Advanced section** *in the Export EPS dialog box contains production controls for creating an EPS file.*

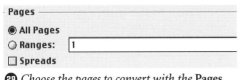

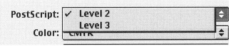

㉙ *Choose the pages to convert with the* **Pages controls** *in the Export EPS dialog box.*

㉚ *Use the* **PostScript menu** *in the Export EPS dialog box to set the type of printing instructions.*

㉛ *Use the* **Color menu** *in the Export EPS dialog box to control the colors in the file.*

Color: CMYK
None
Preview: ✓ TIFF
PICT
Embed Fonts: subset

㉜ *Use the* **Preview menu** *in the Export EPS dialog box to give a preview to the image.*

The PostScript level sets how complex the instructions are that are sent to the printer.

To set the EPS PostScript level:

◆ In the General area, use the PostScript menu to choose the following ㉚:

- **Level 2** is used with older printers.
- **Level 3** is used with newer printers. Use Level 3 only if you know the printer can handle Level 3 PostScript.

You can control the color space in the file.

To set the EPS colors:

◆ In the General area, use the Color menu to choose one of the following options ㉛:

- **CMYK** forces the colors to CMYK. Use this setting for process separations.
- **Gray** converts the colors to their grayscale values. Use this to limit the colors to a black plate.
- **RGB** converts the colors to RGB color space. Use this for onscreen presentation programs.
- **Device Independent** lets the destination printer use color management to control the color in the EPS.

Not all programs can create a preview directly from a placed EPS file. For those that can't, you need to set a preview.

To set the EPS preview:

◆ In the General area, use the Preview menu to choose one of the following options ㉜:

- **None** adds no preview to the file.
- **TIFF** creates a preview that is visible on both the Mac and Windows platforms.
- **PICT** creates a preview that is visible on the Mac only.

Creating EPS Files

Just as you can embed fonts in a PDF file, you can also embed fonts in an EPS file.

To set embed fonts in the EPS file:

◆ In the General area, use the Embed Fonts menu to choose one of the following options 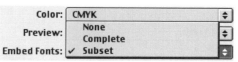:

- **None** does not embed any fonts in the file.
- **Complete** includes all the characters in the fonts.
- **Subset** includes only the characters you have used in the file.

㉝ *Use the* **Embed Fonts menu** *in the Export EPS dialog box to control how many characters in a font are added to the EPS file.*

EPS files need to be formatted with a specific type of data.

To set the data format of the EPS file:

◆ In the General area, use the Data Format menu to choose one of the following options 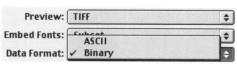:

- **Binary** is acceptable for most instances.
- **ASCII** is used for a PC network that requires ASCII data.

TIP Choose Binary. If you have trouble printing, then switch to ASCII.

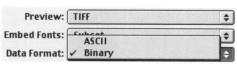

㉞ *Use the* **Data Format menu** *in the Export EPS dialog box to specify the formatting language of the EPS file.*

㉟ *Set the size of the bleed in the* **Bleed fields** *in the Export EPS dialog box.*

Just as you can add a bleed area when printing a document, you can add a bleed to an EPS file. *(See page 311 for additional discussion on creating a bleed.)*

To set the size of a bleed:

◆ In the General area, set each of the bleed fields to create a bleed area **㉟**.

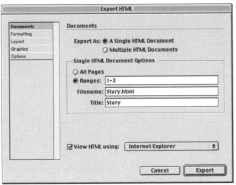

36 *The* **Export HTML dialog box** *lets you convert InDesign documents into Web pages.*

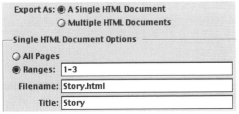

37 *The Export HTML* **categories** list.

38 *The settings to export pages as a* **single** HTML document.

39 *The* **title of a document** *is displayed in the title bar of a browser window.*

Creating Web Files

You may want to use your documents as Web pages. A Web page is a text file with codes from a language called HTML *(hypertext markup language)*.

TIP For intricate Web sites, use a real HTML editor such as Adobe GoLive.

To set the document HTML Options:

1. Choose HTML from the Save as File Type (Win) or Formats (Mac) menu: The Export HTML dialog box appears **36**.

2. Click Documents from the categories on the left of the Export HTML dialog box **37**.

You can export multiple pages as a single HTML page or as multiple HTML pages.

To create a single HTML page:

1. Choose A Single HTML Document from the Export As area. The Single HTML Document Options appear **38**.

2. Choose All Pages to export all the pages.

   or

   Choose Ranges and enter the page numbers you want to export.

   TIP Use a hyphen to export a range of pages such as *4-9* or a comma to export individual pages such as *3, 8*.

3. Enter the name of the exported HTML file in the Filename field.

4. Enter the name for the document in the Title field **39**. This is the name that appears at the top of the browser window when the page is viewed on the Web.

   TIP If you export multiple pages as a single HTML document, a horizontal line is inserted between the pages in the Web browser.

To create multiple HTML pages:

1. Choose Multiple HTML Documents from the Export As area. The Multiple HTML Documents Options appear ❹.

2. Check the pages that you want to export.

3. Select each page and enter the filename.

4. Select each page and enter the name of the exported HTML file in the Filename field.

5. Select each page and enter a title for each page in the Title field. This is the name that appears at the top of the browser window ❸.

You can set InDesign to automatically open the exported HTML file in a Web browser.

To set the browser for the HTML pages:

1. Check View HTML Using. This makes the menu available ❹.

2. Choose a Web browser from the menu ❹.

   or

   Choose Other to navigate to find additional browser.

TIP The browsers listed are gathered from those installed on your machine when InDesign was first installed. If you install a new browser later, you will have to manually add it to the menu.

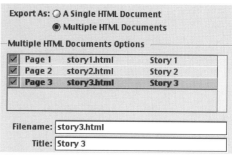

❹ *The settings to export pages as* multiple HTML documents.

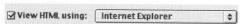

❹ *Check* **View HTML using** *to view the exported HTML pages in a Web browser.*

❹ *Use the* **View HTML using menu** *to choose a Web browser.*

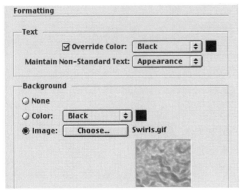

43 *The* **Formatting category** *in the Export HTML dialog box.*

44 *Use the* **Text formatting options** *to control how text is converted HTML.*

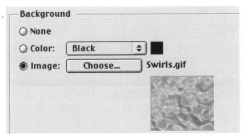

45 *Use the* **Background formatting options** *to change the background color or create a background image.*

46 **A background image** *is repeated behind the page.*

Web pages have different formats than print layouts. For instance, you may want to change the text color so that it is easier to read onscreen. You may also want to set a specific background color or image.

To set the formatting HTML Options:

1. Choose HTML from the Save as File Type (Win) or Formats (Mac) menu. The Export HTML dialog box appears.

2. Click Formatting from the categories on the left of the Export HTML dialog box. This displays the Formatting categories **43**.

To set the text formatting options:

1. Check Override Color to change the color of the text to another color and then choose a text color from the menu **44**.

2. If you have text with special effects or text that is rotated, choose one of the following from the Maintain Non-Standard Text menu:
   - **Appearance** converts the text to a GIF image which preserves the look of the text.
   - **Editability** keeps the text as editable text, but removes all formatting.

To set the background formatting options:

- Choose the Background options as follows **45**:
   - **None** leaves the background as set in the InDesign layout.
   - **Color** allows you to set a color for the background of all the pages.
   - **Image** allows you to choose a GIF or JPEG image that will be repeated as a pattern on all the Web pages **46**.

Creating Web Files

When you convert a print document to HTML, you can choose how the layout of the page is converted.

To set the layout HTML options:

1. Choose HTML from the Save as File Type (Win) or Formats (Mac) menu. The Export HTML dialog box appears.

2. Click Layout from the categories on the left of the Export HTML dialog box. This opens the Layout options **47**.

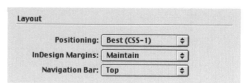

47 *The* **Layout category** *in the Export HTML dialog box.*

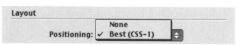

48 *Use the* **Positioning menu** *to arrange how the elements are positioned.*

Positioning controls where the HTML elements are placed on the page.

To set the positioning options:

♦ Choose one of the following from the Positioning menu **48**:

- **None** assembles the pages with text and graphics in separate paragraphs. This may cause elements to shift their position drastically **49**.

- **Best (CSS-1)** uses cascading style sheets to create the closest version of the layout **49**.

TIP CSS-1 requires Netscape or Microsoft browser versions 4.0.

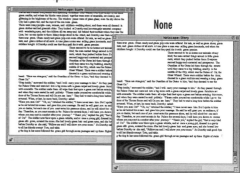

49 *The effect of using* **Cascading Style Sheets (CSS-1)** *when exporting HTML files.*

If you have multiple HTML pages, you can add navigational links to navigate between the pages.

To set the navigation bar options:

♦ Choose the Navigation Bar options as follows **50**:

- **Top, Bottom,** or **Both** add navigational links to the top and/or bottom of the Web page. These links, labeled <PrevNext> allow you to move from one Web page to another **51**.
- **None** adds no links to the pages.

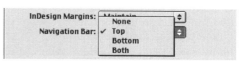

50 *Use the* **Navigation Bar** *to add and position navigation elements on the page.*

51 *The* **navigation links** *let you move from one page to another.*

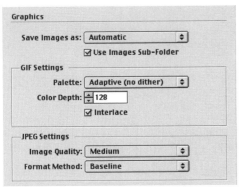

52 *The* **Graphics category** *in the Export HTML dialog box.*

53 *The* **Save Images as menu** *in the Graphics area of the Export HTML dialog box.*

54 *The type of artwork that looks better as a GIF.*

55 *The type of image that looks better as a JPEG.*

When you convert InDesign documents to HTML, there are many elements, such as placed images, lines, frame strokes and fills, and lines that need to be converted into images. The graphics HTML options control how those objects are converted.

To set the graphics HTML Options:

1. Choose HTML from the Save as File Type (Win) or Formats (Mac) menu: The Export HTML dialog box appears.

2. Click Graphics from the categories on the left of the Export HTML dialog box **52**.

You need to choose in what format images will be created for the HTML file. You also need to choose where the images are saved.

To choose the type of images and their location:

1. Choose one of the following from the Save Images As options **53**:
   - **Automatic** lets InDesign choose which type of image, GIF or JPEG, should be used.
   - **GIF** forces all images to the GIF format, which is usually better for artwork that has flat colors or limited shadows and gradients **54**.
   - **JPEG** forces all images to the JPEG format, which is usually better for photographic images **55**.

2. Check Use Images Sub-Folder to place the images in a folder labeled Images.

Where to Save Images for Web Pages?

Your HTML documents contain information about where to retrieve the graphics when the Web browser loads them. So it's important to to create a folder for images because you will need to replicate this hierarchy on the server.

You can use the GIF Settings to set the options for the GIF images ⑤⑥.

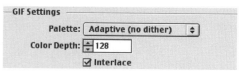

To set the GIF options:

1. Use the GIF Settings Palette menu to control the type of colors in the GIF image as follows ⑤⑦:

   - **Adaptive (no dither)** creates a representative sample of colors. This is the best choice to keep the appearance of the original image.
   - **Web** limits the colors to the 216 Web-safe colors that are present in both the Macintosh and Windows operating systems. This may cause a speckled appearance for some colors.
   - **System (Win)** or **System (Mac)** limits the colors to the built-in colors for the designated computer system.
   - **Exact** uses only those colors that are exactly in the graphic, up to 256 colors.

2. If you choose Adaptive or Exact, set the GIF Settings Color Depth to the number of colors ⑤⑥.

3. Check Interlace to create an image that appears gradually on the page ⑤⑧.

⑤⑥ *The* **GIF Settings** *in the Graphics category in the Export HTML dialog box.*

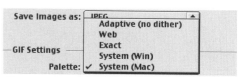

⑤⑦ *The* **Palette menu** *lets you choose the type of colors used in GIF images.*

⑤⑧ *An example of how an* **interlaced GIF** *or a* **progressive JPEG** *image appears.*

You can use the JPEG Settings to set the options for the JPEG images ⑤⑨.

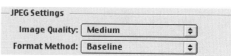

To set the JPEG options:

1. Use the JPEG Settings Image Quality menu to choose the quality of the JPEG image ⑥⓪. The lower the quality, the smaller the file size.

2. Choose a JPEG Settings Format Method as follows ⑥①:

   - **Progressive** creates an image that appears gradually on the page. This is similar to the Interlaced GIF.
   - **Baseline** creates an image that appears all at once, after the entire image has been downloaded.

⑤⑨ *The* **JPEG Settings** *in the Graphics category in the Export HTML dialog box.*

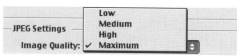

⑥⓪ *The* **Image Quality menu** *controls the size and the quality of JPEG images.*

⑥① *The* **Format menu** *controls how JPEG images are revealed.*

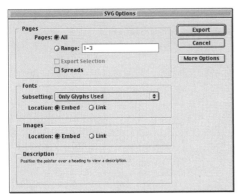

SVG Options

Pages
- Pages: ● All
- ○ Range: 1-3
- ☐ Export Selection
- ☐ Spreads

Fonts
- Subsetting: Only Glyphs Used
- Location: ● Embed ○ Link

Images
- Location: ● Embed ○ Link

Description
- Position the pointer over a heading to view a description.

Export | Cancel | More Options

62 *The* **SVG Options dialog box** *contains the controls for creating SVG and SVG Compressed files.*

Pages
- Pages: ● All
- ○ Range: 1-3
- ☐ Export Selection
- ☐ Spreads

63 *The* **Pages options** *in the SVG Options dialog box lets you control which pages are exported into SVG files.*

SVG or SVG Compressed?

There is no difference between the settings for SVG or SVG Compressed files. However, SVG Compressed files are smaller.

Depending on how you want to use the SVG format, you may not want to compress your SVG files. For instance, the compression may make it harder to edit the SVG file.

Check with your Web designer as to which format you should choose.

Exporting SVG Files

InDesign also lets you export documents in the SVG (scalable vector graphics) format that can be viewed on the Web.

To set the basic SVG options:

◆ Choose SVG or SVG Compressed from the Save as File Type (Win) or Formats (Mac) menu. The SVG Options dialog box appears **62**. *(See the sidebar on this page for the difference between the two SVG options.)*

You can choose which pages or even which selected objects are exported as an SVG file.

To set the pages for an SVG:

1. In the Pages area, select All to export all the pages in the document **63**.

   or

   Select Range to enter specific pages.

   TIP Use the hyphen to select a range of pages such as *4-9*, or use commas to enter individual pages such as *3, 8*.

2. If you have any objects selected, you can check Export Selection to convert just those objects into an SVG file.

3. Check Spreads to keep pages that are within spreads together in the Acrobat file.

SVG files can be changed using database publishing. You may want to embed fonts so that there are characters available for the new text ⑥.

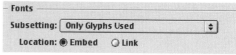

⑥ *The* **Fonts Options** *for creating SVG and SVG compressed files.*

To set the fonts for an SVG file:

1. In the Fonts area, use the Subsetting menu to choose one of the following ⑥:

   - **None (Use System Fonts)** does not embed any characters in the file.
   - **Only Glyphs Used** embeds only the characters in the file. This may limit the ability to edit the text later.
   - **Common English** embeds all the characters in English documents.
   - **Common English & Glyphs Used** adds characters used to Common English.
   - **Common Roman** embeds characters used in Roman language documents.
   - **Common Roman & Glyphs Used** adds characters used to Common Roman.
   - **All Glyphs** uses all characters in a font such as characters in Japanese fonts.

2. For Location, choose Embed to add the characters into the SVG file.

   or

   Choose Linked to have the fonts exist outside the SVG file.

   TIP Use the Linked setting if you expect to have many SVG files that use the same fonts.

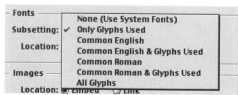

⑥ *The* **Fonts Subsetting menu** *lets you choose how much of a font is embedded in a SVG file.*

⑥ *The* **Images Location controls** *let you choose to embed or link images in the SVG file.*

You can also control how placed images are embedded within an SVG file.

To set the images for an SVG file:

1. In the Images area, choose Embed to add the image into the SVG file ⑥.

   or

   Choose Linked to have the image exist outside the SVG file.

   TIP Use the Linked setting if you have many SVG files that use the same image.

SVG Viewer

If you are interested in working with SVG files on the Web, you will need to install the SVG viewer so that your browser can display SVG files.

Surprise! The SVG plug-in should already be installed on your machine. It is installed along with InDesign 2.

In addition, anyone who downloads and installs Acrobat Reader is also given the option to install the SVG viewer.

You can also download the latest SVG viewer from the Adobe Web site.

Exporting Text

You may find it necessary to export text from InDesign. For instance, you may want to send the text to someone who works with Microsoft Word. You can send them a text file by exporting the text.

To export text:

1. Place an insertion point inside the frame that contains the text. All the text within that story will be exported.

TIP Select an area of text to export only that portion of the text.

2. Choose **File > Export**. This opens the Export dialog box.

3. Choose a text export format:
   - **Rich Text Format** keeps all the styles and text formatting. This format can be opened by most word processors, especially Microsoft Word.
   - **Text** exports only the characters of the text and discards any styles and text formatting. Use this option only if you want to strip out the text formatting or the application you are working with does not support the Rich Text Format.

4. Name the file and choose a destination.

5. Click Save to export the file.

CUSTOMIZING INDESIGN 19

Working with computer software is a personal thing. I'm always impressed with how emotional students are about how their software should work. One student may hate the way a certain feature works; yet another may insist it's his favorite thing in the entire program.

The InDesign team recognizes that some people want the program to work one way, and others want it exactly the opposite. That's why there are many ways to customize the program. You can change the keyboard shortcuts so that they are similar to other software you use. You can change settings for the displays of images and onscreen elements. You can even set the software to automatically update itself so that it is always current.

It's all your choice. You're InControl of InDesign!

Modifying Keyboard Shortcuts

Keyboard shortcuts are the fastest way to invoke program commands. However, if you are used to working with other programs, your fingers may be trained to use those other shortcuts. InDesign lets you change the keyboard shortcuts to keystrokes that match your preferences.

InDesign ships with two sets of shortcuts. The default set is the one that you have when you first use InDesign. This set uses most of the shortcuts found in Adobe products such as Adobe Illustrator or Adobe Photoshop. The other set contains the shortcuts used in QuarkXPress 4.0.

To choose the QuarkXPress shortcut set:

1. Choose **Edit > Keyboard Shortcuts**. The Keyboard Shortcuts dialog box appears ❶.

2. Choose Set for QuarkXPress 4.0 from the Set menu ❷.

3. Click OK. The new shortcuts appear in the menus ❸.

TIP Some keyboard shortcuts are "hard wired" to the program and do not change to match the keystrokes in QuarkXPress. For instance, the Zoom tool does not change to the XPress Control key (Mac) or Ctrl-Spacebar (Win) shortcuts.

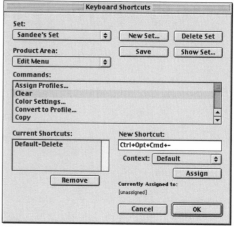

❶ The **Keyboard Shortcuts** dialog box *lets you change the shortcuts used for commands, tools, and palettes.*

❷ The **Set menu** *lets you choose a set of keyboard preferences.*

❸ *You can switch the InDesign default shortcuts to the set for the QuarkXPress 4.0 keyboard commands.*

Modifying Keyboard Shortcuts

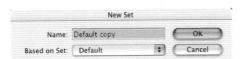

❹ *The* **New Set dialog box** *lets you name a new shortcut set and choose which set it should be based on.*

Creating Your Own Keyboard Shortcuts

I use quite a few different programs from many different software companies. I've taught QuarkXPress for over fifteen years. I work with both Adobe Illustrator and Macromedia FreeHand. I also know both Adobe Photoshop and Macromedia Fireworks. And I use InDesign to layout all my books.

I don't change InDesign's keyboard shortcuts to follow all those other programs. I find it easier to concentrate on learning InDesign's shortcuts. It's the primary program I use when working on a book—so I'd rather remember its shortcuts.

If you work with other programs such as Macromedia FreeHand, you may want to create your own shortcut set.

To create a new shortcut set:

1. Choose **Edit > Edit Shortcuts**.
2. Choose New Set. This opens the New Set dialog box **❹**.
3. Enter a name for the set.
4. Choose a set that the new set will be based on.

TIP Sets must be based on another set so that it starts with some shortcuts. However, if you later change something in the original set, the one that was based on it does not change.

5. Click OK. You can now edit the set as described on the next page.

If you want a list of keyboard shortcuts to print out and post next to your computer, you can create a file with all the shortcuts.

To create a list of the keyboard shortcuts:

1. Choose **Edit > Edit Shortcuts**.
2. Use the menu to choose the set.
3. Click the Show Set button. This opens the list of shortcuts.

TIP The list of shortcuts is opened in the following applications:
   • Simple Text (Mac OS 9)
   • Notepad (Win)
   • TextEdit (Mac OS X)

4. Print the text file.

You can change the shortcut applied to a command. However, ot all commands have shortcuts assigned to them. So you can also assign a shortcut to commands.

TIP You can change the keyboard command shortcuts for any set except the Default or QuarkXPress sets.

To change or assign a shortcut:

1. Choose a shortcut set in the Keyboard Shortcuts dialog box.

   or

   Create a new set.

2. Use the Product Area menu to choose the part of the program that contains the command to which you want to assign a shortcut 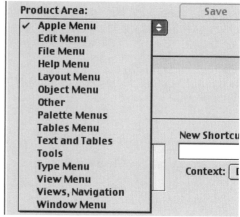.

3. Choose a command from the list under the Product Area menu 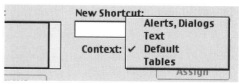.

4. Use the Context menu to choose in what area the keystroke will work 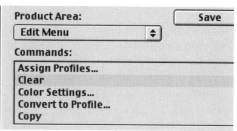.

5. Click inside the New Shortcut field to make that field active.

6. Press the keys on the keyboard that you want to assign to invoke the command.

TIP If the keystroke is already assigned to another command, the command that uses the shortcut is listed in the Currently Assigned To area 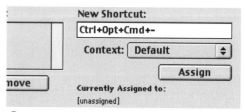.

7. Change the keys if necessary by selecting them and typing a new combination.

   or

   Click Assign to apply the new shortcut.

8. Click Save to save the set as modified.

To delete a set:

1. Use the Set menu to choose the set you want to delete.

2. Click the Delete Set button.

The Product Area menu lets you choose which parts of the program you want to change.

The Commands field contains a list of the commands available for a specific product area.

The Context menu lets you choose in which context a keyboard shortcut is applied.

The Currently Assigned to area shows what command a keystroke is assigned to.

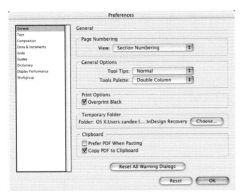

⑨ *The* **Preferences dialog box** *set to the General category.*

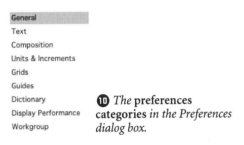

⑩ *The* **preferences categories** *in the Preferences dialog box.*

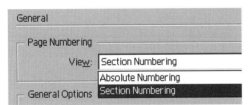

⑪ *The* **Page Numbering View menu** *lets you choose the section numbers or absolute numbers.*

Setting the Preference Categories

InDesign has nine different categories that let you customize how the program works.

To choose a preference category:

1. Choose **Edit** > **Preferences** and then choose one of the preferences categories (Mac OS 9 or Win). This opens the Preferences dialog box **⑨**.

   or

   Choose **InDesign** > **Preferences** and then choose one of the preferences categories (Mac OS X).

   TIP Click the categories on the left side of the dialog box to open a new category **⑩**.

Setting the General Category

The General category let you control various options in the program such as page numbering. Ordinarily, you want page numbers to be displayed in the Pages palette according to their section numbers *(see page 206)*. However, if you have several sections in the same document, they both could have a page number 1. The page numbering preferences change how the page numbers are displayed.

To set the page number preferences:

1. Choose one of the following from the Page Numbering View menu **⑪**:
   - **Absolute Numbering** ignores any section numbers and uses the physical placement number of the page in the document.
   - **Section Numbering** uses the numbers set from the section options.

   TIP If you have several sections with the same page number, use Absolute Numbering if you want to print a single page with a number that appears in two separate sections.

The General Options lets you configure the Tools palette and control how fast Tool Tips appear.

To set the general options:

1. Use the Tool Tips menu to choose one of the following 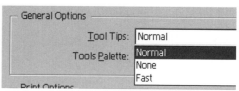:

   - **Normal** waits a moment before displaying the tip.
   - **None** turns off the display of the tips.
   - **Fast** displays the tips almost immediately after the cursor pauses over the tool or feature.

   TIP Tool Tips are explanations and notes that appear when you pause your cursor over a tool or onscreen element.

2. Use the Tools palette menu to choose how the Tools palette is displayed :

   - **Single Column** displays the palette in a single vertical column.
   - **Double Column** displays the palette in two vertical columns.
   - **Single Row** displays the palette in a single horizontal row.

   TIP You can also change the shape of the Tools palette by clicking the control in the Tools palette title bar. *(See Chapter 1, "Getting Started" for changing the shape of the Tools palette.)*

The Print Options control how InDesign prints documents.

To set the print options:

- Choose Overprint Black to have all black ink automatically overprint any other colors it passes over . *(See Chapter 17, "Output" for more information on preparing a file for printing.)*

The **Tool Tips menu** *lets you control the display of the electronic tips.*

The **Tools Palette menu** *lets you choose the configuration of the Tools palette.*

The **Print Options** *let you set the color black to overprint other colors.*

Setting the General Category

⓯ *Click the* **Temporary Folder button** *to specify the folder that holds recovered documents.*

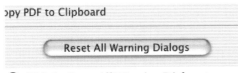

⓰ *Use the* **Clipboard controls** *to set the format for data copied from or pasted into InDesign.*

ɔpy PDF to Clipboard

Reset All Warning Dialogs

⓱ *Click the* **Reset All Warning Dialogs** *to show the alerts that have been set to be ignored.*

If InDesign crashes or the computer is shut down without saving the InDesign documents, a file is created that contains the recovered document. You can choose where that recovered document is located. This lets you specify a folder on a drive that has more space than the one that contains the InDesign application folder.

To set the temprary folder:

1. Click the Choose button in the Temporary Folder area ⓯.

2. Use the dialog box to choose the location of the recovered documents.

The clipboard contains the information stored during a copy or cut command. You can choose the format for data in the clipboard. This is important when copying and pasting between applications.

To set the clipboard format:

1. Check Prefer PDF when pasting to have PDF information come into InDesign ⓰. Do not check this if you want to edit paths from Illustrator or Photoshop.

2. Check Copy PDF to Clipboard ⓰. This lets you copy data as complete PDF files.

Every once in a while you may see a dialog box that warns you about doing something. These alerts have boxes you can check so you never see the warning again. If you've turned them off, you can reset them all.

To reset the warning dialog boxes:

◆ Click the Reset All Warning Dialogs button at the bottom of the General preferences ⓱. An alert box informs you that you will now see the warnings.

Setting the Text Category

The Text category sets the preferences for how the text is displayed and formatted 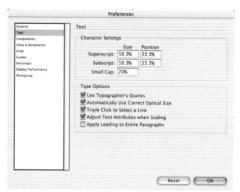. The Character Settings control the size and position of superscript, subscript, and small cap characters **⑲**. *(See page 47 for working with the superscript, subscript, and small cap characters.)*

⑱ *The Preferences dialog box set to the Text category.*

To set the character settings preferences:

1. Enter amounts in the Size field to control the size of the characters.

2. Enter amounts in the Position field to control how far above or below the baseline the characters are positioned.

TIP The percentage amount is based on the total space between the two lines.

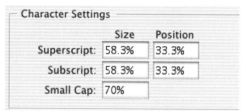
⑲ *The Character Settings control the size and position of superscript, subscript, and small cap characters.*

Use the Type Options controls for working with text **⑳**.

To set the type options preferences:

1. **Use Typographer's Quotes** automatically changes typewriter quotes into the proper curly quote characters **㉑**.

2. **Automatically Use Correct Optical Size** sets the correct value for the optical size of Multiple Master fonts.

3. **Triple Click to Select a Line** does the following:
   - Three clicks selects a line.
   - Four clicks selects a paragraph.
   - Five clicks selects the story.

TIP If this option is unchecked, three clicks selects the paragraph and four clicks selects the story.

4. **Adjust Text Attributes when Scaling** lets the text increase or decrease when scaled.

5. **Apply Leading to Entire Paragraphs** lets InDesign work more like QuarkXPress.

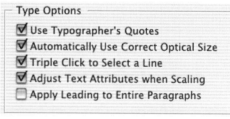
⑳ *The Type Options let you change the preferences for how text is set.*

"The Wizard of Oz" Off
"The Wizard of Oz" On
㉑ *An example of using typographer's quotes.*

Setting the Text Category

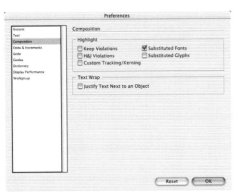

22 *The Preferences dialog box set to the* **Composition category.**

low bricks one by one. She
started slowly at first, but
then started to walk faster

23 *An example of text with a* **highlight** *applied.*

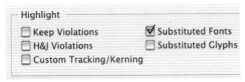

24 *The* **Highlight controls** *in the Composition category.*

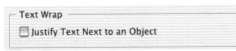

25 *The* **Text Wrap controls** *in the Composition category.*

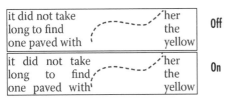

26 *The effect of setting the Justify Text Next to an Object.*

Setting the Composition Category

The Composition category controls how text is displayed and composed **22**. The Highlight settings let you control which parts of the text are highlighted to indicate composition or typographic violations or substitutions **23**.

To set the highlight options:

◆ Set the Highlight options as follows **24**:

- **Keep Violations** displays lines that have been broken in violation of the Keep With settings that you choose for the paragraph options *(see page 286)*.

- **H&J Violations** highlights those areas that have been set in violation of the hyphenation or justification controls *(see page 290)*.

TIP H&J Violations occur when there is no other way to set the text except to break the H&J controls.

- **Custom Tracking/Kerning** highlights the text that has had tracking or kerning applied to it *(see page 48)*.

- **Substituted Fonts** highlights characters that are substituted for a font that is not installed in the computer system *(see page 285)*.

TIP If the shape of the uninstalled font exists in the Adobe Type Manager database, the shape of the font is approximated. If not, a default font is used.

- **Substituted Glyphs** highlights Open Type characters that have been substituted with alternate glyphs *(see page 297)*.

You can also control how text wraps around objects **25**.

To set the text wrap options:

◆ **Justify Text Next to an Object** forces text next to an object to be justified if it wraps around an object inside the frame **26**.

Setting the Units & Increments Category

The Units & Increments category is divided into the Ruler settings and the Keyboard increments **27**. *(See Chapter 2, "Document Setup" for more information on working with the grids preferences.)*

To set the ruler units:

1. Use the Origin menu to select one of the following **28**:
   - **Spread** sets the horizontal ruler to stretch across the pages in a spread.
   - **Page** sets the horizontal ruler to reset for each individual page in a spread.
   - **Spine** sets the horizontal ruler to stretch across the spine of the document.

2. Use the Horizontal or Vertical menus to set the unit of measurement for each of the rulers **29**. *(See page 20 for more information on setting the ruler units.)*

There are several keyboard shortcuts *(see the Appendix)* you can use to move objects, or increase text settings. The keyboard increments control how much the objects move or the text changes **30**.

To set the keyboard increments:

- ◆ Enter an amount in the fields as follows:
   - **Cursor Key** lets you choose the amount that the arrow keys should nudge objects.
   - **Size/Leading** controls the amount that the type size and leading changes.
   - **Baseline Shift** lets you set the amount that the baseline shift changes.
   - **Kerning** controls the amount that the kerning changes.

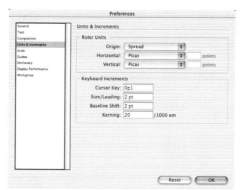

27 *The Preferences dialog box set to the **Units & Increments** category.*

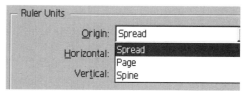

28 *The **Ruler Units Origin** menu in the Units & Increments category.*

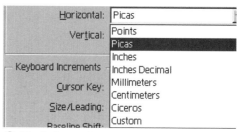

29 *The **Ruler Units Horizontal** menu in the Units & Increments category.*

Keyboard Increments

Cursor Key:	0p1
Size/Leading:	2 pt
Baseline Shift:	2 pt
Kerning:	20 /1000 em

30 *The **Keyboard Increments** fields in the Units & Increments category.*

Setting the Units & Increments Category

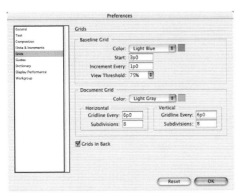

❸① *The Preferences dialog box set to the* **Grids** *category.*

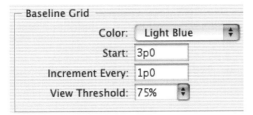

❸② *The* **Baseline Grid controls** *in the Grids category.*

❸③ *The* **Document Grid controls** *in the Grids category.*

❸④ *The* **Grids in Back control** *in the Grids category.*

Setting the Grids Category

The Grids category controls the colors and increments of the baseline and document grids **❸①**. *(See Chapter 2, "Document Setup" for more information on the grids preferences.)*

To set the baseline grid options:

1. Use the Color menu to choose a color for the baseline grid **❸②**.

2. Enter a value for each of the fields as follows:
   - **Start** positions where the grid should start on the page.
   - **Increment Every** sets the distance between the lines of the grid.
   - **View Threshold** sets the lowest magnification at which the grid is visible at.

To set the document grid preferences:

1. Use the Color menu to choose a color for the document grid **❸③**.

2. Enter a value for the Horizontal and Vertical fields as follows:
   - **Gridline Every** sets the distance between the major lines of the grid.
   - **Subdivisions** sets the number of secondary lines of the grid.

To set the positioning of the grids:

- ◆ Check Grids in Back to position the grids behind graphics and text **❸④**.

Setting the Guides Category

The Guides category controls the colors and behavior of the margin and column guides ㉟. *(See Chapter 2, "Document Setup" for more information on the grids preferences.)*

To set the margins color:

◆ Use the Margins Color menu to set the color for the margin guides ㊱.

To set the columns guides color:

◆ Use the Columns Color menu to set the color for the column guides ㊲.

To set the guide options:

1. Use the Snap to Zone field to set how close the objects should be when they snap to guides ㊳. This amount is set in pixels.

2. Check Guides in Back to hide the guides when they appear behind objects ㊳.

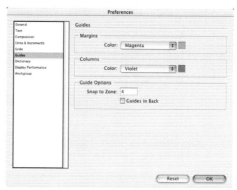

㉟ *The Preferences dialog box set to the* **Guides** **category.**

㊱ *The* **Margins Color menu** *in the Guides category.*

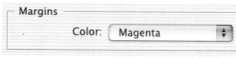

㊲ *The* **Columns Color menu** *in the Guides category.*

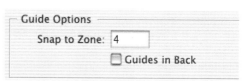

㊳ *The* **Guide Options** *in the Guides category.*

Setting the Guides Category

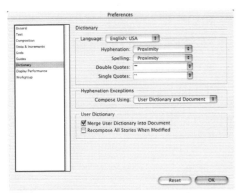

39 *The Preferences dialog box set to the* **Dictionary category**.

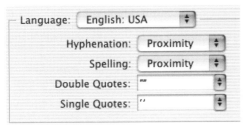

40 *The* **Language controls** *in the Dictionary category.*

Double quote choices

Single quote choices

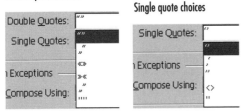

41 *The* **Quote menus** *in the Dictionary category.*

Setting the Dictionary Category

The Dictionary category lets you choose the default language settings and hyphenation controls **39**. The language settings are used for checking spelling as well as hyphenation and quotation marks **40**.

To set the language options:

1. Use the Language menu to set the default.

TIP If you want to choose other languages, you need to do a custom install from the InDesign installer CD.

2. If you have installed special hyphenation preferences, choose a preference from the Hyphenation menu.

3. If you have installed special spelling preferences, choose a preference from the Spelling menu.

4. Use the Double Quotes menu to choose the characters for double quotation marks.

5. Use the Single Quotes menu to choose the characters for single quotation marks.

TIP The Quotes menus list the quotations used for different languages, such as Spanish and French. Or you can enter your own special characters in the field **41**.

The hyphenation exceptions let you choose to apply the hyphenations created by editing the Dictionary *(see page 294)* or those built into the application.

To set the hyphenation exceptions:

♦ Choose one of the following from the Compose Using menu 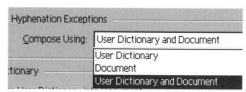:

- **User Dictionary** uses only the hyphenation exceptions set by editing the Dictionary.
- **Document** uses the hyphenation exceptions list stored inside the document. *(See the next exercise for how to add the user dictionary hyphenation exceptions into a document.)*
- **User Dictionary and Document** merges the exceptions in both the document and the user dictionary. This is the default setting.

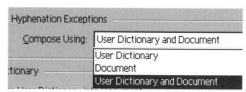

The Compose Using menu in the Hyphenation Exceptions area.

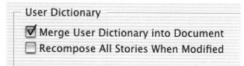

The User Dictionary controls in the Dictionary category.

The User Dictionary options let you merge hyphenation exceptions into a document and create new hyphenation exceptions that affect the document 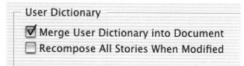.

To set the user dictionary preferences:

1. **Merge User Dictionary into Document** adds the hyphenation exceptions in the user dictionary into the document. This is on by default.

TIP This is especially useful if you send the native InDesign document to a service bureau for output.

2. **Recompose All Stories When Modified** applies the new exceptions in the user dictionary to to all the stories in the document.

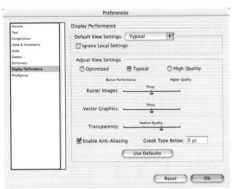

The Preferences dialog box set to the Display Performance *category.*

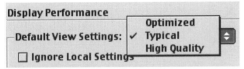

The Default View Settings *controls in the* Display Performance *category.*

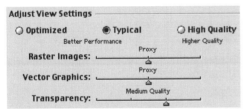

The Adjust View Settings *in the Display Performance category.*

Setting the Display Performance Category

Display Performance controls how placed images appear onscreen . *(See Chapter 8, "Imported Graphics" for more information on how to set each of the options in the Display Performance category.)*

The default view is the view that is used when documents are first opened.

To set the default view:

1. Use the Default View Settings menu to choose which of the display performance settings is automatically applied new graphics .

2. Check Ignore Local Settings to override any individual settings applied to graphics *(see page 174)*.

The Adjust View Settings controls how images appear onscreen for each of the three view choices . *(See page 175 for more information on working with the Adjust View Settings.)*

To choose the options for Adjust View Settings:

1. Click one of the radio buttons to choose a view setting.

2. Drag the slider controls to set the quality for raster images, vector graphics, and the transparency effects.

3. Repeat for the other two view settings.

TIP It takes longer for the screen to redraw if you choose the highest quality previews.

Anti-aliasing is the term used to described the soft edge applied to either text or graphics. Most designers keep anti-aliasing turned on. However, if you want, you can turn off the anti-aliasing to speed screen redraw ❹❼.

To control the anti-aliasing of text and graphics:

◆ Check Enable Anti-Aliasing to add a soft edge to the type and graphics displayed on the monitor ❹❽.

Greeking is the term used to describe the gray band that is substituted for text characters ❹❾. When text is greeked it improves how fast the screen is displayed.

To set text to be greeked:

◆ Enter an amount in the Greek Type Below field. This sets the size below which the text characters will be substituted onscreen with gray bands.

Setting the Workgroup Category

You can also use InDesign as part of a workgroup. This allows files to be checked in and out of a server. The Workgroup controls ensure that files are not accidentally modified. Because setting the workgroup preferences is so important, it is suggested that you check with your workgroup administrator for how to set the Workgroup category ❺⓿.

❹❼ *The controls for anti-aliasing, greeking type, and resetting the defaults in the Display Performance category.*

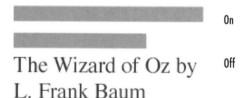

❹❽ *The effect of applying* **anti-aliasing** *to type.*

❹❾ *The effect of applying* **greeking** *to type.*

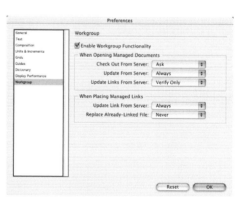

❺⓿ *The Preferences dialog box set to the* **Workgroup category.**

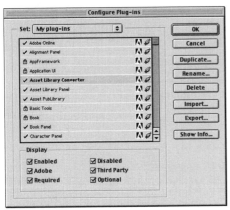

⑤ *The* **Configure Plug-ins** *dialog box.*

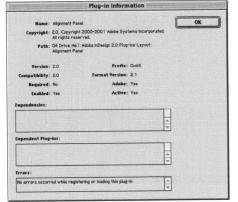

⑤ *The* **Plug-in Information** *dialog box.*

Configuring Plug-ins

InDesign uses a large set of plug-ins as its core set of commands and features. You can also get plug-ins from other companies that add other features to the program. If you have many plug-ins, you may want to control which plug-ins are installed each time you launch the program. This allows you to maintain sets that require less system memory or avoid plug-in conflicts.

To select the plug-ins set:

1. Choose one of the following to open the Configure Plug-ins dialog box **⑤**:
   - **Apple > Configure Plug-ins** (Mac OS 9).
   - **InDesign > Configure Plug-ins** (Mac OS X).
   - **Help > Configure Plug-ins** (Win).
2. Choose a set from the Set menu.

TIP InDesign ships with three default sets:
   - All Plug-ins
   - Adobe Plug-ins
   - Required Plug-ins

To modify a plug-in set:

1. Select the plug-in set.
2. If the set is one of the three default sets, choose Duplicate to make a copy of the set.
3. Click the checkbox column to the left of the name to enable or disable the plug-in from the set.
4. Use the Display checkboxes to see certain types of plug-ins such as those from Adobe third-party companies.

To see the information about a plug-in:

◆ Click the Show Info button in the Configure Plug-ins dialog box. This opens the Plug-in Information dialog box **⑤**.

Updating with Adobe Online

One of the benefits of using InDesign is that it is entirely modular. This means that Adobe can send out updates or replacements to various parts of the program via the Internet. You use the Adobe Online application controls to set up how these updates are received.

53 *The* **Adobe Online Preferences** *dialog box.*

To set the online controls:

1. Choose **Edit** > Preferences > **Online Settings** (Mac OS 9 or Win). This opens the Adobe Online Preferences dialog box **53**.

   or

   Choose **InDesign** > Preferences > **Online Settings** (Mac OS X).

2. Choose one of the following from the Update Options menu **54**.

5. Choose how often you want to update from the Refresh menu:

   • **Never** turns off all automatic updates.
   • **Once a Day, Once a Week,** or **Once a Month** automatically connects to Adobe Online.

TIP If you choose Never, you can click the Update button to manually check for InDesign updates.

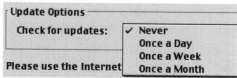

54 *The* **Check for updates** *menu lets you choose when to have InDesign perform an automatic update.*

KEYBOARD SHORTCUTS

As you become more familiar with the various InDesign features, you should start to use the keyboard shortcuts for the commands you use most often. For instance, rather than use the mouse to choose File > Place, it is much faster and easier to press the keyboard shortcut Cmd/Ctrl-D.

This appendix lists the shortcuts for the Default set of InDesign menu commands. This is the set that is turned on when you first open InDesign. As shown on pages 252—254, you can change these keyboard commands.

Many of these shortcuts are displayed along with the command on the menus. So you can look at these pages or refer to the menus to learn new shortcuts.

Some of the shortcuts are context-sensitive—that is, they work only in a certain context. For instance, the shortcut to show or hide all the palettes is listed as the Tab key. However, that shortcut works only if your insertion point is not in a text frame. If it is in a text frame, pressing the Tab key enters a tab stop.

Macintosh Keyboard Shortcuts

Macintosh Keyboard Shortcuts

The following are the keyboard shortcuts for the Macintosh platform. These are the abbreviations used for the keys.

Cmd	Command
Opt	Option
Up	Up key
Down	Down key
Left	Left key
Right	Right key
Space	Spacebar

Edit Menu

Clear	Delete
Copy	Cmd-C
Cut	Cmd-X
Deselect All	Cmd-Opt-A
Copy	Cmd-Opt-Shift-D
Find Next	Cmd-Opt-F
Find/Change	Cmd-F
Paste	Cmd-V
Paste in Place	Cmd-Opt-Shift-V
Paste Into	Cmd-Opt-V
Preferences: General	Cmd-K
Redo	Cmd-Opt-Z
Select All	Cmd-A
Step and Repeat	Cmd-Opt-V
Undo	Cmd-Z

File Menu

Close	Cmd-W
Document Setup	Cmd-Opt-P
Export	Cmd-E
New: Document	Cmd-N
Open	Cmd-O
Package	Cmd-Opt-Shift-P
Place	Cmd-D
Preflight	Cmd-Opt-Shift-F
Print	Cmd-P
Quit	Cmd-Q

Save	Cmd-S
Save a Copy	Cmd-Opt-S
Save As	Cmd-Opt-S

Help Menu

InDesign Help	Help

Layout Menu

First Page	Cmd-Opt-Page Up
Go Back	Cmd-Page Up
Go Forward	Cmd-Page Down
Last Page	Cmd-Opt-Page Down
Next Page	Shift+Page Down
Previous Page	Shift+Page Up

Object Menu

Bring Forward	Cmd-]
Bring to Front	Cmd-Opt-]
Send Backward	Cmd-[
Send to Back	Cmd-Opt-[
Clipping Path	Cmd-Opt-Shift-K
Compound: Make	Cmd-8
Compound: Release	Cmd-Opt-8
Corner Effects	Cmd-Opt-R
Drop Shadow	Cmd-Opt-M
Center Content	Cmd-Opt-E
Fit Proportionally	Cmd-Opt-Shift-E
Fit Content to Frame	Cmd-Opt-E
Fit Frame to Content	Cmd-Opt-C
Group	Cmd-G
Lock Position	Cmd-L
Text Frame Options	Cmd-B
Ungroup	Cmd-Opt-G
Unlock Position	Cmd-Opt-L

Other

New index entry	Cmd-Opt-U
New index entry (reversed) . . .	Cmd-Opt-F8
Add New Page	Cmd-Opt-P
Clear Local Display Settings . . .	Cmd-Opt-F2
Close all	Cmd-Opt-Shift-W

Close document . . . . Cmd-Opt-W
Create outlines . . . . Cmd-Opt-Shift-O
Decrease size / scale by 1% . . . . . . Cmd-,
Decrease size / scale by 5% . . . . Cmd-Opt-,
Increase size / scale by 1% . . . . . . Cmd-.
Increase size / scale by 5% . . . . . Cmd-Opt-.
New default document . . . . . Cmd-Opt-N
Nudge down . . . . Down
Nudge down .1 . . . . Cmd-Opt-Down
Nudge down .1 copy . Cmd-Opt-Shift-Down
Nudge down copy . . . . Opt-Down
Nudge down x10 . . . . Shift-Down
Nudge down x10 copy . . . Opt-Shift-Down
Nudge left. . . . . Left
Nudge left 1/10 . . . . Cmd-Opt-Left
Nudge left 1/10 copy . . . Cmd-Opt-Shift-Left
Nudge left copy. . . . . Opt-Left
Nudge left x10 . . . . Shift-Left
Nudge left x10 copy . . . . . Opt-Shift-Left
Nudge right. . . . . Right
Nudge right 1/10 . . . . Cmd-Opt-Right
Nudge right 1/10 copy . Cmd-Opt-Shift-Right
Nudge right copy. . . . . Opt-Right
Nudge right x10 . . . . Shift-Right
Nudge right x10 copy . . . . Opt-Shift-Right
Nudge up . . . . Up
Nudge up 1/10 . . . . Cmd-Opt-Up
Nudge up 1/10 copy . . . . Cmd-Opt-Shift-Up
Nudge up copy . . . . Opt-Up
Nudge up x10 . . . . Shift-Up
Nudge up x10 copy . . . . . . Opt-Shift-Up
Open index entry dialog. . . . . Cmd-U
Save all . . . . Cmd-Opt-Shift-S
Select all guides. . . . . Cmd-Opt-G
Select bottom object . . . . . Cmd-Opt-Shift-[
Select next object above . . . . . Cmd-Opt-]
Select next object below . . . . . . Cmd-Opt-[
Select top object . . . . . . Cmd-Opt-Shift-]

Palette Menus

Redefine Style . . . . Cmd-Opt-Shift-C
All Caps. . . . . Cmd-Opt-K
Small Caps . . . . Cmd-Opt-H
Strikethrough. . . . . Cmd-Opt-/
Subscript . . . . Cmd-Opt-Shift-=
Superscript . . . . Cmd-Opt-=
Underline. . . . . Cmd-Opt-U
Hyphenation . . . . Cmd-Opt-H
Justification. . . . . Cmd-Opt-Shift-J
Keep Options. . . . . Cmd-Opt-K

Tables Menu

Cell Options: Text . . . . Cmd-Opt-B
Delete: Column . . . . Shift+Delete
Delete: Row. . . . . Cmd-Delete
Insert Table . . . . Cmd-Opt-Shift-T
Insert: Column Cmd-Opt-9
Insert: Row Cmd-9
Select: Cell . . . . Cmd-/
Select: Column Cmd-Opt-3
Select: Row Cmd-3
Select: Table. . . . . Cmd-Opt-A
Table Setup . . . . Cmd-Opt-T

Text and Tables

Align center. . . . . Cmd-Opt-C
Align force justify . . . . Cmd-Opt-F
Align justify. . . . . Cmd-Opt-J
Align left . . . . Cmd-Opt-L
Align right . . . . Cmd-Opt-R
Align to baseline grid . . . . Cmd-Opt-Shift-G
Apply bold . . . . Cmd-Opt-B
Apply italic . . . . Cmd-Opt-I
Apply normal. . . . . Cmd-Opt-Y
Auto leading . . . . Cmd-Opt-Shift-A
Auto-hyphenate on/off . . . Cmd-Opt-Shift-H
Clear . . . . Delete
Decrease baseline shift. . . . Opt+Shift+Down

Decrease baseline shiftx5 Cmd-Opt-Shift-Down
Decrease kerning/tracking. . . . . . . Opt+Left
Decrease kerning/trackingx5 . . Cmd-Opt-Left
Decrease leading . . . . Opt+Up
Decrease leadingx5. . . . . . . Cmd-Opt-Up
Decrease point size. . . . . Cmd-Opt-,
Decrease point sizex5 . . . . Cmd-Opt-Shift-,
Decrease word space . . . . . Cmd-Opt-Delete
Decrease word spacex5 Cmd-Opt-Shift-Delete
Find Next. . . . . Shift+F2
Increase baseline shift . . . . . . Opt+Shift+Up
Increase baseline shiftx5 . . Cmd-Opt-Shift-Up
Increase kerning/tracking . . . . . . Opt+Right
Increase kerning/trackingx5 . . . Cmd-Opt-Right
Increase leading . . . . Opt+Down
Increase leadingx5 . . . . . . Cmd-Opt-Down
Increase point size . . . . Cmd-Opt-.
Increase point sizex5 . . . . . Cmd-Opt-Shift-.
Increase word space . . . . Cmd-Opt-\
Increase word spacex5 . . . . Cmd-Opt-Shift-\
Load Find and Find Next instance . . Shift+F1
Load Find with selected text Cmd-F1
Load Replace with selected text Cmd-F2
Move Down . . . . Down
Move down one line . . . . Down
Move Left. . . . . Left
Move Right . . . . Right
Move to beginning of story . . . . Cmd-Home
Move to end of story. . . . . Cmd-End
Move to First Cell in Column . . Opt+Page Up
Move to First Cell in Row . . . . . Opt+Home
Move to First Row in Frame. . . . . Page Up
Move to Last Cell in Column Opt+Page Down
Move to Last Cell in Row . . . . . . Opt+End
Move to Last Row in Frame . . . . . Page Down
Move to Next Cell . . . . Tab
Move to Previous Cell . . . . Shift+Tab
Move to the end of the line . . . . End
Move to the left one character . . . . . . Left
Move to the left one word . . . . . . Cmd-Left

Move to the next paragraph. . . . Cmd-Down
Move to the previous paragraph . . . Cmd-Up
Move to the right one character. . . . . Right
Move to the right one word . . . . Cmd-Right
Move to the start of the line. . . . . . Home
Move Up . . . . Up
Move up one line. . . . . Up
Normal horizontal text scale . . . Cmd-Opt-X
Normal vertical text scale . . Cmd-Opt-Shift-X
Recompose all stories . . . . Cmd-Opt-/
Replace with Change To text Cmd-F3
Reset kerning and tracking . . . . Cmd-Opt-Q
Select Cells Above . . . . Shift+Up
Select Cells Below . . . . Shift+Down
Select Cells to the Left . . . . Shift+Left
Select Cells to the Right . . . . . Shift+Right
Select line. . . . . Cmd-Opt-\
Select one character to the left . . . Shift+Left
Select one character to the right . Shift+Right
Select one line above. . . . . Shift+Up
Select one line below. . . . . Shift+Down
Select one paragraph before. . . Cmd-Opt-Up
Select one paragraph forward Cmd-Opt-Down
Select one word to the left . . . . Cmd-Opt-Left
Select one word to the right . . Cmd-Opt-Right
Select to beginning of story . Cmd-Opt-Home
Select to end of story. . . . . . Cmd-Opt-End
Select to the end of the line . . . . Shift+End
Select to the start of the line. . . . Shift+Home
Toggle Cell/Text Selection . . . . Escape
Toggle Quotes preference . . Cmd-Opt-Shift-'
Update missing font list . . . Cmd-Opt-Shift-/

Tools

Add Anchor Point Tool . . . . =
Apply color. . . . . ,
Apply default fill and stroke colors . . . . . D
Apply gradient . . . .
Apply None. . . . . /, Num /
Convert Direction Point Tool . . . . . . Shift+C

Delete Anchor Point Tool . . . . -
Direct Selection Tool. . . . . A
Ellipse Tool L
Eyedropper Tool I
Free Transform Tool . . . . E
Gradient Tool. . . . . G
Hand Tool . . . . H
Line Tool . . . . \
Path Type Tool . . . . Shift+T
Pen Tool. . . . . P
Pencil Tool . . . . N
Rectangle Frame Tool . . . . F
Rectangle Tool . . . . M
Rotate Tool . . . . R
Scale Tool . . . . S
Scissors Tool C
Selection Tool V
Shear Tool . . . . O
Swap fill and stroke activation X
Swap fill and stroke colors. . . . . . . Shift+X
Toggle Text and Object Control. . . . . . . J
Toggle view between default and preview . . W
Type Tool . . . . T
Zoom Tool . . . . Z

Type Menu

Character . . . . Cmd-T
Character Styles . . . . Shift+F11
Check Spelling . . . . Cmd-I
Create Outlines. . . . . Cmd-Opt-O
Insert Column Break . . . . Enter
Insert Forced Line Break. . . . . Shift+Return
Insert Frame Break. . . . . Shift+Enter
Insert Page Break. . . . . Cmd-Enter
Insert Auto Page Number . . . . . Cmd-Opt-N
Insert Discretionary Hyphen . . . Cmd-Opt--
Insert Indent to Here . . . . Cmd-\
Insert Next Page Number . . Cmd-Opt-Shift-]
Insert Nonbreaking Hyphen . . . Cmd-Opt--
Insert Previous Page Number . Cmd-Opt-Shift-[

Insert Right Indent Tab . . . . Shift+Tab
Insert Section Name . . . . . Cmd-Opt-Shift-N
Insert Em Space . . . . Cmd-Opt-M
Insert En Space. . . . . Cmd-Opt-N
Insert Figure Space. Cmd-Opt-Shift-8
Insert Hair Space. . . . . . . Cmd-Opt-Shift-I
Insert Nonbreaking Space . . . . . Opt+Space
Insert Thin Space . . . . Cmd-Opt-Shift-M
Paragraph. . . . . Cmd-M
Paragraph Styles F11
Show Hidden Characters . . . . Cmd-Opt-I
Tabs . . . . Cmd-Opt-T

View Menu

Display Master Items . . . . Cmd-Y
Entire Pasteboard Cmd-Opt-Shift-0
Fit Page in Window Cmd-0
Fit Spread in Window Cmd-Opt-0
Hide Frame Edges . . . . Cmd-H
Hide Guides . . . . Cmd-;
Hide Rulers. . . . . Cmd-R
High Quality Display . . . . . . Cmd-Opt-H
Lock Guides . . . . Cmd-Opt-;
Optimized Display. . . . . Cmd-Opt-O
Show Baseline Grid . . . . Cmd-Opt-'
Show Document Grid . . . . Cmd-'
Show Text Threads. . . . . Cmd-Opt-Y
Snap to Document Grid. . . . . . Cmd-Opt-'
Snap to Guides . . . . Cmd-Opt-;
Typical Display. . . . . Cmd-Opt-Z
Zoom In . . . . Cmd-=
Zoom Out . . . . Cmd--

Views, Navigation

200% size Cmd-2
400% size Cmd-4
50% size. Cmd-5
Access page number box. . . . . Cmd-J
Access zoom percentage box . . . Cmd-Opt-5
Activate last-used field in palette . . . . Cmd-`

Actual Size Cmd-1
First spread . . . . Opt+Shift+Page Up
Fit Selection in Window . . . . . . Cmd-Opt-=
Force redraw . . . . Shift+F5
Go to first frame . . . Cmd-Opt-Shift-Page Up
Go to last frame . Cmd-Opt-Shift-Page Down
Go to next frame . . . . Cmd-Opt-Page Down
Go to previous frame . . . Cmd-Opt-Page Up
Last spread . . . . Opt+Shift+Page Down
Next spread . . . Opt+Page Down, Cmd-Right
Next window Cmd-F6
Previous spread . . . Opt+Page Up, Cmd-Left
Previous window Cmd-Opt-F6
Scroll down one screen . . . . . . Page Down
Scroll up one screen . . . . Page Up
Show/Hide palettes . . . . Tab
Show/Hide palettes except toolbox . Shift+Tab
Toggle between views Cmd-Opt-2
Toggle Measurements . . . . Cmd-Opt-Shift-U

Window Menu

Align F8
Color F6
Hyperlinks . . . . Shift+F7
Index . . . . Shift+F8
Layers F7
Links . . . . Cmd-Opt-D
Pages F12
Stroke F10
Swatches F5
Table . . . . Shift+F9
Text Wrap . . . . Cmd-Opt-W
Transform F9
Transparency . . . . Shift+F10

Windows Keyboard Shortcuts

The following are the keyboard shortcuts for the Windows platform. These are the abbreviations used for the keys.

Ctrl . . . . Control key
Alt . . . . Alt key
Up . . . . Up key
Down . . . . Down key
Left . . . . Left key
Right . . . . Right key
Space . . . . Spacebar

Edit Menu

Clear . . . . Backspace/Delete
Copy . . . . Ctrl-C
Cut . . . . Ctrl-X
Deselect All . . . . Ctrl-Shift-A
Copy . . . . Ctrl-Alt-Shift-D
Find Next . . . . Ctrl-Alt-F
Find/Change . . . . Ctrl-F
Paste . . . . Ctrl-V
Paste in Place . . . . Ctrl-Alt-Shift-V
Paste Into . . . . Ctrl-Alt-V
Preferences: General . . . . Ctrl-K
Redo . . . . Ctrl-Shift-Z
Select All . . . . Ctrl-A
Step and Repeat . . . . Ctrl-Shift-V
Undo . . . . Ctrl-Z

File Menu

Close . . . . Ctrl-W, Ctrl-F4
Document Setup . . . . Ctrl-Alt-P
Exit . . . . Ctrl-Q
Export . . . . Ctrl-E
New: Document . . . . Ctrl-N
Open . . . . Ctrl-O
Package . . . . Ctrl-Alt-Shift-P

Place. . . . . Ctrl-D

Preflight. . . . . Ctrl-Alt-Shift-F

Print. . . . . Ctrl-P

Save . . . . Ctrl-S

Save a Copy. . . . . Ctrl-Alt-S

Save As . . . . Ctrl-Shift-S

Help Menu

InDesign Help F1

Layout Menu

First Page . . . . Ctrl-Shift-Page Up,

Go Back. . . . . Ctrl-Page Up

Go Forward. . . . . Ctrl-Page Down

Last Page . . . . Ctrl-Shift-Page Down

Next Page . . . . Shift+Page Down

Previous Page. . . . . Shift+Page Up

Object Menu

Bring Forward . . . . Ctrl-]

Bring to Front . . . . Ctrl-Shift-]

Send Backward . . . . Ctrl-[

Send to Back . . . . Ctrl-Shift-[

Clipping Path. . . . . Ctrl-Alt-Shift-K

Compound: Make Ctrl-8

Compound: Release Ctrl-Alt-8

Corner Effects . . . . Ctrl-Alt-R

Drop Shadow. . . . . Ctrl-Alt-M

Center Content. . . . . Ctrl-Shift-E

Fit Content Proportionally . . Ctrl-Alt-Shift-E

Fit Content to Frame . . . . Ctrl-Alt-E

Fit Frame to Content . . . . Ctrl-Alt-C

Group. . . . . Ctrl-G

Lock Position. . . . . Ctrl-L

Text Frame Options . . . . Ctrl-B

Ungroup . . . . Ctrl-Shift-G

Unlock Position . . . . Ctrl-Alt-L

Other

Add index entry . . . . Ctrl-Alt-U

Add index entry (reversed) Ctrl-Shift-F8

Add New Page . . . . Ctrl-Shift-P

Clear Local Display Settings. . . Ctrl-Shift-F2

Close all. . . . . Ctrl-Alt-Shift-W

Close document . . . . Ctrl-Shift-W

Create outlines . . . . Ctrl-Alt-Shift-O

Decrease size/scale by 1% . . . . Ctrl-,

Decrease size/scale by 5% . . . . . . Ctrl-Alt-,

Increase size/scale by 1% . . . . Ctrl-.

Increase size/scale by 5% . . . . . . Ctrl-Alt-.

New default document . . . . . . Ctrl-Alt-N

Nudge down . . . . Down

Nudge down .1 . . . . Ctrl-Shift-Down

Nudge down .1 copy . . . Ctrl-Alt-Shift-Down

Nudge down copy . . . . Alt+Down

Nudge down x10. . . . . Shift+Down

Nudge down x10 copy . . . . Shift+Alt+Down

Nudge left. . . . . Left

Nudge left .1 . . . . Ctrl-Shift-Left

Nudge left .1 copy . . . . . Ctrl-Alt-Shift-Left

Nudge left copy. . . . . Alt+Left

Nudge left x10 . . . . Shift+Left

Nudge left x10 copy . . . . . . Shift+Alt+Left

Nudge right. . . . . Right

Nudge right .1 . . . . Ctrl-Shift-Right

Nudge right .1 copy . . . . Ctrl-Alt-Shift-Right

Nudge right copy. . . . . Alt+Right

Nudge right x10 . . . . Shift+Right

Nudge right x10 copy . . . . Shift+Alt+Right

Nudge up . . . . Up

Nudge up 1/10 . . . . Ctrl-Shift-Up

Nudge up 1/10 copy . . . . . Ctrl-Alt-Shift-Up

Nudge up copy. . . . . Alt+Up

Nudge up x10 . . . . Shift+Up

Nudge up x10 copy . . . . . . Shift+Alt+Up

Open index entry dialog. . . . . Ctrl-U

Windows Keyboard Shortcuts

Save all . . . . Ctrl-Alt-Shift-S
Select all guides. . . . . Ctrl-Alt-G
Select bottom object . . . . . . Ctrl-Alt-Shift-[
Select next object above . . . . . . Ctrl-Alt-]
Select next object below . . . . . . Ctrl-Alt-[
Select top object . . . . Ctrl-Alt-Shift-]

Palette Menus

Redefine Style . . . . Ctrl-Alt-Shift-C
All Caps. . . . . Ctrl-Shift-K
Small Caps . . . . Ctrl-Shift-H
Strikethrough. . . . . Ctrl-Shift-/
Subscript . . . . Ctrl-Alt-Shift-=
Superscript . . . . Ctrl-Shift-=
Underline. . . . . Ctrl-Shift-U
Redefine Style . . . . Ctrl-Alt-Shift-R
Hyphenation . . . . Ctrl-Alt-H
Justification. . . . . Ctrl-Alt-Shift-J
Keep Options. . . . . Ctrl-Alt-K
Paragraph Rules . . . . Ctrl-Alt-J

Tables Menu

Cell Options: Text . . . . Ctrl-Alt-B
Delete: Column . . . . Shift+Backspace
Delete: Row. . . . . Ctrl-Backspace
Insert Table . . . . Ctrl-Alt-Shift-T
Insert: Column Ctrl-Alt-9
Insert: Row Ctrl-9
Select: Cell . . . . Ctrl-/
Select: Column Ctrl-Alt-3
Select: Row Ctrl-3
Select: Table. . . . . Ctrl-Alt-A
Table Options: Table Setup . . . . . Ctrl-Alt-T

Text and Tables

Align center. . . . . Ctrl-Shift-C
Align force justify . . . . Ctrl-Shift-F
Align justify. . . . . Ctrl-Shift-J
Align left . . . . Ctrl-Shift-L

Align right . . . . Ctrl-Shift-R
Align to baseline grid . . . . . Ctrl-Alt-Shift-G
Apply bold . . . . Ctrl-Shift-B
Apply italic . . . . Ctrl-Shift-I
Apply normal. . . . . Ctrl-Shift-Y
Auto leading . . . . Ctrl-Alt-Shift-A
Auto-hyphenate on/off . . . . Ctrl-Alt-Shift-H
Clear . . . . Backspace
Decrease baseline shift. . . . Shift+Alt+Down
Decrease baseline shiftx5 Ctrl-Alt-Shift-Down
Decrease kerning/tracking. . . . . . Alt+Left
Decrease kerning/trackingx5 . . . Ctrl-Alt-Left
Decrease leading . . . . Alt+Up
Decrease leadingx5. . . . . Ctrl-Alt-Up
Decrease point size. . . . . Ctrl-Shift-,
Decrease point sizex5 . . . . . Ctrl-Alt-Shift-,
Decrease word space. . . . Ctrl-Alt-Backspace
Decrease word spacex5 Ctrl-Alt-Shift-Backspace
Delete. . . . . Delete
Find Next. . . . . Shift+F2
Increase baseline shift . . . . . Shift+Alt+Up
Increase baseline shiftx5 . . . Ctrl-Alt-Shift-Up
Increase kerning/tracking . . . . . Alt+Right
Increase kerning/trackingx5. . . Ctrl-Alt-Right
Increase leading . . . . Alt+Down
Increase leadingx5 . . . . Ctrl-Alt-Down
Increase point size . . . . Ctrl-Shift-.
Increase point sizex5. . . . . . Ctrl-Alt-Shift-.
Increase word space . . . . Ctrl-Alt-\
Increase word spacex5 . . . . . Ctrl-Alt-Shift-\
Load Find and Find Next instance . . Shift+F1
Load Find with selected text Ctrl-F1
Load Replace with selected text. . . . Ctrl-F2
Move Down . . . . Down
Move down one line . . . . Down
Move Left. . . . . Left
Move Right . . . . Right
Move to beginning of story . . . . Ctrl-Home
Move to end of story. . . . . Ctrl-End

Move to First Cell in Column . . .	Alt+Page Up	Select to the end of the line	Shift+End
Move to First Cell in Row	Alt+Home	Select to the start of the line. . . .	Shift+Home
Move to First Row in Frame.	Page Up	Toggle Cell/Text Selection	Escape
Move to Last Cell in Column .	Alt+Page Down	Toggle Quotes preference . . .	Ctrl-Alt-Shift-'
Move to Last Cell in Row	Alt+End	Update missing font list	Ctrl-Alt-Shift-/

Move to First Cell in Column . . . Alt+Page Up
Move to First Cell in Row . . . . . Alt+Home
Move to First Row in Frame. . . . . Page Up
Move to Last Cell in Column . Alt+Page Down
Move to Last Cell in Row . . . . . . Alt+End
Move to Last Row in Frame . . . . . Page Down
Move to Next Cell . . . . Tab
Move to Previous Cell . . . . Shift+Tab
Move to the end of the line . . . . End
Move to the left one character . . . . . . Left
Move to the left one word . . . . . . Ctrl-Left
Move to the next paragraph. . . . . Ctrl-Down
Move to the previous paragraph . . . Ctrl-Up
Move to the right one character. . . . . Right
Move to the right one word . . . . . Ctrl-Right
Move to the start of the line. . . . . . Home
Move Up . . . . Up
Move up one line. . . . . Up
Normal horizontal text scale . . . Ctrl-Shift-X
Normal vertical text scale . . . Ctrl-Alt-Shift-X
Only Align First Line To Grid . [none defined]
Recompose all stories . . . . Ctrl-Alt-/
Replace with Change To text Ctrl-F3
Reset kerning and tracking . . . . . Ctrl-Alt-Q
Select Cells Above . . . . Shift+Up
Select Cells Below . . . . Shift+Down
Select Cells to the Left . . . . Shift+Left
Select Cells to the Right . . . . . . Shift+Right
Select line. . . . . Ctrl-Shift-\
Select one character to the left . . . Shift+Left
Select one character to the right . Shift+Right
Select one line above. . . . . Shift+Up
Select one line below. . . . . . . Shift+Down
Select one paragraph before. . . Ctrl-Shift-Up
Select one paragraph forward Ctrl-Shift-Down
Select one word to the left . . . . Ctrl-Shift-Left
Select one word to the right . . Ctrl-Shift-Right
Select to beginning of story . Ctrl-Shift-Home
Select to end of story. . . . . . Ctrl-Shift-End

Select to the end of the line . . . . . Shift+End
Select to the start of the line. . . . Shift+Home
Toggle Cell/Text Selection . . . . Escape
Toggle Quotes preference . . . Ctrl-Alt-Shift-'
Update missing font list . . . . Ctrl-Alt-Shift-/

Tools

Add Anchor Point Tool . . . . =
Apply color . . . . ,
Apply default fill and stroke colors . . . . . . D
Apply gradient . . . .
Apply None. . . . . Num /, /
Convert Direction Point Tool . . . . . . Shift+C
Delete Anchor Point Tool . . . . -
Direct Selection Tool. . . . . A
Ellipse Tool L
Eyedropper Tool I
Free Transform Tool . . . . E
Gradient Tool. . . . . G
Hand Tool . . . . H
Line Tool . . . . \
Path Type Tool . . . . Shift+T
Pen Tool. P
Pencil Tool . . . . N
Rectangle Frame Tool . . . . F
Rectangle Tool . . . . M
Rotate Tool . . . . R
Scale Tool . . . . S
Scissors Tool C
Selection Tool V
Shear Tool . . . . O
Swap fill and stroke activation X
Swap fill and stroke colors. . . . . Shift+X
Toggle Text and Object Control. . . . . J
Toggle view settings . . . . W
Type Tool . . . . T
Zoom Tool . . . . Z

Windows Keyboard Shortcuts

Type Menu

Character . . . . Ctrl-T
Character†Styles . . . . Shift+F11
Check Spelling . . . . Ctrl-I
Create Outlines. . . . . Ctrl-Shift-O
Insert Column Break . . . . Num Enter
Insert Forced Line Break. . . . . Shift+Enter
Insert Frame Break. . . . . Shift+Num Enter
Insert Page Break. . . . . . . Ctrl-Num Enter
Insert Auto Page Number . . . . . Ctrl-Alt-N
Insert Bullet Character . . . . Alt+8
Insert Copyright Symbol . . . . Alt+G
Insert Discretionary Hyphen . . . Ctrl-Shift--
Insert Double Left Quotation . . . . . Alt+[
Insert Double Right Quotation . Shift+Alt+[
Insert Ellipsis. . . . . Alt+;
Insert Em Dash. . . . . Shift+Alt+-
Insert En Dash . . . . Alt+-
Insert Indent to Here . . . . Ctrl-\
Insert Next Page Number . . . Ctrl-Alt-Shift-]
Insert Nonbreaking Hyphen . . . . Ctrl-Alt--
Insert Paragraph Symbol . . . . Alt+7
Insert Previous Page Number . Ctrl-Alt-Shift-[
Insert Registered Trademark Symbol. . . Alt+R
Insert Right Indent Tab . . . . . . Shift+Tab
Insert Section Name . . . . . Ctrl-Alt-Shift-N
Insert Section Symbol . . . . Alt+6
Insert Single Left Quotation . . . . . . Alt+]
Insert Single Right Quotation . . Shift+Alt+]
Insert Trademark Symbol . . . . Alt+2
Insert Em Space . . . . Ctrl-Shift-M
Insert En Space. . . . . Ctrl-Shift-N
Insert Figure Space. Ctrl-Alt-Shift-8
Insert Hair Space. . . . . . . Ctrl-Alt-Shift-I
Insert Nonbreaking Space. . . . . Ctrl-Alt-X
Insert Thin Space . . . . . . Ctrl-Alt-Shift-M
Paragraph. . . . . Ctrl-M
Paragraph†Styles. F11

Show Hidden Characters . . . . . . Ctrl-Alt-I
Tabs . . . . Ctrl-Shift-T

View Menu

Display Master Items . . . . Ctrl-Y
Entire Pasteboard Ctrl-Alt-Shift-0
Fit Page in Window Ctrl-0
Fit Spread in Window Ctrl-Alt-0
Hide Guides . . . . Ctrl-;
Hide Rulers. . . . . Ctrl-R
High Quality Display . . . . Ctrl-Alt-H
Lock Guides . . . . Ctrl-Alt-;
Optimized Display. . . . . Ctrl-Alt-O
Show Baseline Grid . . . . Ctrl-Alt-'
Show Document Grid . . . . Ctrl-'
Show Frame Edges. . . . . Ctrl-H
Show Text Threads. . . . . Ctrl-Alt-Y
Snap to Document Grid. . . . . . Ctrl-Shift-'
Snap to Guides . . . . Ctrl-Shift-;
Typical Display. . . . . Ctrl-Alt-Z
Zoom In . . . . Ctrl-=
Zoom Out . . . . Ctrl--

Views, Navigation

200% size Ctrl-2
400% size Ctrl-4
50% size. Ctrl-5
Access page number box. . . . . Ctrl-J
Access zoom percentage box Ctrl-Alt-5
Activate last-used field in palette . . . . Ctrl-`
Actual Size Ctrl-1
First spread . . . . Shift+Alt+Page Up
Fit Selection in Window. . . . . . Ctrl-Alt-=
Force redraw . . . . Shift+F5
Go to first frame . . . . Ctrl-Alt-Shift-Page Up
Go to last frame . . Ctrl-Alt-Shift-Page Down
Go to next frame . . . . . Ctrl-Alt-Page Down
Go to previous frame . . . . Ctrl-Alt-Page Up
Last spread . . . . Shift+Alt+Page Down

Next spread. . . .   Alt+Page Down, Ctrl-Right
Next window Ctrl-F6
Previous spread . . . .   Alt+Page Up, Ctrl-Left
Previous window. Ctrl-Shift-F6
Scroll down one screen Page Down, Page Down
Scroll up one screen . . . . .   Page Up, Page Up
Show/Hide palettes . . . .   Tab
Show/Hide palettes except toolbox .   Shift+Tab
Toggle between views Ctrl-Alt-2
Toggle Measurements . . . . .   Ctrl-Alt-Shift-U

Window Menu

Align F8
Color F6
Hyperlinks . . . .   Shift+F7
Index . . . .   Shift+F8
Layers F7
Links . . . .   Ctrl-Shift-D
Pages F12
Stroke F10
Swatches F5
Table . . . .   Shift+F9
Text Wrap. . . . .   Ctrl-Alt-W
Transform F9
Transparency . . . .   Shift+F10

Windows Keyboard Shortucts

INDEX

E

Index

Index